Writings From Life

Fourth Edition

Tom Tyner

Breadan Publishing

Breadan Publishing

Writings from Life
Fourth Edition
Tom Tyner

Publisher, English	Pat Nishimura
Editor, Writing	Susan Wiesick
Marketing	Lori Jones

Address for Domestic and International Orders

Breadan Publishing
4706 N. Quail Lake Dr.
Clovis, CA 93619

Website: www.breadanpublishing.com
Telephone: 559-291-2152
Fax: 559-291-1978

Printed in the United States of America ISBN: 978-0-692-33800-1

Breadan Publishing

Preface

Writings from Life is a process-oriented writing textbook that helps students continue to grow and improve as writers. Students learn by writing, and the textbook provides a variety of writing assignments that require students to develop and apply different writing and thinking skills as they progress through the book.

Writing Process

In each unit, students use the writing process in the text to develop their paper. The basic process of prewriting, drafting, revision, and editing is repeated in each unit, with new instructional elements introduced in each section that apply to the type of writing the students are doing. The process is repeated in each unit so that students become familiar and comfortable with the approach to use for any writing they may do.

      The text also recognizes the individual differences among writers. For some writers, prewriting may involve detailed planning while for others, it may involve coming up with an idea to get started. The text acknowledges such differences and allows for individual flexibility within the writing process rather than a one-size-fitsall model. The textbook also recognizes that some students come to the course with considerable writing experience, and they are encouraged to meld what they learn from the text with their previous experiences to create the most effective personalized writing process.

Writing Assignments

The title *Writings from Life* indicates the kind of writing students will do: writings based on their personal experiences, interests, observations, knowledge, beliefs, and opinions. They write about aspects of their lives, and the world around them, that they find most important, significant, and interesting. They use the writing process in the textbook, along with the instructional guides, to develop and express their ideas most effectively.

Writing as Communication

Writings from Life also emphasizes writing as a form of communication. To that end, students write for different reading audiences, such as their classmates, and for a particular purpose: to inform, entertain, influence, educate, or move readers to action. The writing assignments in the text are real in that they are written for others and for a purpose, which is more meaningful than writing as a textbook exercise.

Importance of Revision

Writings from Life also strongly emphasizes the role of revision in the writing process. Throughout the text, students work on revising and improving their writing in a number of areas: wording, organization, content development, paragraphing, openings and conclusions, transitional wording, and so on. The text provides specific revision guidelines for the type of writing students do in each unit.

New to Fourth Edition

Some exciting changes have been made in this fourth edition of *Writings from Life*. First, the textbook has been converted to a workbook format with perforated pages and space for students to complete many activities within the book. The new format should make the book more "user friendly" for both students and instructors. Second, the number of end-of-unit readings, essays written by professional writers, has increased from eleven to twenty-six. The added readings provide more interesting reading material, a wide variety of writing models, and a range of provocative topics for students to discuss.

Finally, a new unit – "Making Decisions" – has been added. The writing emphasis in this unit is on comparing and contrasting similar subjects and making decisions based on that comparison. This new Unit Six is a valuable addition to the book, providing students with a different writing experience to help them further develop their writing and thinking skills.

Writing Correctness

As the last step in the writing process in each unit, students proofread and edit their papers to eliminate errors. Correct writing is emphasized as the best way to showcase a writer's ideas, as a courtesy to readers, as a goal that all writer share.

Within each unit, the text provides instruction in the areas of punctuation, grammar usage, and spelling where writers have the most problems: run-on sentences and comma splices, sentence fragments, comma usage, subject-verb agreement, and so on. Students are also taught to proofread a paper several times, looking for a different kind of error each time. In addition, the text provides an editing checklist in each unit for students to apply to the paper they are working on.

Writing Samples

Throughout the text are writing samples that students use in number of ways: to get ideas for their writing, to see how writers develop, organize, and paragraph their papers, to read and evaluate different openings and conclusions, to see how writers develop a thesis statement, to see how writers work dialogue into their writing effectively, and so on. The sample writings provide models for the type of writing that students are doing and material for class or group discussion.

Contents

Unit Three
Interests

Unit Four
Beliefs and Values

Unit Five
Problems and Solutions

Unit Six
Making Decisions

Unit Seven
Discoveries

Readings
Unit One: Experiences

Unit Two: Influences

Unit Three: Interests

Unit Four: Belief and Values

Unit Five: Problems and Solutions

Unit Six: Making Decisions

Unit Seven: Discoveries

2

example, make critical judgments about job candidates based on their writing ability, often selecting the person with the best-written resume over all others.

3. Writing can be a rewarding activity. Whether people write journals, fiction, letters to the editor, or e-mails to friends, they often derive enjoyment and a sense of accomplishment from their writing.

4. There are not many jobs today that don't require some writing, particularly those that require at the least a four-year college degree or a two-year degree or certification. Report writing, self-evaluations, memos, e-mail communications, work-site improvement suggestions, questionnaires, inventory assessments, research write-ups, grant requests, letters to customers, suppliers, or clients, in-house studies, analysis of competitors, and marketing studies are commonplace writing tasks across the job market.

5. The age of electronic mail has put an added emphasis and value on writing. With the ease of e-mailing, more written communication is occurring today than ever, both personal and business. Never in recent times has the ability to write effectively been more useful or important.

6. Writing is often the most effective mode of communication, and in many instances, the best means to an end. People use writing for many purposes: to inquire into a health insurance billing; to request copies of college transcripts; to rally supporters for a peace demonstration; to convince trustees not to raise tuition; to provide experiences and work attributes to a potential employer. The written word is a powerful tool for which people find many uses.

7. Writing well builds self-confidence. Writers who are confident in their ability welcome educational and professional situations where writing is required. They are more apt to take courses that involve writing and to consider professions where writing skills are an asset. As writers improve their skills, they find more and more doors that open to them.

8. Writing well leads to college success. Good writers are at a great advantage in the classroom, often performing well in the many courses across the curriculum that require writing.

9. Good writing and sound thinking go together. Though some people can get by verbally with more style than substance, writers have only the quality of their thoughts and their ability to express them to rely upon. When an illogical thought sits on the page, no stylish flourishes can hide it from discerning readers. With writing, weak thinking is most easily exposed and sound thinking most highly valued. Writing also helps to develop sound thinking as writers learn to support their ideas convincingly, dissect an unsound argument, and organize and express their thoughts effectively.

Writing Process

As you write your first paper, you will be using a writing process that is similar for most writers and that involves *prewriting, drafting, revising,* and *editing* steps. While all writers don't follow

Our lives are made up of thousands of experiences, most of which we forget over time. However, some experiences remain etched in our minds, forever memorable due to the impact they made on our lives.

Such experiences are a valuable part of our backgrounds, often shaping the way that we think and feel about life. For writers, life experiences are a rich source for writing, one that you will tap for your writing assignment in this unit.

Experiences can have a powerful effect on us for different reasons. They may be painful, thrilling, disappointing, fulfilling, frightening, or amusing, or trigger a range of different emotions. They may affect us in ways that we are very aware of and in other more subtle ways. Analyzing the impact of a particular experience is a valuable part of the writing process.

Writing about a personal experience, called narrative writing, is your first writing assignment for several reasons. First, since you have a number of experiences to draw from, finding a topic should not be too difficult. Second, since you will select an experience that you remember well, you can draw on your recall of the experience to write the paper. Third, you will write about the experience chronologically, in the time order that it occurred, one of the most natural organizations fora paper. Fourth, writing about a personal experience allows you to tell, or narrate, a "true" story in a vivid, interesting way, and to analyze the impact that it had on you. Finally, narrative writing provides readers with an interesting story, a glimpse into the life of the writer, and an experience that they may relate to or learn from.

The papers that you write during the course will be for a reading audience, frequently your own classmates, along with your instructor. One writing consideration will be the impact that your writing may have on others: what they may find interesting, what they may learn, how they may react or respond, or how they may relate. As a writer, you share your thoughts with readers in ways that may affect their own lives.

Why Write?

Writing texts often launch into writing activities without answering a question that is on some students' minds: why write? While the value of effective writing may be evident to some students, it isn't to all, and some may say, "I'm not going to write much beyond school, so why should I waste my time now? Writing has little to do with my future." Such concerns certainly deserve a response, and there are good reasons for all students, and for people in general, to develop their writing skills. Here are a few you may or may not have considered:

1. Being able to write well is one mark of an educated person. All students should leave college with the writing skills to communicate effectively. If students don't develop these skills in college, they may always struggle with their writing.

2. For better or worse, other people judge us by the way that we write. Employers, for

the same process, and may combine and configure parts of the process in individual ways, there are enough similarities about how people write to conclude that writing, at its best, is a process-oriented task.

The writing assignment for each unit will be divided into different parts beginning with pre-writing activities and followed by writing a first draft, revising and improving the draft, proofreading and editing the draft to eliminate errors, and writing the final paper. In each unit, you will be introduced to new writing considerations based on the writing task at hand, but the process itself will be duplicated and become a natural part of how you write.

The text also assumes that you have had other writing experiences both in school and out. The process approach in the text may be similar to your current writing practices, or it may extend or alter what you are doing. In the end, you may take what is most useful from the process approach in the text, combine it with what already works for you, and create a most effective writing process. If you have done little writing in the past, or have not used a process approach, the text will provide you with a writing process that will serve you well for most writing that you may do.

4

Prewriting

In each prewriting section, you prepare to write the first draft of your paper by selecting a topic to write on and giving some thought to what you may want to include in your paper. In the prewriting sections of the text, you will use a variety of prewriting strategies that you will find useful for different writing tasks.

Writing Assignment 1

The title of this text, *Writings from Life,* indicates the kind of writing you will do for the course: papers that are based on your experiences, interests, beliefs, and opinions. You are writing about aspects of your life, and the world around you, that you find important and significant. This first writing assignment begins your exploration.

You will select a particular experience that you remember well and that has had an impact on you. As you recall memorable experiences, consider those that you remember best and that have most affected you. Through such experiences, you may have experienced a variety of emotions: excitement, joy, shock, anger, sadness, disappointment, regret, satisfaction, relief, shame, or a mixture of feelings. You will write about one particular experience that stands out and analyze its impact on you.

Focusing Your Topic

As you consider possible experiences to write about, focus on specific experiences that you could relate in detail in an essay. Think of single events or occurrences that stand out in your life as being particularly memorable.

For example, during the 7th grade, a student had attended a summer music camp held at a nearby college. She considered the week of experiences that she had – meeting new people, staying overnight in the dorms, practicing and playing with older students – and hit upon one experience that stuck in her mind. As a seventh grader, she had to play the clarinet in a trio with a more experienced high school and college student at the end-of-week recital for relatives and friends. It was a terrifying experience for her and one that didn't end up at all as she had expected. She chose this specific experience to write about.

To narrow your writing focus to a specific experience, ask yourself questions such as these:

A bad football season (What was a particular experience that stands out?)

A wonderful vacation (What was the most memorable single experience?)

A lousy job (What specific experience reveals how bad the job was?)

Senior night at Disneyworld (What specific occurrence best reflects your experience?)

The student who had gone through a bad football season ended up writing about this specific experience:

As defensive end, I was running downfield to cover a punt return and concentrating on the guy who was receiving the punt. All of a sudden I felt something hit me on the helmet. It was the football. Maybe the only people that weren't laughing were me and the coach. I didn't want to return to the sidelines.

As you consider different experiences to write about, narrow your potential topics down from the general to the specific, focusing your essay on a single event or experience.

Free Writing

Free writing is a prewriting activity that helps writers decide what experience to write about, what they may want to write about the experience, and how much they may remember about it. When you free write, you write whatever comes to your mind without concern for order, logic, or correctness. Free writing allows you to put your thoughts on paper without being judged on your writing, and you take from your free writing whatever might help you write your paper.

Prewriting Activity 1.1

Write freely for ten minutes or so on three or four different experiences that you remember well and that made an impact on your life. You may write about experiences from any time in your life. Write without hesitation or concern for what you are putting on paper. From your free writing, you may decide on a topic for your first paper and create some material that you will use in your first draft.

Sample free writing:
#1

When I was in grade school, my mom came home one afternoon and said my sister was in the hospital. She had had some seizures which had hurt her brain. I didn't know what a seizure was or what to expect when Emily came home. I was shocked when I finally saw her. This wasn't the sister I had known. My fun-loving, talkative sister had been replaced by someone who couldn't talk or even walk. She had to have therapy to regain her normal abilities, and I kept waiting for my real sister to come back to life. Unfortunately, that never happened, and I went through a terrible time of being lonely, angry, and frightened. Eventually I grew to realize that the sister in front of me was the only sister I would ever have. As a young child, all I could do was selfishly think of the effects of Emily's condition on me. Later I came to realize that the real tragedy had befallen Em.

#2

In elementary school I was never one of the best students in the class. If I got B's and C's on my report card I was doing well. We had four awards assemblies a year and all the students who had received the best grades or read the most books or got student of the quarter for their class got to go up on the stage and get their awards. I never got to go up and felt kind of lousy along with all of the rest of us who never got an award. Then one assembly in the fourth grade I got a real shock. I was sitting as always through all of the awards and all of the students streaming up to the stage and I was daydreaming. All of a sudden the girl sitting next to me elbowed me and said, "Maggie, go up there. They called your name." Everyone around me was looking at me and smiling, and someone said, "You're student of the quarter!" I don't remember walking up or receiving my award or anything, but it was the proudest day of my school life.

#3

When I was a senior in high school I got pregnant and had a hard decision to make. I didn't want to get married and neither did the father, and I wanted to go to college. I didn't feel I was ready to raise a baby. I thought about an abortion or adoption. My parents weren't against an abortion, and that seemed like the easiest way out. However, the thought of killing my unborn baby was too strong and I couldn't do it. As the months went by and I felt my baby growing inside and then felt it kicking, I began to realize that I wanted this baby, that it was a part of me. I made the decision to keep the baby, and it didn't ruin my life. It was the best decision I could make.

#4

When I was a young child, my cousin had a little electric car that he rode on top of. It was a little car, but it would go almost five miles an hour. Riding up and down in front of his house, he made it look easy, so I wanted to try. My uncle showed me how to use the hand throttle and break and warned me not to turn the hand throttle hard because the car would jump forward and go up on its back tires. I got on and slowly moved forward. I went down the street a ways, turned around, and then went back by my uncle the other way. I started to turn around again to come back, and somehow I turned the throttle handle hard. The car jumped forward and I slid off the back. Trouble was, I held onto the handle bars, so I was dragging on the street behind the moving car. It stopped when it hit the curb, and my uncle ran over. I was in shock and crying, and my legs and stomach were burning. I ended up with some good road burns and more pain than I'd ever experienced. To this day I remember that accident clearly and the days that followed in the doctor's office and the long nights when I couldn't sleep. I learned a painful lesson.

Prewriting Activity 1.2

Take some time to reflect on your free writing and also on other experiences that you may have not included. In the end, select an experience to write about following these suggestions.

1. Choose an experience that you want to write about and that you remember clearly.

2. Choose an experience that readers -your classmates -may find interesting or get something out of.

3. Choose an experience that had a powerful effect on your life, or that may still affect you.

Prewriting Activity 1.3

After you have decided upon a particular experience to write about, spend some time thinking about the impact of that experience on your life. Consider what you may have learned from it, how it may have changed you or your life circumstances, what you may have learned about yourself or other people, or how it may have changed your way of thinking about someone or something. Then write freely for a few minutes about the impact the experience has had on you, and include anything that comes to your mind.

Sample Freewriting
From #1

Emily's sickness changed my life forever. I had lost the sister I had always known, my talkative, fun-loving best friend. A loneliness remains with me today for that lost sister. But I came to understand that what happened to Em wasn't her fault and that she had suffered the greatest tragedy, not me. Because of Em, I grew less self-centered, I learned to love more deeply, and I discovered that helping others had its own rewards. I'm a better person because of my sister, and I treasure the time that we have together. I hope that she is in my life for a long time.

From #2

Getting student of the quarter didn't dramatically change my life, but it made me feel better about myself and lifted my spirits about going to school. It also made me appreciate my friends at school who were happy for me. It made me realize that although I wasn't one of the best students in class, there was more to being successful than just getting the best grades. I had gotten student of the month, I think, for being a good girl in class, for respecting my classmates, and for trying my best. If I couldn't be the best student, there were things I could continue doing to be successful, and I tried to make that effort.

From #3

I learned some things about myself, like I'm a stronger person than I thought I was. Going through pregnancy and staying in school was tough, but I finished up in continuation school the last semester and graduated. I also knew that the baby's father and I didn't have a future together and that I'd be raising the baby on my own, with my mom's help. That's something I've been able to do, and I love my daughter and try to be the best mom I can. You also find out who your real friends are when you get in a tough situation. I had some friends who never judged me and were there for me whenever I needed them. They really helped me get through my pregnancy. Finally, I realized what a great mom I have, although I already knew that but the way she's helped me is more than I could ask for. Thanks to her I'm able to attend college while she takes care of my baby. She also said I always have a place to stay with them as long as I need to, which may be quite a while. She's been a second mom to my baby, and I know she will always be a big part of my daughter's life.

From #4

The pain I think is what I remember the most. I knew as a young child that I didn't want to experience that kind of pain again. I was afraid to ride any kind of a motorized car or bike or scooter after that, and I still am. I realized as I got a little older that it only takes one bad fall to really mess you up, and you never know when that's going to happen. So I've been pretty cautious because of that experience, and I still am today. It took me longer than most kids to learn to ride a bike, and I never got good on a skateboard or a scooter, probably because I was so cautious and anxious about falling. I realized that an accident like that, even at an early age, can stay with you for a long time, maybe a lifetime. I know it will also affect how I raise my own children if I have any. I know I'm not going to let them do anything like I did with that car. I also know that when they do ride a bike or something, they're going to wear helmets and pads and long pants, all the things I didn't have on when I took my spill. I can still remember the feeling of getting dragged along the street behind that car and it was like I wasn't able to let go of the handles. That was one scary experience for a six year old.

First Drafts

After you have completed your prewriting work, you are ready to write the first draft of your paper. This draft is the first version of your paper, the first time you put the complete experience into words. It will be followed by a second revised draft, and other subsequent drafts may follow until you are satisfied with the finished product. Writing drafts is a part of the writing process for most writers, and the writing usually improves with each draft.

Why do writers write drafts of a paper? Writing is a complex task, and seldom can any writer create a final, polished paper in one writing. The complexities of writing include choosing the best words to express your thoughts, organizing your thoughts in the most effective manner, including the best details and examples to develop your thoughts, adding new ideas as you write that you hadn't previously considered, assessing the impact of your writing on readers, and making sure that your paper is free of spelling, punctuation, or grammar errors.

Even the most experienced writers can't accomplish everything they want in a single writing. The drafting process is the natural way that many people improve their writing. Writers create drafts because that is how they write best. We have learned that through years of research that analyzed how people write, including effective student writers.

Of course, writing drafts without understanding how to improve them from one draft to the next is rather a waste of time. During this course, you will be provided specific revision guidelines to help you change and improve your drafts. Revision is a critical part of the writing process, and it leads ultimately to the best paper you can write.

First Draft Guidelines

As you begin writing the first draft of your paper, keep the following in mind.

1. The purpose of your first draft is to get the experience on paper as clearly as you recall it. Don't worry about how you word your sentences or whether you make an occasional error.

    Writing is a recursive activity, where writers continually go back and reread what they have written in a previous sentence or sentences to help them decide what to write next. Rereading sentences is not a waste of time; it provides you the momentum to continue writing and to make sure your next sentence follows logically from the previous ones.

2. Providing some background information is helpful to prepare readers for the experience lying ahead. You might include your age at the time and describe where the experience took place and what occurred leading up to it.

3. As you write, you are leading to the heart of the experience: whatever happened that made the impact on your life. Try to bring the experience to life for readers by describing it in detail.

4. The experience no doubt was an emotional one. Include your feelings and thoughts during the experience as you recall them so that readers can sense what you went through.

5. You might include some dialogue in your draft if what you said, or what others said, is an important part of the experience. If you or someone else is speaking in your draft, insert quotation marks (" ") before and after the spoken words, and identify the speaker: "I'll

never trust you again to borrow my car," I told my brother. (See how the writer uses and punctuates dialogue in the sample draft "Emily" in Drafting Activity 1.4.)

6. Conclude the draft with what happened as a result of the experience, and your analysis of why the experience was so memorable: the impact it had on your life.

7. Write your draft in paragraphs, changing paragraphs as you move to something new in your paper: a different time, a different place, a different aspect of the experience.

8. Your reading audience for this paper is your classmates, and of course, your instructor. Keep them in mind as you write.

9. Title your draft in a simple manner that indicates what it is about.

Drafting Activity 1.4
Write the first draft of your paper following the guidelines presented. You may first want to read the following sample draft.

Sample First Draft: Emily
When I returned home from 3rd grade one afternoon, I was greeted with the news that my younger sister was sick and in the hospital. I could tell by my mother's looks that she was concerned, and she said I would be staying with granda some evenings while she was at the hospital. I asked if I could go and see Emily at the hospital, and mom said, "Not right now, honey. But you can see her in a few days."

For the next days it was very lonely in the house without my sister, who was my best friend and playmate. My mom was somber most of the time, and I would hear her talking with grandma in low voices. In bits and pieces I learned that my sister had had a high fever and had a seizure, in fact several of them. Mom said that the doctors were helping Emily and controlling the seizures, but that her brain had been hurt. I didn't really understand what any of it meant except that it seemed serious and I became very worried. "Emily may not seem like her old self for awhile," mom warned me. "It will take her time to recover."

I learned much later, when I was old enough to understand, that Emily was a victim of status epilepticus, a relatively rare condition resulting in multiple seizures which can severely impair the brain. She would have seizures on and off for the rest of her life, the frequency and severity controlled by medication, but it was that initial series of seizures that she had as a six-year old that caused the damage. Apparently no one knows what causes the condition or why one child in thirty thousand is afflicted. We will never know why it happened to Emily.

When Emily finally came home from the hospital, I was shocked by her condition although mom had tried to prepare me. Em just lay in bed, a blank stare on her face that I had never seen. She couldn't talk or walk, and she didn't even seem to recognize me. Mom said because of Emily's illness, she would have to relearn much of what her brain sickness had erased: being able to talk, walk, and recognize people. A therapist from the hospital started coming to the house three days a week to help Emily with her recovery.

Very slowly, Em began to recover some motor skills, first sitting up, then standing, then taking a few halting steps. She also began making noises although they didn't form into words. Her eyes began to focus better and when she looked at me, I could see some recognition in her eyes. She also began to smile sometimes and with mom or me helping her, walk slowly around her room. Mom was encouraged by the progress she was making, hoping that every day would bring more improvement.

I however was hoping for a miracle. Every day I woke up I would hope that I'd walk into Em's room and my real sister would be there, the fun, active, loving sister I knew. I missed that sister so much and sometimes I would become angry at that "imposter" who had taken my real sister from me. I also resented that mom's life now seemed to revolve around Emily and that I was never the center of her attention. As a self-absorbed child, all I could think of was how Em's illness had affected my life and how lonely I was without Em to play with and talk to. I was also fearful that what happened to Emily could happen to me, and I was sometimes afraid to go to sleep at night, worried that I might wake up like Emily.

After months and then years, it became apparent that Emily was never going to be the person she had been. My mom, the doctors, the therapists, and the special needs teachers did everything possible to bring Em to her highest developmental level, but there was just too much permanent brain damage for her to recover greatly. She could walk in her shuffling gate and seemed to enjoy walking from room to room around the house. She never talked but made noises which made it clear when she was happy and when she wasn't, but she had a good temperament. She had a good appetite and enjoyed eating. She also grew to know her family again, and was always happy to see me when I came home from school. Thankfully, my mom said that Em knew nothing of her previous life or what she had been like before her illness. The only life she knew was the one she now lived, so thankfully, her great loss was much more painful to our family than to her.

As I grew older, I learned to accept my sister as she was. I always carried a sadness for the sister that I had lost and for the normal life that was taken away from her. It was truly a great tragedy, and at some point I knew that it was important to help make Em's life as happy as it could be. Sometimes I would feel guilty at relative gatherings when I was having fun playing with the cousins and Em would be curled up on the sofa staring out the window, but mom assured me that Em's situation didn't mean that I shouldn't enjoy my life and have fun. "I don't want you to live your life for Emily, honey," she said. "Emily would want you to have the best life possible, and so do I."

My life with Emily grew into a routine. I would come home from school and she would be happy to see me. She'd often take my hand and we would walk around the house for a while. Then we would sit on the sofa, and often she would put her head on my shoulder and stroke my hand. With all of the abilities that her illness had taken away from her, she had not lost perhaps the greatest: the ability to love. "I love you Em," I would tell her every day, and the words came from my heart. She never had to say a word to show her love.

Our family's life changed dramatically eleven years ago when Em became sick. It's been hard at times on everyone as we've all changed our routines and given up something of our more active lives to care for my sister. And the fact that Emily will never have a normal life weighs on all of us at times. Seeing her sitting on the sofa cuddling her baby doll can bring tears to my eyes, thinking what her life might have been like. But I've learned that dwelling on such thoughts doesn't help anything.

We don't know how long we will have Emily with us, as someone in her condition may not live long into adulthood. There was a time when I spent time with Em more out of a sort of free-floating guilt, a feeling that I somehow bore some blame for Em's condition. I also had moments when I wondered, "Why her and not me," and felt the guilt of being the "normal" person that my sister couldn't be. Today, however, I spend time with Em out of love, a love that has grown more deeply as I have gotten older and want to appreciate every moment that I have with her.

While there is little that I do for Em but spend time with her, there is a lot that she has done for me. I am no longer the self-absorbed person who was mainly concerned with how anything that happened affected me and my happiness. Through my relationship with my sister, I have grown more patient, more caring, and more loving. I don't always have to be doing for myself to find happiness or contentment. I may also have found my professional calling in life: working with people with disabilities, perhaps as a therapist or speech pathologist. Because of Em, I'd like to think that I've become a better person.

Revision

Now that you have written your first draft, you are ready to take a look at it to see what you might improve. In each unit, you are given some specific guidelines for revising your drafts, based on the type of writing you are doing and the revision emphases for that unit. As you work through the text, you will develop a mental checklist that will help you revise any writing you may do.

The purpose of revision is simple: to make a paper better. Improving a draft seldom means a major overhaul of what you've written. Instead, it might include adding a detail here or an example there to develop a thought, rewording some sentences to make them clearer or smoother, dividing an overly long paragraph into two, moving a particular sentence to a more effective location, or strengthening the opening or conclusion of the paper to make a greater impact on readers.

In this first "Revision" section, you will concentrate on three particular areas: providing description, improving your wording, and paragraphing your paper. These considerations are common to all writers, and you will focus on them throughout the course.

Providing Description

In a paper relating an experience, writers often describe the sights, action, people, and feelings involved to heighten the readers' interest and understanding. This does not mean bogging the paper down in a minutia of details but rather using vivid description to capture the essence of the experience and help the reader visualize what happened.

The following suggestions will help you provide effective description as you revise your paper.

1. Use details to describe the setting for readers and help them see and hear what is happening during the experience.

    From a sample first draft:

    We gathered at my house to decide how to handle the situation. We made a lot of noise and caught my dad's attention.

    Revised first draft:

    My four high school friends and I gathered in my small bedroom to decide whether to tell the coach about our drinking before he found out himself. We yelled a lot because we were all scared and couldn't agree, and soon my dad stood in the doorway shouting, "What's going on in here?"

2. Use details to describe your thoughts and feelings as the experience occurred.

    From sample first draft:

    In a ceremony at city hall, I was given a medal by the chief of police for helping pull a child out of a canal. I put the medal in a drawer.

14

Revised first draft:

In a ceremony on the steps of city hall, I was given a medal by the chief of police for helping pull a child out of a shallow, dirt-banked canal. I didn't feel like a hero because I just jumped in the water without thinking, and I knew I wasn't risking my life. I was embarrassed when anyone called me a hero, and I put the medal in a drawer and never looked at it again.

3. Use details to describe something or someone when that description is important to understanding the experience.

From sample first draft:

I had never been in a fight in my life, but as I sized up Maria, I felt she knew how to fight.

Revised first draft:

I had never been in a fight in my life, but as I sized up Maria, her face contorted in an angry mask, her muscled legs taut and ready to spring, I knew I was in for trouble.

4. In general, use details to describe anything that will help bring your experience to life for readers.

From sample first draft:

Henry was too busy to notice that his son had climbed onto the roof and was making motions with his arms.

Revised first draft:

His head stuck under the hood of his '68 Chevy, Henry was too occupied to notice that his eight-year old son had climbed atop the tin shed roof and was flapping his arms like he was going to fly off.

Revision Activity 1.5

Read the following first draft paragraph. With a classmate, note places in the draft where you would recommend that the writer add a particular detail to improve the paragraph. Be prepared to discuss your suggestions with the class.

I'll never forget my quinceanera party. My court of friends looked wonderful, and I wore a white gown that made me feel like a princess. Our back yard was turned into a wonderland, and lanterns flickered in the trees like fireflies. For one night, I was the center of attention, which embarrassed me but also made me feel special. I'll never forget dancing with my father, the changing of the shoes, or the delicious food. It was all like a dream, and the look on my mother's face said everything.

Revision Activity 1.6

Read your first draft looking for places where you might include some detail to help readers see, hear, and feel what you went through. If you are revising on a computer, add the details into the draft. If you are revising a written draft, write in the details above the lines where you want to add them.

When you finish, share drafts with a classmate, or a small group of classmates, and make suggestions if there are places in your classmate's draft where some added description would help you visualize or better understand the experience.

Paragraphing

As you probably know, most writing is divided into paragraphs to make it easier for readers to follow the writer's thoughts. As writers move from one idea, example, place, or time to another, they frequently change paragraphs to indicate to readers that something has concluded and something new is beginning.

Paragraphing is not an exact science, and there is no absolute right or wrong way to paragraph a paper. Paragraphing is effective when it moves readers smoothly through a writer's thoughts, and the best paragraphing is so natural that it is hardly noticeable.

Paragraphing Guidelines

The following guidelines will help you paragraph your papers effectively.

1. As a general definition, a paragraph is a group of related sentences focusing on one idea, point, example, or thought.

2. You change paragraphs as you move to something new in your paper: a different idea, a new example, a different part of an experience, a different time or place.

3. You change paragraphs to avoid overly long paragraphs that readers can get bogged down in, ending a paragraph at a natural break in your thoughts.

4. If you find yourself writing series of short paragraphs -two or three sentences each -you need either to combine the paragraphs or to develop them further.

5. Effective paragraphing is not that difficult. When you read a draft and concentrate on its paragraphing, you can often see where a long paragraph can be divided into two or where some short, related paragraphs can be combined. If you remind yourself to change paragraphs as you conclude one thought and move to another, you will paragraph your papers effectively.

16

Revision Activity 1.7

With a partner, analyze the paragraphing of the following paper. Discuss the content of each paragraph, and decide why the writer changes paragraphs when she does. Then paragraph the next two papers by marking off the beginning of each new paragraph.

Almost Like Flying

There was one special day in the 8th grade when I almost felt like I could fly. It was the best day of high jumping I ever experienced, and to this day I still remember the feeling.

I had been high jumping since grade school, and I was always pretty good at it. I never had any coaching, so I just learned how to jump by doing it. I was so involved in high jumping that the summer after my 6th grade year my dad bought a big foam pad and built a high jump pit in our back yard. I practiced a lot at home the next couple years.

In the 8th grade we had a regular track team that competed against other schools. I was not the best high jumper in the area but usually got around 3rd place in the district track meets. I would jump close to 5 feet and occasionally cleared 5 feet or 5 feet 1 inch. There were a couple of boys from other schools that could regularly jump over 5 feet, and sometimes up to 5 feet 2 or 5 feet 3, and that motivated me to want to jump higher.

One afternoon I was at school practicing in the high jump pit, which was located in a large dirt area north of the school's track. I was doing my regular routine, starting at the lower heights and working my way up. I wasn't having any trouble with the lower heights and I felt a good spring in my legs that day, so I was hopeful I'd have some good jumps.

I kept raising the bar higher and continued to leap over it without a problem. A couple of my teammates had come over to the high jump area to watch me and raise the bar as I'd clear a new height. Soon the bar was raised to 5 feet, which was always a great challenge for me. However, on this day it wasn't a problem. I leaped over the bar with room to spare, and it had never felt so easy. It was a great feeling.

Soon the coach had wandered over and a few more teammates as they saw me jumping. The bar had been raised to 5 feet 2 inches, and the coach measured it with his tape measure just to make sure that it was correct. I'd never jumped 5 feet 2 inches in my life, but as I stood about 40 feet from the bar, ready to make my approach, my confidence had never been higher. I took my normal run, pushed off my right leg, and sailed over the bar without touching it. My teammates let out a whoop and my coach was all smiles. It was the best feeling I had ever had in sports.

Amazing to me, I still wasn't finished that day, and ended up clearing 5 feet 4 inches, which was a new school record. It didn't count as a record, however, because you had to do it at a track meet. However, that didn't matter to me. Nothing could dampen my spirits after having jumped higher than I could have ever imagined.

I never jumped as high or felt as light and springy as I did on that day. It was just one unbelievable day in my life when, for some reason, I was a different high jumper. I'll never forget that day, the way it felt to soar over the bars and have my teammates and coach cheer me on. On one warm spring day, I had done something special.

The Big Scare

I remember I was six years old, in kindergarten, and living in Hanford the day my brother scared the heck out of me. It was such a big scare that I've never forgotten it, and my brother laughs about it to this day. It wasn't funny at the time, and I hated my brother for it. My brother was two years older, and we were alone at our house for a couple hours while my parents went shopping on a Saturday morning. I had a pretty lively imagination back then, and it didn't take a whole lot to scare me. I always slept with a light on, and the slightest sound could send me out of my bed and down the hall to my parents' room. My brother knew I was a bit of a scaredy cat, and with my parents gone, he had the perfect opportunity to scare me. I had to go bathroom that morning, so I went into our one bathroom, closed the door, and sat on the toilet. It didn't take long before my brother ran to the bathroom door, opened it, and screamed, "There's a lion in the house. Run for your life!" And he ran for his life, leaving me sitting on the toilet. As a six year old in a moment of panic, I didn't think for a second about the illogic of a lion being in our house or the possibility of my brother trying to scare me. All I knew was that there was a lion in the house and it was probably coming to eat me. I jumped off the toilet seat, pants around my ankles, and ran out of the bathroom, down the hall, and towards the back door, falling every few steps as my pants tripped my ankles. Finally I made it to the back door, knowing the lion must be only a few steps behind me, opened the door and ran out, immediately falling down the back steps onto the yard. Then I heard my brother's howling laugh as he saw me lying on the ground, pants around my ankles, naked bottom in the air, toilet paper still stuck you know where. I knew in an instant that my brother had made it all up to scare me as he had done many times before. He was a little devil and I hated him at that moment, but all I could do was lie on the ground and cry. Even at the young age of six, the humiliation of being tricked, of falling down the steps, and of lying half naked on the ground was too much to take. I wailed like I had been stung by a hive of bees. Eventually my parents came home, and I couldn't wait to tell on my brother. He got punished good, but I knew it was never enough to keep him from doing it again. Tormenting me was one of his greatest pleasures. Today I can see the humor others get out of picturing me running out of the bathroom bare butted, toilet paper flying, falling every few steps, but at the time the feeling was pure terror. To this day when I go into the bathroom, my brother will occasionally say, "Watch out for the lion," the old tormenter's grin on his face. I still don't find it funny.

An Important Lesson

In high school when I was a senior, my friends wanted to punish a girl because she had taken my friend's boyfriend from her. My friend Eva was in love with the guy, and they had plans to get married and have a big family. She was always talking about how happy she was going to be when she became the wife of the man she loved. One shocking phone call from Emmanuel destroyed that dream forever. One Sunday Eva called me crying, telling me that Emmanuel had broken up with her and was with another girl. The girl was from another town and Eva didn't even know her. She said that she didn't want to live without him, that he was everything to her. For days, she was devastated. She did not eat or talk to anyone; all she did was cry. I felt awful for her. What could we do to help her? I thought. Perhaps taking her out to a dance to try and have some fun would help. Eva, however, was in no mood to cooperate. Instead, she wanted revenge on the girl that had taken the only man she loved. That scared me because all of our friends agreed with her that revenge was justified, except for me. However, I didn't want to tell them that I wouldn't go along with their plans. I didn't want to let my friends down because they would think I was betraying them. Besides, I didn't know what kind of revenge Eva was talking about, perhaps just telling the other girl that Emmanuel still loved Eva or sending the girl an anonymous card saying that Emmanuel was cheating on her. When I heard them say that they should kill the girl so Emmanuel would return to Eva, it left me numb. Oh my God, I thought. Is Eva really capable of doing something like that to someone that had done her no personal harm? Are my friends so crazy that they would even consider killing the girl and not consider the consequences? There is no way I am going to go along with them, I thought, and I told them so. I backed out, and I wanted nothing to do with the problem. The next day Eva called and informed me that she had bought the gun to kill Emmanuel's new girl friend. I tried to talk to her and tell her that what she was doing was wrong, but there was no way of talking her out of it. This was not the person I had grown up with. It was liked she had been possessed by an evil spirit. I decided I couldn't let my friend ruin her life forever, so I called Emmanuel and told him what Eva was planning on doing. At first he thought I was joking, but I convinced him otherwise. He called the police, and the police conducted an investigation, including talking to Eva and all of her friends and confirming that Eva had bought a gun. She ended up going to jail for six months for plotting a potential murder. Eva has not seen me or spoken to me since I called Emmanuel. That bothers me because we were best friends, but at least she is out of jail and won't spend the rest of her life in prison for killing someone. Eva may thank me someday for what I have done for her. Thank God that I did not go along with her plan. What would have become of my life? The last thing I heard was that her family moved out of the area. I hope and pray that Eva learned that an obsession for somebody else can destroy your life. I believe that when a person doesn't love you, you just have to let go, as hard as that may be. If Emmanuel didn't love Eva anymore, I wondered, why did she even want to be with him? I also learned to trust my own instincts and not go along with my friends if I know they are wrong. What I did was hard for me, but it was the right thing to do. I have a clear conscience, and I hope that someday I'll see my friend again.

Revision Activity 1.8

Check the paragraphing in your paper. If you did no paragraphing, paragraph your paper similarly to how you paragraphed the sample papers, changing paragraphs as you moved to something new in your draft. If you paragraphed your paper, see what changes might be made to improve your paragraphing, including dividing overly long paragraphs or combining two or more short paragraphs. Share papers with a classmate and evaluate each other's paragraphing based on how smoothly it moved you through the writer's thoughts.

Improving Sentence Wording

In a first draft, you word your thoughts as they come to you the first time. As with most writers, your thoughts don't always translate into written words as smoothly or clearly as you would like. Among your first draft sentences, you will usually find some that are wordy - overly long to make your point - and others that are a little awkward, not quite sounding the way you want. Sentence revision is a task shared by all writers, and the first draft of a sentence is often a beginning point for crafting a really good sentence.

For example, let's say a writer wants to express her feelings about global warming and our government's lack of action in addressing the situation and starts out with a sentence like this:

The effects of global warming throughout the world can be disastrous, including the flooding of cities and millions of people displaced and homeless, and our government is doing nothing to solve the problem but in fact is adding to the problem by ignoring it.

The sentence contains a lot of good information, but it is also rather long and unwieldy. A revision of the sentence might read something like this:

Global warming can have disastrous effects throughout the world, such as flooded cities and millions of people losing their homes, and our government just adds to the problem by ignoring it.

The revised sentence is clearly more readable and less wordy, and no meaning has been lost. This final revision may improve the sentence further:

Flooded cities and millions of homeless people are just two of the disastrous effects that global warming can wreak on the world, and our government makes matter worse by doing nothing.

Whether you favor the last sentence or the previous one is a matter of choice, with each about the same length and providing similar information with a different emphasis. Clearly, there is more than one way to revise and improve any sentence.

Sentence Wording Guidelines

The following suggestions will help you revise and improve your first draft sentences.

1. First draft sentences often contain more words than necessary. Ideally, every word in a sentence is needed to complete the thought. Look for sentences that appear overly wordy or that repeat the same words or phrases, and see what can be eliminated or reworded.

    Example:

    The current below the ocean's surface, which is called an undertow, is flowing outward, and it is dangerous because it makes it difficult for a swimmer to get back to the shore.

    Revised:

    An undertow, a current flowing outward below the ocean's surface, is dangerous because a swimmer must struggle against it to get back to shore.

2. Sentences that seem awkward to you will probably have the same effect on readers. Revising an awkward sentence often requires moving words or phrases around, eliminating

unnecessary words, and replacing questionable words with better choices.
Example:

The mother cat behind the washing machine hid her kittens, which was in the garage.

Revised:

The mother cat hid her kittens behind the washing machine in the garage.

3. Finding the best word to express a particular thought, feeling, or action is challenging for any writer. As you revise, replace any word that doesn't clearly convey your ideas with a more appropriate one.

    Example:

    Gretchen felt downtrodden by the bad behavior of her best friend.

    Revised:

    Gretchen was badly hurt by the cruel behavior of her best friend.

4. Some first draft sentences are rather vague, leaving readers in doubt as to what the writer meant. Such sentences need to be revised, sometimes dramatically, to clarify their meaning.

    Example:

    For positive reinforcement to work, you must factor in the child's positive reinforcement history and any over-reliance thereon.

    Revised:

    If a child is constantly praised for even the smallest accomplishment, positive reinforcement becomes meaningless.

5. Some first draft sentences may contain slang - informal words that are more suitable for conversation. Replace slang words and phrases - *cool, neat, hang out, hassle, dude* - with more appropriate ones.

    Example:

    I give that dude his props for always sticking by his friends.
    Revised:

    I respect Frank for being loyal to his friends.

Revision Activity 1.9

Revise the following first-draft sentences to make them clearer, smoother, and more concise by eliminating unnecessary words, replacing awkward wording, moving words or phrases around, and improving word choice. Try out different wording options until you are satisfied with the wording of each sentence.

Example:

First draft: The moon was rounder and brighter and bigger last night than I had ever seen it.

Revised: Last night's moon was round, bigger, and brighter than ever.

1. The parking lot was full and overflowing with cars for the Beyonce concert at the SaveMart Center, so cars that were still coming in were directed to a large, huge dirt area south of the parking lot for the SaveMart Center to park.

2. The crowd inside of the SaveMart center was filled with all ages of people from young children with their parents to teenagers to young adults to older people all coming to see Beyonce.

3. Long lines of people inside of the Savemart Center were lined up at the souvenir booths to purchase all kinds of things with Beyonce's name or picture on them like t-shirts, sweat shorts, coffee mugs, and posters.

4. The crowd, which were watching the warm-up group before Beyonce, grew restless waiting for Beyonce to come out, which took over an hour from the time the warm-up group began singing.

5. Many of the adults in the crowd were sipping on daiquiris, which cost $15.00, which is a ridiculous price for a daiquiri, but they were big enough to last the entire concert to the end of it.

6. When Beyonce finally came out onto the stage of the SaveMart Center, the crowd jumped to their feet and erupted in cheers and shouts and whistling that lasted for at least a good two minutes.

7. When Beyonce performed her faster songs, which happened quite often, most of the crowd would dance at their seats and seemed to obviously be having a great time.

8. Looking around the SaveMart Center arena, it looked like there were thousands of fireflies twinkling brightly around the Savemart Center arena, and these fireflies were actually the flash of cellphone cameras going off all the time.

   _____

   _____

9. When Beyonce launched into one of her hit songs which she sang like "Single Ladies," most of the ladies in the crowd, and especially the ladies that were a bit younger, sang along so that you could still hear Beyonce but you could also hear the singing crowd of ladies around you.

   _____

   _____

10. Beyonce went through about ten costume changes at the least, and it was always fun to see which costume she would wear as she came back on the stage from changing costumes.

    _____

    _____

    _____

Revision Activity 1.10

Read your first draft, looking for sentences whose wording can be improved. Eliminate unnecessary words, reword awkward phrases, replace questionable word choices, and clarify vague sentences. Read the sample draft in Revision Activity 1.11 to see how the writer revised her sentences.

Revision Activity 1.11

Write the second draft of your paper, including all improvements you made in description, sentence wording, and paragraphing. In addition, if you discover other things to change or add to improve the draft, feel free to do so. Then exchange second drafts with a classmate. Read each other's draft to see if there is anything you don't understand or if you have questions that the draft leaves unanswered. Give suggestions to your classmate, and based on your classmate's input, revise your draft further if you feel it can be improved, incorporating all changes into your second draft.

Revision excerpts from sample first draft "Emily:" *(deletions lined out; additions in bold)*

When Emily finally came home from the hospital, I was shocked by her condition although mom had tried to prepare me. ~~Em~~ **She** just lay in bed~~, a blank stare on her face that I had never seen~~ **staring blankly at the ceiling.** She couldn't talk or walk. ~~and~~ **Most heartbreaking to me,** she didn't even seem to recognize me. Mom said because of Emily's ~~illness~~ **brain damage**, she would have to relearn ~~much of what her brain sickness had erased~~ **what she had lost:** being able to talk, walk, recognize people, **and take care of herself.** A **physical** therapist from the hospital started ~~to come~~ **coming** to the house three days a week to help Emily with her recovery. **I just waited for my "real" sister to return.**
(Note: Revisions were made to provide clearer description, to improve sentence wording, to add information, and to share the writer's feelings.)

Very slowly, Em began to recover some motor skills, first sitting up, then standing, then talking a few halting steps **with help**. She also began making noises **like she was trying to talk,** ~~although~~ **but** they didn't form into words. Her eyes began to focus better, and when she looked at me, I ~~could see some recognition in her eyes~~ **believed that she recognized me.** She also began to smile ~~sometimes~~ occasionally, **which brought me moments of joy,** and with mom or me ~~helping her~~ **steadying her balance,** walk slowly around the room. Mom was encouraged by ~~the~~ **her** progress ~~she was making~~, hoping that every day would bring more improvement.
(Note: Revisions were made to add detail, improve sentence wording, add the writer's feelings, and providing more accurate description.)

Editing

The final step in completing your paper is to proofread it for errors and correct any that you find. This is the editing phase of the writing process, where you eliminate all errors from your paper, and it comes at the end of the writing process after you have made your changes in content and wording. The goal of the editing phase is to produce a polished, error-free final draft.

Of course, if you have been running the spelling check on your computer as you wrote, you may have few spelling errors. In addition, although the emphasis in the writing process has not been on correcting errors, if you found a flagrant error in spelling, punctuation or grammar usage earlier, you may have already corrected it.

The editing phase, however, is the first time you will systematically scrutinize your paper for errors, looking for the types of errors that are most frequently found in writing. When you proofread your paper -scouring it thoroughly for errors -few will escape your detection.

In each "Editing" section, you focus on different kinds of error correction, covering the most typical errors that writers make. By the end of the text, you will have covered most errors that frequently appear in writing and learned to detect and correct them if they appear in your own writing. In this section, you work on eliminating run-on sentences and on using correct irregular verb forms.

Correcting Run-on Sentences

A common error that writers make is running two sentences together rather than separating them with a period. Writers often run two relatively short sentences together whose content is related.

Readers can have problems with run-on sentences. They have expectations that a sentence will end with a period, and they rely on those periods to help move them from one thought to another. Run-on sentences can confuse readers, distracting them from the writer's ideas.

When run-on sentences are brought to most writers' attention, they can see where the period belongs to end the first sentence and make the correction. Run-on sentences are a solvable problem, one that most writers can eliminate from their papers once they are made aware of them.

Guidelines for Correcting Run-on Sentences

The following guidelines will help you avoid run-on sentences in your writing.

1. A sentence is a group of words expressing a complete thought. The end of a sentence is designated by an end mark, most frequently a period.

    Example: The best place to park on campus in the late morning is behind the library.

2. A run-on sentence most frequently involves two sentences run together as a single sentence without a period ending the first sentence. A run-on sentence is an incorrect sentence form that needs editing.

    Example: The best place to park on campus in the late morning is behind the library I frequently park there between ten and eleven.

Corrected: The best place to park on campus in the late morning is behind the library. I frequently park there between ten and eleven.

3. One form of a run-on sentence, called a *comma splice*, has a comma between the two sentences rather than a period. A comma splice is not a correct sentence form and needs to be edited.

Example: The grass in the meadow was dry and brown, it hadn't rained all summer.

Corrected: The grass in the meadow was dry and brown. It hadn't rained all summer.

4. Anytime you find a run-on sentence or a comma splice in your writing, you need to correct it. To correct a run-on or comma splice, you can do one of two things:

   a. Separate the sentences by ending the first sentence with a period and beginning the second sentence with a capital letter.

   Example: Joanna excels in track and field and plays stringed instruments, her brother Theo has the same interests.

   Corrected: Joanna excels in track and field and plays stringed instruments. Her brother Theo has the same interests.

   b. Combine the two sentences that are run together with a joining word such as *and, but,* or *because* to form one complete sentence.

   Example: I enjoyed the Beyonce concert very much, Maria thought it lasted too long.

   Corrected: I enjoyed the Beyonce concert very much, but Maria thought it lasted too long.

   c. As a general rule, separate longer run-on sentences with a period and combine shorter ones with a joining word.

   Example: Alyssa had one complaint about working in a store that sold incense she couldn't get the smell out of her hair.

   Corrected: Alyssa had one complaint about working in a store that sold incense. She couldn't get the smell out of her hair.

   Example: Harold liked working as a security officer, he drove a new car around all day.

   Corrected: Harold liked working as a security officer because he drove a new car round all day.

Editing Activity 1.12

Identify and correct any run-on or comma-splice sentences. Separate longer sentences with a period and connect shorter sentences with a joining word.

Example: Global warming is raising the sea level in all major oceans on the planet there is a serious risk of coastal towns and farmlands being permanently flooded within the next two decades.

Corrected: Global warming is raising the sea level in all major oceans on the planet. There is a serious risk of coastal towns and farmlands being permanently flooded within the next two decades.

1. Global warming is caused by industrial and automotive emissions that remain in the atmosphere, these gases trap the sun's heat, gradually raising temperatures.

2. Melting glaciers are one indication of global warming radical weather patterns are another.

3. Some politicians deny that man-made global warming exists despite much scientific evidence to the contrary, they have frequently blocked legislation to reduce emissions.

4. Farmers are beginning to see the effects of global warming drought conditions are more prevalent, and the warmer weather ripens crops earlier than usual.

5. Many scientists attribute milder winters to global warming, such winters have an impact on both agriculture and winter resort areas.

6. Man has been emitting carbon dioxide into the atmosphere since the Industrial Revolution as a consequence, the planet has warmed more in the past two-hundred years than in the previous fifty-thousand years.

7. It will take a world-wide effort to reduce global warming the U.S. needs to take a leading role.

8. The earth's ozone layer is being replenished successfully due to a sharp reduction in the emission of ozone-destroying hydrocarbons through legislation a similarly aggressive approach must be taken if we are to turn the global warming situation around.

Editing Activity 1.13

The following paragraphs contain some run-on sentences and comma splices. Correct these sentences by separating longer sentences and combining shorter sentences.

Example: The overflow from the river had left large puddles of water along the river bank that turned stagnant the puddles became prime breeding grounds for mosquitoes. Families living around the river attended meetings of the county board of supervisors to alert them to the problem.

Corrected: The overflow from the river had left large puddles of water along the river bank that turned stagnant. The puddles became prime breeding grounds for mosquitoes. Families living around the river attended meetings of the county board of supervisors to alert them to the problem.

Casual Dress

Over the years, the way that Americans dress has become more casual and informal. A good example was the way that people were dressed at my grandfather's church last Sunday I went with him as I was visiting for the weekend. As always, my grandfather dressed in a coat and tie as he has done all his life. However, he was the only person at the church in a tie, only a few were wearing coats. The majority of men wore colorful short-sleeved shirts not tucked in. Quite a few wore shorts instead of long pants, there were also a number in sandals. Although I didn't see many men in t-shirts, I wouldn't be surprised to see more in the future. While the women appeared to be dressed somewhat better than the men, most of them wore pants instead of dresses.

The minister obviously embraced the casual dress, his outfit included khaki pants, an open-necked shirt, and loafers. You couldn't distinguish him from the churchgoers until he stood before us. The casual dress also contributed to the loose, laid-back atmosphere inside the church and the relaxed, informal church service that took place. This was very different from the church my grandfather grew up in, where everything was very formal and solemn, he hasn't completely adjusted to the change. He also has no intention of removing his coat and tie to fit in.

Editing Activity 1.14

Proofread your latest draft for any run-on sentences or comma splices, and correct any you find by inserting periods or combining sentences with joining words. Then exchange papers with a classmate and proofread each other's drafts for run-ons and comma splices.

Irregular Verbs

Since you wrote your paper about a past experience, you no doubt wrote in the past tense, the verb tense used to write about things that have already occurred. While most writers have little trouble with the regular past tense verbs, which uniformly end in ed (e.g. walked, talked, climbed, baked), there are a group of verbs called irregular verbs that follow no rules and form their past tenses in different ways (e.g. slept, drank, driven, won).

Irregular verb forms give writers some problems since they don't follow a single pattern and must be committed to memory. Many irregular verbs also have two different past tense forms: one for the simple past tense, and one for the past participle, a form which includes a helping verb before the main verb (e.g. had drunk, have driven, has eaten, have swum).

Irregular Verb List

The following list of irregular verbs includes the most commonly used and misspelled verbs. The verbs are grouped by similarities in their spelling in the past tense and past participle forms.

The following verbs have the same form for the past tense and past participle:

Present Tense	Past Tense	Past Participle
bring	brought	brought
build	built	built
burst	burst	burst
catch	caught	caught
cut	cut	cut
find	found	found
has	had	had
lay (place down)	laid	laid
lead	led	led
quit	quit	quit
read	read	read
set	set	set
sit	sat	sat
think	thought	thought

The past participle of the following verbs ends in "en:"

choose	chose	chosen
drive	drove	driven
eat	ate	eaten
fall	fell	fallen
get	got	gotten
give	gave	given
ride	rode	ridden
rise	rose	risen

Present Tense	Past Tense	Past Participle
speak	spoke	spoken
take	took	taken
write	wrote	written

From the past tense to the past participle, one vowel changes from a to o or from a to u in the following verbs.

become	became	become
come	came	come
begin	began	begun
drink	drank	drunk
ring	rang	rung
run	ran	run
shrink	shrank	shrunk
sing	sang	sung
swim	swam	swum

For the following verbs, the past tense ends in ew and the past participle ends in own, with the exception of drawn.

blow	blew	blown
draw	drew	drawn
fly	flew	flown
grown	grew	grown
know	knew	known
throw	threw	thrown

The following commonly used irregular verbs follow no particular pattern.

do	did	done
go	went	gone
see	saw	seen
lie (lie down)	lay	lain

Past Tense and Past Participle

The following distinctions between the past tense and past participle verb forms will help you use and spell them correctly.

1. The past tense verb form is used to write about an action that occurred or a condition that existed in the past. It is not preceded by a helping verb.

   Examples: Yesterday I *wrote* an e-mail to my cousin.
   Last Friday *was* the hottest day of the summer.

2. The past participle verb form is used to write about an action that occurred or a condition that existed over a period of time, and that may continue in the present and the future. The past participle verb form is always preceded by a helping verb such as *has, have,* or *had.*

   Examples: I *have written* an e-mail to my cousin every week this month.
   Julie *has taken* care of her invalid aunt for several weeks.
   Miles *had grown* tomatoes on his apartment balcony every summer.

3. Whether you use the past tense or past participle depends what you are expressing in a particular sentence. For example, note the distinction in meaning between the three following sentences.

   Yesterday I *drove* to school for the first time in a month.
   I *have driven* to school more than I *have ridden* my bike this semester.
   I *had driven* to school every Friday until my roommate started giving me rides.

The first sentence uses the past tense verb *drove,* and indicates an action that occurred in the past. The second sentence uses the past participle verb *driven* with the present tense helping verb *has,* and indicates an action that occurred over a period of time and may continue into the future. The third sentence uses the past participle verb *driven* with the past tense helping verb *had,* and indicates an action that occurred over a period of time but no longer occurs. As you can see, past tense and past participle verb forms carry different meanings, and writers use them in different situations.

Editing Activity 1.15

Fill in the blanks in the following sentences with appropriate irregular verbs from the list. All of the sentences require *past tense* or *past participle* verbs forms; do not use the *present tense* verbs. Remember to use the past participle verb form when the blank is preceded by a helping verb (*has, had, have*).

Example: No one has <u>driven</u> as many miles to school this semester as you have.

1. I have _____ great care not to tear my new disposable contact lenses.

2. No American has _____ the English Channel in the last twenty years.

3. A flock of geese have _____ over our apartment every day this month.

4. The concert _____ with a tribute band playing Jimmy Hendrix' music.

5. I have _____ to doubt your interest in sharing an apartment with him.

6. Mona had _____ to work with her brother until his car broke down.

7. Home prices had _____ more in 2005 than at any time in the past twenty years.

8. My T shirt _____ two sizes when I washed it in hot water.

9. Homer's young daughter gleefully _____ into the room.

10. I hadn't _____ too far into my calculus homework until I realized that I had no idea what I was doing.

11. The enrollment of new students has _____ very smoothly since the college established its on-line enrollment site.

12. I _____ your doorbell several times before you heard me.

13. Have you _____ everything possible to get the cheapest airplane tickets?

14. Rudy hadn't _____ a solo before an audience since junior high.

15. No one has _____ more letters to her state senator than Alma.

16. I should have _____ that it would be impossible to find a parking space around the ferry building.

17. You _____ a very difficult major, but you are certainly up to the challenge.

18. Franklin hasn't _____ in a restaurant for over a year.

19. We _____ the horses down the rocky trail rather than try to ride them.

20. I _____ your sweater back that I borrowed last week.

21. Have you _____ any thought to subletting your back room?

22. Gretchen _____ the musical Hairspray in four different cities.

23. I have never _____ so many squirrels in one area of Central Park.

24. Juliette had _____ down for a nap this morning, but by late afternoon, she was already drowsy.

_____

Editing Activity 1.16

Proofread your latest draft for errors involving irregular verbs and make the necessary corrections. Then run a final spell check on your paper and proofread your paper carefully for spelling errors and make corrections. Finally, exchange papers with a classmate and give them a final proofreading for errors.

Editing Activity 1.17

Write the final corrected draft of your paper to share with classmates.

Applying the Writing Process

Now that you have written a personal experience paper following the step-by-step process in the unit, you are ready to apply what you have learned to writing a second paper more independently. The purpose of this second writing assignment is to give you more writing practice, an opportunity to write on a second life experience, and a chance to work through the writing process on your own.

Writing Assignment 2

Select a second experience to write about that you remember well. Select a very different experience from your first topic, one that made a different kind of impact, evoked different emotions, and occurred at a different stage in your life.

Working independently, follow a similar writing process that you used to develop your first paper:

> Select a personal experience to write about.
> Do some free writing on your topic.
> Write a first draft.
> Revise the draft by focusing on descriptive detail, sentence wording, paragraphing, and overall effectiveness.
> Edit the draft by correcting any errors that you find.
> Write the final paper.

Before revising, share first drafts with a classmate or two, and ask each other questions about anything that seems unclear in the draft or that you'd like to know more about. Consider your classmates' input as you revise your paper.

Readings

In the Face of Adversity
by Nelson Mandela

One night, toward the end of May, a warder came to my cell and ordered me to pack my things. I asked him why, but he did not answer. In less than ten minutes, I was escorted down to the reception office where I found three other political prisoners: Tefu, John Gaetsewe, and Aaron Molete. Colonel Aucamp curtly informed us that we were being transferred. Where? Tefu asked. Someplace very beautiful, Aucamp said. Where? said Tefu. "*De Eiland,*" said Aucamp. The island. There was only one. Robben Island.

The four of us were shackled together and put in a windowless van that contained only a sanitary bucket. We drove all night to Cape Town, and arrived at the city's docks in the late afternoon. It is not an easy or pleasant task for men shackled together to use a sanitary bucket in a moving van.

The docks at Cape Town were swarming with armed police and nervous plainclothes officials. We had to stand, still chained, in the hold of the old wooden ferry, which was difficult as the ship rocked in the swells off the coast. A small porthole above was the only source of light and air. The porthole served another purpose as well: the warders enjoyed urinating on us from above. It was still light when we were led on deck and we saw the island for the first time. Green and beautiful, it looked at first more like a resort than a prison.

The island takes its name for the Dutch word for seal, hundreds of which once cavorted in the icy currents that wash the island's shores. It became a prison in the early 1800's and later was turned into a leper colony, a lunatic asylum, and a naval base. The government had only recently turned the island back into a prison.

We were met by a group of burly white warders shouting: "*Dis die eiland. Hier gaan julle vrek!*" (This is the island. Here you will die.) Ahead of us was a compound flanked by a number of guard houses. Armed guards lined the path to the compound. It was extremely tense. A tall, red-faced warder yelled at us: "*Hier is ek jou baas!* (Here I am your boss!) He was one of the notorious Kleynhans brothers, known for their brutality to prisoners. The warders always spoke in Afrikaans. If you replied in English they would say, "*Ek verstaan nie daardie Kafferboetie se taal nie.*" (I don't understand that kaffir-lover's language.)

As we walked toward the prison, the guards shouted, "Two-two! Two-Two!" ---
meaning we should walk in pairs, two in front, two behind. I linked up with Tefu. The guards started screaming "*Haas! Haas!*" The word *hass* means to move in Afrikaans, but it is customarily reserved for cattle.

The warders were demanding that we jog, and I turned to Tefu and under my breath said that we must set an example; if we gave in now we would be at their mercy. Tefu nodded his head in agreement. We had to show them that we were not everyday criminals but political prisoners being punished for our beliefs.

I motioned to Tefu that we two should walk in front, and we took the lead. Once in front, we actually decreased the pace, walking slowly and deliberately. The guards were incredulous. "Listen," Kleynhans said, "this is not Johannesburg, this is not Pretoria, this is Robben Island, and we will tolerate no insubordination here. "*Haas! Haas!*" But we continued at our stately pace. Kleynhans ordered us to halt, and stood in front of us. "Look man, we will kill you, we are not fooling around, your wives and children and mothers and fathers will never know what happened to you. This is the last warning. *Haas! Haas!*"

To this I said, "You have your duty and we have ours." I was determined that we would not give in, and we did not, for we were already at the cells. We were ushered into a rectangular stone building and taken to a large, open room. The floor was covered with water a few inches deep. The guards yelled, "*Trek uit! Trek uit!*" (Undress! Undress!) As we removed each item of clothing, the guards would grab it, search it quickly, and then throw it in the water. Jacket off, searched, thrown in the water. Then the guards commanded us to get dressed, by which they meant for us to put on our soaking clothes.

Two officers entered the room. The less senior of the two was a captain whose name was Gericke. From the start, I could see that he was intent on manhandling us. The captain pointed to Aaron Molete, the youngest of the four of us and a very mild and gentle person, and said, "Why is your hair so long?" Aaron said nothing. The captain shouted, "I'm talking to you. Why is your hair so long? It is against regulations. Your hair should have been cut. Why is it long . . ." and then he paused and turned to me, and said ". . . like this boy's!" I began to speak, "Now, look here, the length of our hair is determined by the regulations . . ."

Before I could finish, he shouted in disbelief, "Never talk to me that way, boy!" and began to advance. I was frightened; it is not a pleasant sensation to know that someone is about to hit you and you are unable to defend yourself.

When he was just a few feet from me, I said, as firmly as I could, "If you so much as lay a hand on me, I will take you to the highest court in the land and when I finish with you, you will be as poor as a church mouse." The moment I began speaking he paused, and by the end of my speech, he was staring at me in astonishment. I was a bit surprised myself. I had been afraid, and spoke not from courage, but out of a kind of bravado. At such times, one must put up a bold front despite what one feels inside.

"Where's your ticket?" he asked, and I handed it to him. "What's your name?" he said. I nodded to the ticket and said, "It's written there." He said, "How long are you in for?" I said again, gesturing at the ticket, "It is written there." He looked down and said, "Five years! You are in for five years and you are so arrogant? Do you know what it means to serve five years?" I said, "That is my business. I am ready to serve five years but I am not prepared to be bullied. You must act within the law."

No one had informed him who we were, or that we were political prisoners, or that I was a lawyer. I had not noticed it myself, but the other officer, a tall, quiet man, had vanished during our confrontation. I later discovered that he was Colonel Steyn, the commanding officer of Robben Island. The captain then left, much quieter than he had entered.

Questions for Discussion
1. Although Mandela wasn't told why he was being transferred to Robben Island prison, why do you think he and the other political prisoners were transferred there? What was the South African government's intent?

2. Why did Mandela refuse to abide by the warder's order to jog? Why do you think the warder did nothing about Mandela's disobedience other than to threaten?

38

3.   Why do you think Mandela's strong verbal responses to the captain kept him from taking any physical action? Why do you think Colonel Steyn, the commanding officer at Robben Island, vanished from the room during Mandela's confrontation with the captain?

4.   Mandela showed great courage in the face of life-threatening situations despite his fear. Discuss situations where you or others you know have had to overcome fear and show courage.

Escape
by Park Ji Woo

I was born in North Ham-Gyong province, North Korea, which is located in the far northeast of the country. It is extremely cold in winter. When the North Korean food distribution system collapsed in the early 1990s, my father, who was a doctor and the breadwinner for my family, couldn't bring us food anymore. Like other North Koreans, my parents had no idea how to get food when they stopped being paid at their jobs. They sold the family's furniture, television, and radio, but we still didn't have enough money for food and clothes.

My younger sister and I were always hungry, particularly in the winter. Since there was no food on the farms during winter, the price of food was unbelievably high. It goes without saying, my parents had no money to buy warm winter coats and shoes for us. My younger sister and I wore a pair of cotton, rubber-soled shoes during the winter that were not warm and got wet easily after being out in the snow. Our feet were always frozen and my mother forbid us from riding sleds, but we insisted on going outside to enjoy the snow. As a result, we suffered from frostbitten feet and hands.

One day, my sister and I had so much fun riding the sled that I didn't realize my shoes fell off. I looked for them for a long time, but I couldn't find them. I was frightened because I knew my mother would be really mad at me. I walked home on bare feet in the snow. When my mother saw me, she said nothing and just wiped my feet because my left heel was bleeding. She put my feet into a container with cold water. That was a well-known remedy for frostbite in North Korea because it made your feet warm up fast even though it was really painful. I screamed as the cold water became red with my blood. My mother cried. The next day, she gave me her winter shoes and she wore her flats, which were thin shoes meant for the summer. She didn't have money to buy new winter shoes for me. That winter, her feet were frostbitten, too.

By the summer of 1996, the famine was even worse than expected. The government still didn't give us any food. I vividly remember that many people died in the street because of hunger. I saw many children who were my age begging for food in Jang-ma-dang (North Korean Market), even stealing food. We only had one meal a day for three months. Even my 6-year-old younger sister, the youngest person in my family, wasn't spared starvation.

One morning, somebody knocked on our door quietly when my younger sister and I were eating our only meal of the day. I thought that it was my mother, who had gone to the farm to look for food. I opened the door happily, but there stood a short, skinny girl. She looked about 8 years old, same as me. She had a pale and frightened face. Behind her, a little boy was smiling at me. He looked about five years old and had a red, dirty face. They wore ragged clothes. The girl finally said, "Would you please lend us some food? We haven't had anything to eat since two days ago. My parents went to Cheng-jin to get food and said they would be back in 3 days, but they haven't come back yet. When they come back, we will have food to eat and I can give you back your food. I swear."

I looked at her earnest face and said, "I am hungry, too. I have no food to give you." I closed the door coldly and locked it quickly. Even though the girl kept knocking on the door desperately for a while, we ate all the corn porridge, which was all we had for the whole day. Now I feel sorry for them. Sometimes it makes me cry. I don't know where they went and if anyone gave them food. However, at that time, sharing food was a crazy behavior for me and for most North Koreans because everyone knew that one day we would die in the street of hunger if we didn't save as much food as we could. We had to compete for getting one more ear of corn. Sympathy was an extravagance for us.

On top of the hunger, my father contracted typhoid from his patients in the hospital. My mother sold everything we had, even the linens that my grandmother hand made for her when she got married. They were not only wedding gifts, but also an expression of a mother's love for her daughter. My father was hospitalized for 3 weeks, where he regained his health speedily. But after his hospitalization, he was a changed man. He often yelled at my mother and complained about the food. My mother tried to endure all his anger and complaints. She usually skipped her one meal a day because she wanted to save more money to buy meat for my father. Like most North Korean women, she made great sacrifices for her husband and family. I asked her why father was always angry about everything. She said hunger and poverty made my father more sensitive and aggressive.

Despite all the effort that my mother put in, she and my father decided to divorce. That day was my 9th birthday. I woke up earlier than usual and I saw my mother was packing her things. My father told me I should stay with him and younger sister would live with my mother. My mother said, "We decided to live separately and I will live in your aunt's house. You can come visit and see your sister and mom any time." I didn't know what to say. It was my birthday. How could my parents tell me they were going to get a divorce instead of saying "Happy birthday" to me? At that moment, I hated both of them. I thought they were brutal.

One evening in late December, 1998, my mother came to my house and told me she was going to China to restart her life. She said if I wanted to go with her, she would take me to China. She also told me my father had made the difficult decision to allow her to take me to China and that he would raise my younger sister instead. I was only 9 years old. All I knew about China was that it was a rich place full of delicious food and warm clothes. I was not old enough to know what it meant to escape from North Korea. I happily said "Yes" without any hesitation. I would go anywhere to be with my mother. My father cried a lot but said nothing.

I left the apartment that I had lived in since I was 5. I turned my head slowly and looked up at the window to our apartment. My father stood there in tears. My mother told my younger sister that she was going to my grandmother's house and she would come back tomorrow. With a smile on her face, my sweet, trusting younger sister said "Bye-bye, mommy and older sister." My mother kissed her forehead and said nothing, like my father did to me.

At midnight, my mother and I walked to the border. It took us almost 5 hours. The night was cold and my feet were freezing. I asked to stop and rest at times but she said that we must keep going. I didn't realize the danger that we were in if we were caught. As we walked, our bodies were hidden by the forest close to the Tumen River.

Suddenly, a soldier was running toward us and waving his hands. My mother said, "Run as fast as you can!" I didn't know what was happening. I just ran like crazy. When my mother finally stopped running, I realized that the river had frozen over and there was no one following us. My mother told me we had already crossed the border into China.

I asked her who the soldier was. "I gave him money to guide us to China. I promised him we would be back in two days. I lied to him. We will never go back to our country. Do you understand?" she said quietly but firmly. I didn't understand what she was saying and told her that it seemed like I could go back home whenever I wanted to because North Korea and China were so close. But mother said "No, we can't," so seriously that it made me terribly sad. I realized at that moment that I may never see my sister or father again. That thought haunted my dreams for a long time.

I stared at the frozen river. My home, North Korea, was already behind us. What lay ahead of us I couldn't imagine. I gripped my mother's hand tightly as we walked towards the light of morning.

Questions for Discussion

1. What details does the author provide to show the effects of the famine on her life?

2. What conditions led to the disintegration of her family? Why do you think her mother took the drastic step of leaving for China?

3. In what ways did being so young – nine years old – protect the author from the realities of what was happening? Discuss any traumatic events in your earlier years that had a profound effect on your life.

Living with the Mystery of Headache
by Sallie Tisdale

My headache began on a Monday afternoon around three o'clock. The pain centered on my left temple and eye, constant, gnawing, broken only by sudden waves of sharper pain. My doctor was on vacation, but after several days I decided I couldn't wait and took the next available appointment. By the time I made it to her office I could hardly walk across the room in a straight line.

The physician's assistant was attentive, working down the neurological checklist: reflexes, balance, gait, grip strength, and cranial-nerve function, which affects swallowing, eye movement, sensation, facial expression, and more. Everything was normal, except for the pain. Finally, with a grunt of satisfaction, she decided that I must be dehydrated. I knew that I was dehydrated because I couldn't eat, and that I couldn't eat because I had a headache that would not stop. By then the headache had so eroded my ability to think that I didn't even comment; I just waited in a darkened room while she wrote a prescription for Vicodin.

When my doctor returned a week later, she was also attentive, and took her time: reflexes, balance, gait, grip strength, cranial-nerve function. The Vicodin had given me no relief. I was tremulous, ill defined. The feeling was hard to describe; my words failed, trailing off.

"I'm sure it's not migraine," she told me. Migraines rarely last more than a few days. "But I'm not sure what it is." Although severe headaches are only rarely a sign of something dire, like a ruptured aneurysm or a brain tumor, she recommended an MRI to be sure.

"There is a medication that sometimes works for headaches like these," she said, and suggested I try indomethacin, an anti-inflammatory drug in the same class as ibuprofen. Usually reserved for arthritis, it's a nasty medication, known for causing stomach ulcers and gastrointestinal bleeding, cardiac arrhythmia and heart failure. I started taking twenty-five milligrams twice a day — started as soon as the pharmacist handed me the bottle — along with a daily dose of omeprazole, an acid-reducing drug, to protect my gut. The pain retreated but didn't disappear. I complained in private but mostly I kept my headache to myself, shivering my way through conversations. I had work and a class to teach and my son was getting married in a month.

The indomethacin tamped down my constant pain, but every hour or so I had sudden tides of sharp pain that I began to call surges. They were always on the left side of my head above the eye and in the temple, with swells of tingling and electrical sensations. They made my eye squint and blink; sometimes my jaw ached, or I found myself leaning to the left in my chair.

Indomethacin is singularly diagnostic for an uncommon headache I had never heard of called hemicrania continua. The pain of hemicrania continua centers around the eye and forehead. (A number of people with HC experience "foreign body" syndrome, the sense that there is something in the eye.) HC may seem to wax and wane, but it never disappears; in fact it is layered: the moderate, relentless foundation, a kind of water torture of headache, overlaid with bursts of sharp, even blinding, pain. Many people with hemicrania (and "many" is the wrong word; it is rarely diagnosed, though some researchers think it is less rare than once believed) also have "migrainous" symptoms, like my occasional nausea and sensitivity to light.

How quickly I was willing to take on the risks of indomethacin! I felt dizzy, clumsy, weak, but whether this was the medication or the headache is hard to say. The continual pain faded into the background, turning into a kind of internal pressure, as though the headache were pushing on the inside of my head, trying to get out. The surges diminished in frequency, and then in intensity, but didn't cease. Beneath the business of preparing for my son's wedding, a monotone of dull pain; on top of the happiness and cheer, the faint perfume of indomethacin. After a few weeks, I found myself sinking to the bottom of Maslow's hierarchy of needs: in danger. One night my heart began to skitter and twitch; I lay in bed and hoped they wouldn't take my medicine away.

I didn't tell my doctor about my heart, but still she refused to increase my dose, instead referring me to Dr. N., a neurologist with a weeks-long waiting list. Together they decided to start me right away on a low dose of gabapentin, an anticonvulsant.

Almost immediately, my heart settled down. But that week of weaning myself off the indomethacin gave me a headache that seemed to fill the world. When I woke each morning, I couldn't think clearly. *What time is it?* I would wonder. *What's going on?* Eventually I would rise, going straight for the morning dose, then dip my head under the faucet before climbing into the shower, pulling on clothes, and careening into the kitchen to line my stomach for the pills. Within an hour of each dose, I'd feel better. I've never needed medication in this acutely timed way before; it seemed the first sign of a fatal erosion. I resented the needing of it.

I waited three weeks for the next appointment and went back to Dr. N., who was not smiling. "I've reached my limit on headaches," he told me. "I'm a general neurologist. If you had Parkinson's disease? Multiple sclerosis, epilepsy — that's what I do."

I had reached a point of feeling almost infinitely strange. I still had a headache all the time, though it was masked; I was depersonalized. Something almost like an aura ebbed and flowed away — the feeling of a crucial piece broken wild and loose, the cotter pin of control. After a particularly bad day, when my skin felt like fuzzy wool and I was afraid to drive and I couldn't get an appointment with anyone, I cut back on my medication; I had plenty now, and I had reached the point of prescribing for myself. Soon my thinking cleared up, but the surges renewed — pain, and a frisson of electricity around the eye, into the cheek, a vague tingle. I found myself getting used to it.

Dr. P.'s headache clinic was just off a busy freeway exit at the junction of two overgrown suburbs of Portland, a cheap second-story office with a few small rooms and cardboard boxes piled in one corner next to a few chairs near the secretary's desk.

First we talked: the entire history of the headache, my family medical history, the medications I'd taken, how I felt right then. When I tried to explain that I sometimes felt like I had a headache without actually having pain, she knew what I meant. She heard this a lot — that something feels wrong in the head in an uncertain way. All she does is headaches; the only patients she sees are patients like me, struggling to explain the way it feels inside our heads, stumbling over words because each thought is work. It was only after we had talked for forty-five minutes that she examined my reflexes, balance, gait, grip strength, cranial-nerve function.

Finally, she pressed on my shoulders for a moment and stepped back. "I'm quite sure this is hemicrania. The indomethacin didn't work perfectly because you couldn't take a high enough dose." She had seen it before. We discussed alternative drugs, one of which, topiramate, is known to cause memory and speech problems. She suggested lamotrigine, another anticonvulsant, instead, noting that I would have to increase the dose very slowly. Lamotrigine has interesting side effects — behavioral changes, nausea, double vision, and the rare Stevens–

44

Johnson syndrome, a widespread inflammatory reaction in which large sections of skin blister and slough off. Lamotrigine can also cause headaches.

I winced at her description. "How long do I need to take it?" "I hope I can talk you into a year," she answered. "Sometimes hemicrania just burns itself out. Sometimes it doesn't." The quiet paring of disease, the fraying at the edges of liver and heart, the vision slowly blurring, the cough that sticks around. Sometimes we can only rely on a kind of maladaptation. We get used to it.

I'm on a drug that is not benign; I've gained some weight, and my blood pressure has gone up a bit. I am still occasionally dizzy, and, for the first time in my life, I'm sensitive to the sun. Only months after I began taking lamotrigine did I suddenly remember that it is sometimes used for mood disorders; now and then I wonder how much of my sense of well-being is just the chemical. But it helps.

Reading my journal from the spring, I find it hard to accept my fragile handwriting, the daily recording of what felt like slow destruction. I don't have a headache most of the time now, and not having a headache is like being twenty years younger. I have energy and good cheer and I can hike and travel. I can write again, at last. Then the surge comes. I stop, hold my hand against my temple, cupping my eye. I stand still for a moment, feeling the pain scrape across the bone above my eye and fade. And then I forget again.

Questions for Discussion

1. How according to Tisdale does the pain of an excruciating headache differ from other physical pains? Does that differentiation make sense to you?

2. Based on Tidale's experiences with doctors and medications in seeking out help, how do you view the process of medical diagnosis and prescription? What is your experience?

3. Have you had personal experience or know of others who have experienced severe headaches? How is your experience different from or similar to Tisdale's?

Overcoming Abuse - My Story
by Shawna Platt

Where do I begin? I grew up in an environment of alcoholism. This environment was filled with physical abuse, emotional abuse, neglect, anxiety and most importantly….denial. We weren't allowed to discuss what went on in our home. It was to be swept under the rug, like the dirty little secret it was.

I can't count how many times we had to silently put the house back together while my dad slept it off on the couch. I guess it was simply easier to pretend it didn't happen. I guess not acknowledging it meant we didn't have to deal with it. But we did have to deal with it and not discussing it didn't make it go away…it allowed it to continue.

I could start with the emotional issues domestic violence causes. Or the anxiety and panic attacks. The issues of trust and constantly being guarded. Always looking over your shoulder, waiting for the next bomb to drop. The effort to accept and forgive…at least enough to move on and live a normal daily life. I could start with the importance of breaking the cycle so this doesn't move on to the next generation. Or the importance of releasing the anger and becoming a productive human being. These are all important topics that need to be addressed and I will try to include them all.

I could start with some of my own personal experiences. The constant physical fights. The yelling and screaming. The broken "things." Being picked up by the throat while my mom stood by and did nothing. Watching my mom get shoved through a kitchen window by the hair, pulled back through, and pushed out the door onto the porch. Then being told by my dad that if we tried to let her in, he'd shoot us.

I could talk about the small travel trailer that was pulled from place to place, sometimes with no running water and illegally wired electricity. Relocating was a constant. There was no need to feel secure, because in no time at all, we'd be on the move again.

I could discuss the countless times my parents left us with people we didn't even know, sneaking out when they thought we weren't aware. And there were times those people made it very clear that we were not wanted there. I could never understand how I could be placed somewhere I wasn't truly wanted. But it happened time and time again. I remember my brother and I spending some time on the porch because we weren't allowed to enter the house while the other kids got to have their bowl of ice cream.

I remember wearing the same clothes every day and let me tell you…other kids aren't afraid to remind you of it. I could also talk about the sexual abuse I endured from one of my dad's drunk friends when I was five years old. I could dwell on my mom's attitude of, "If I can't beat him, I'll join him" and how she spent her share of time on the bar stool beside him while we were left at home alone, probably because no one would take us for the night. And of course, there's my mom's denial and how, "My kids always came first."

I started taking care of my sister when she was a baby. I was ten years old and had no idea how to care for an infant. I recall the first time I was left alone with her. I stood out at the end of the driveway, looking up the street, begging them to come back. That was the day something shifted in me.

I became hard as survival issues kicked in. When my parents would conveniently find a different sitter for the night, I always seemed to run them off. I literally had babysitters walk out on me because I made their experience with us a living hell. Who did they think they were, coming into my home and telling me what to do, thinking they could take care of my baby sister better than I could? I've been handling things just fine, thank you very much. I certainly didn't need them. Over time, my mom told me since I kept running them off, I would just do it on my own. Like I hadn't been doing that already. My sister wouldn't respond to anyone but me anyway.

I was never shown how to change a diaper or make a bottle. I guess it was assumed I would figure it out. After all, they would only be gone "a couple of hours." What could possibly go wrong? But those couple hours always turned into a day-long event, usually extending into the early morning hours, which would end with them coming home in a fight. Do you realize how scary it is to a ten year old child to be left at home alone, with an infant, especially when it gets dark? We rarely had a phone, so I never had any way of checking in to see when they'd be home. I was forced to learn to deal with it.

These few examples I've shared are only the tip of the iceberg. The emotional issues from domestic abuse could fill a book. The programming that comes from living in an abusive household is devastating to the human mind. In order to survive, the mind has to adapt and it becomes programmed to work in a certain way. It remembers everything and protects against danger in ways we still don't understand. The human mind literally has the ability to protect itself and it does this by altering what we think, which affects the way we see things. When our programming changes the way we think, it also affects the way we feel because the mind and body are tightly connected. What affects one affects the other.

Emotional abuse is one of the hardest to overcome because of the programming done to the mind. You can reprogram the mind to think and operate in a different manner, but it takes time and a lot of hard, heavy and deep soul searching, which is hardly a walk in the park.

Anxiety and panic attacks are also experiences that come from abuse. In most cases, the attacks are chronic because the mind/body are used to working in a fight or flight mode. When the mind is trained to live this way, it will continue to do so, even when there is no reason for it. It simply doesn't know any different. I've been experiencing anxiety since I was five years old and it wasn't until a few years ago that I finally figured it out. I still get anxious from time to time, but I've learned to deal with attacks.

Growing up in an abusive environment made me hard, guarded and non-trusting. You'll never see me cry. It doesn't mean I don't…it just means you won't see it. I view life differently and I respond to it differently. I don't drink. How could I? Drinking is what caused my childhood to be the way it was. The thought of putting alcohol in my system makes me physically ill and brings on anxiety instantly.

I've had to overcome serious trust issues. How could I possibly believe what you tell me? You're not really going to be there for me, so I simply won't count on it. I've learned to survive and I can take care of myself. I've learned to accept certain things and I've learned to forgive. I've done this for ME. Not for my parents, not for the bullies I encountered, not for the other adults who treated me as less than the trash in their garbage…but for ME. For my own sanity and well-being. For my own piece of mind. I'm happy with the person I've become and I've become that person on my own.

I decided a long time ago that I would not remain a victim and I would not become a product of my environment. I decided I would forgive as much as I could. Does that mean the circumstances I encountered were justified? Not for a second! But where do I place blame? With my father, who didn't know how to stop? With my mother, who allowed it to happen? I feel they both should be held responsible. But I'm no longer a victim of their circumstance. Their life is theirs to live as they choose. I simply choose to move in a difference direction.

I decided the cycle stops with me. It will not be passed on to the next generation that I brought into this world. Which means my kids won't pass it on to theirs and nothing makes me happier! At least I can sleep at night knowing that.

Questions for Discussion

1. The author detailed her years of abuse as a child. What incidents stand out In your mind as the most destructive? How was the author able to survive the abuse?

2. Many abused children end up as abusers themselves as adults. How do you think the author was able to stop the "cycle" and raise her own children differently?

3. Discuss any childhood abuse that you or others you know have gone through. How has it affected your (or their) life, and how have you dealt with it?

Unit Two
Influences

Throughout our lives we encounter people who influence us in different ways: parents, grandparents, spouses, siblings, friends, teachers, coaches, co-workers, supervisors, clergy, and so on. Some times the influence is obvious and direct, and other times it is more subtle, affecting us in ways we may not fully understand until later in life.

Writers often write about people who have helped shape their lives, for better or for worse: a wonderful grandmother, an absent father, a caring teacher, a trouble-making friend, a special older brother, an impossible boss. In this unit you will write about one such person, someone who has made an indelible imprint on your life.

In writing this paper, you will bring a person to life for readers and reveal your relationship with him or her by providing examples that capture that relationship. You will also analyze and share with readers the influence this person has had on you and the impact that he or she has made in your life.

There are several purposes for this writing assignment. First, it allows you once again to draw on your own background and experiences to write your paper. Second, it provides you a different writing experience from Unit One. You are now focusing your writing on another person rather than yourself, and you are analyzing a relationship rather than a personal experience. Third, you employ a new type of writing development: using examples from life to help characterize your subject and show your relationship with him or her. This unit's writing assignment provides some new challenges that will add to your growth as a writer.

As in the first unit, you use the writing process in the text to prepare, write, and improve your drafts, beginning with prewriting activities and concluding with proofreading and editing. In each section you are also introduced to new elements of effective writing and review what was covered in the previous unit. The purpose of the regular review activities is to ingrain in your mind key elements of effective writing so that they become a natural part of your writing process.

Prewriting

During each "Prewriting" section, you prepare to write the first draft of your paper. Prewriting activities can help you accomplish a number of things: selecting a topic, developing some material for your draft, analyzing your thoughts and feelings about the topic, and deciding how you might organize your thoughts on paper.

Topic Selection

To help you decide on a person to write about, think about some of the people who have been important in your life: family members, friends, teachers, co-workers, supervisors, coaches, and so on. Keep in mind those people who have made the biggest impact on your life and that you would most like to write about.

The following examples of individuals that students have written about may give you some ideas of whom you might like to consider:

- The wrestling coach who made me believe in myself
- The person that raised me to be who I am today
- The one friend that I could always count on
- The bully that made my life miserable for two years
- The daughter that changed my life forever

Free Writing

As you did in Unit One, you will do some free writing to consider different people you might want to write about and develop some material for your paper. Free writing is a good way to recall memories about people, explore your feelings, and decide whom to write about.

Prewriting Activity 2.1

Free write for ten minutes on two or three people that have made an impact on your life. The purpose of the free writing is to help you decide on a topic, generate some material for your paper, and think about your relationships with different people.

Sample Free Writing
#1

I guess everyone has a teacher that they had a crush on when they were little. I still remember the name of my third grade teacher, Mrs. Sinclair. It may have been Miss Sinclair, I don't remember. She was pretty and young and had dark shiny hair. She wa slender and wasn't very tall, and I remember that she smiled a lot. She was nice to all the kids in the class, and she was nice to me all the time and I really liked her a lot. One time though I did something to upset her and I felt crushed. Kids were going to the front of the room one at a time to do something, recite a poem and make a short speech or tell what we did on the weekend or something. When it was my turn, rather than just get up and walk to the front of the room, I tried to be funny and make everyone laugh. Mostly I think I was trying to impress Mrs. Sinclair, but it didn't turn out that way. I'd walk half way to the front of the room then say something like, Oops, I forgot something, and run back to my seat and pretend to get a piece of paper. Then I'd walk back about half way and say Oops I forgot something, and ran back again. By now the kids were laughing and I was laughing and I figured Mrs. Sinclair must be laughing, but when I stopped to run back to my seat the third time, she said sternly, "Hector, stop that right now and get to the front of the class. I don't want any more clowning around from you." I was shocked and I could feel my face burning. My eyes were beginning to water and I fought back the tears. I went to the front of the class and meekly did whatever I was supposed to and then walked back, my head down. I felt humiliated and sick to my stomach and I didn't think Mrs. Sinclair liked me any more. I actually remember going home for the next few nights and having trouble sleeping because of what happened and how Mrs. Sinclair had jumped on me. So in school I tried extra hard to be good and win her over, and of course, all the big problems were just built up in my mind and she hadn't given it a second's thought. She was her nice self again and I didn't give her any trouble the rest of the year. I think I liked her even more after that incident and I remember liking her for the whole year. It was a real childhood crush.

#2

Growing up, my mother was the most important person in my life. I didn't think much about it at the time, but she did everything for me. She made me breakfast, she always had my clothes clean and laid out for me, she took naps with me in the afternoon, and she took care of me when I got sick. She was also always there to give me a hug or a good night kiss. When I had a problem, it was mom I always went to. One time I got in trouble with another kid in the neighborhood. She had a new doll and was showing it off to us kids, so I took it to look at it, and when she wasn't looking, I buried it in the dirt on the lot we were playing in. I just did it as a joke, but when I went back to dig it up, I couldn't find it. She was furious and I was in big trouble, so I ran home. Mom came back to the lot with me with a shovel and dug around until she uncovered the doll, and we returned it to her. That's the kind of mom she was. And I don't ever remember her getting mad at me, even when I did something like that. She was my hero, and as long as she was around, I always felt safe and loved. Every kid should grow up with a mom like mine.

#3

One person that comes to mind almost immediately was my dad's friend Bow Wow, who had an unpronounceable Polish name. He was a real character, a bigger-than-life type of guy who would bound into your life and then bound out again. He had all of this energy and enthusiasm and you couldn't help but like him. He was far from perfect, however, and he'd have these big dreams and launch into something but seldom finish anything. He was also someone who was full of surprises and you'd never know what to expect from him next. He was actually famous in his own way, or at least glommed onto some well-known people, but he was also a bit of a loser. It was that huge gap between what he projected and who he really was that was both fascinating and disturbing. I really never knew who the real Bow Wow was.

Prewriting Activity 2.2
Select a person to write about from your free writing or a different person that has come to mind. Select someone that you would like to write about, that you have clear memories of, and that has been influential in your life.

Clustering

Clustering, aka "branching" or "mapping," is a structured prewriting technique that helps you generate ideas for a particular topic and consider how those ideas are related. Beginning with a central topic, in this case the person you are writing about, you write a down a few general things that come to mind about this person - e.g. personality traits, characteristics, abilities, certain memories - and circle or draw a square around each idea. These initial ideas may trigger more specific thoughts related to each main idea. As you write down these thoughts, you create a clustering diagram, drawing lines to connect related ideas:

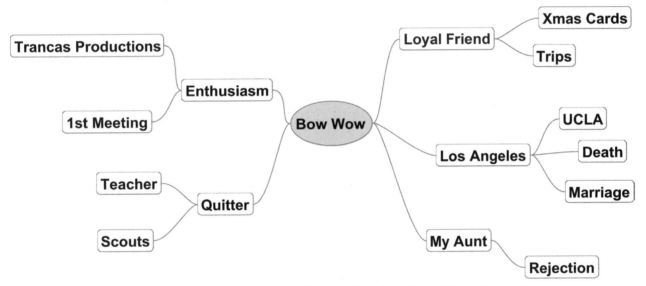

Notice that the writer began with five central ideas related to Bow Wow - loyal friend, my aunt, Los Angeles, quitter, and enthusiasm - and then added more specific thoughts for each central idea that would help develop it.

From your own clustering diagram you may generate some main ideas for your paper and some supporting ideas, examples, and details to develop your paragraphs. While clustering may not provide you with everything you eventually include in a paper, it will help you generate ideas and consider how you may organize and develop them.

Prewriting Activity 2.3
To generate ideas for your upcoming paper, create a clustering diagram for the person you are writing your paper on.

Sample clustering diagram:

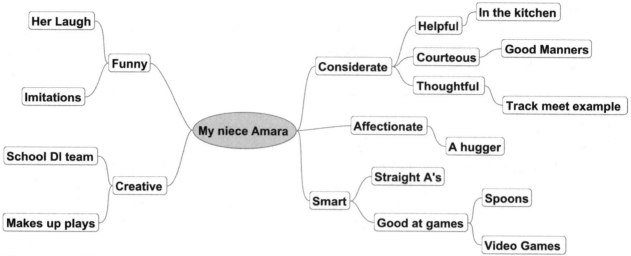

Clustering Diagram:

First Drafts

Now that you have selected a person to write on and done some free writing on your subject, you are ready to write the first draft of your paper. One of your challenges is to bring this person to life for readers, to make him or her distinct from anyone else. One way to do this is to provide examples from life that best characterize your subject, which is a focus for this paper.

Providing Examples

As you write your first draft, you will include qualities that your subject possesses and the relationship that you have with him or her. In both cases, the best way to help distinguish this person from others is to provide examples from life that set him or her apart. Providing examples helps to personalize your paper, creates interest for readers, and presents the clearest picture of your subject and your relationship with him or her.

For example, it is not uncommon for a student to write, "My grandma has always been there for me whenever I needed help." Of course, this statement could be written about many people and doesn't distinguish one grandma from others. By itself, the statement doesn't mean a lot to readers.

However, if this statement were followed by a specific example from life, we would understand a great deal more about the person and her relationship with the writer. For example, consider the following two paragraphs that begin in the same manner.

My best friend Sylvia has always been there for me when I needed help. Once I got pretty drunk at a party, it was very late, and I was going to drive my car home. Sylvia said, "There's no way you're going to drive home like that. Give me your keys." Like drunk people often do, I said something like, "I'm fine. I can drive. There's no problem," but she wouldn't listen. She took my keys, got me in the passenger side, and drove me home. Being drunk, I just stumbled into the house and said goodby, not even wondering how she was going to get home. As it turned out, she walked home, about six blocks, at 2:00 a.m. in the morning. That's the amazing kind of friend that Sylvia was.

My best friend Wyndell has always been there for me when I needed help. I was always the little guy with a chip on his shoulder. I decided when I was pretty young that I didn't like getting picked on because I was little. I was little, but I was tough, so I wouldn't take any bull off anyone. Luckily, my buddy Wyndell was usually around, and he wasn't a fighter, but he was a peacemaker. More than once I took on more than I could handle, standing up to a guy who was twice my size, and Wyndell, who was a big guy himself, would step in before any punches were thrown. He'd say something like, "Come on guys, let's go throw the football," or he'd laugh and say, "Come on. I'll fight both of you with my eyes closed." Usually guys like to find a way out of a fight without losing face, and Wyndell had a knack of stopping a fight without putting anyone down. Of course, I was the one he was doing it for, and he kept me out of a lot of fights until I got older and didn't have to prove myself to anyone.

As you can see, the two very different examples in the paragraphs are what bring meaning to the first sentence in each paragraph. They bring people to life, create interest for readers, show the relationships between subjects and writers, and reveal the unique characteristics of people that make us all different.

Guidelines for Using Examples

The following guidelines will help you use examples effectively in your writing.

1. Provide examples to show a particular quality that a person possesses.

   Example:

   Mr. Fritz had more energy than any teacher I'd ever had. It seemed like he bounced into class rather than walked. His whole face would just light up with enthusiasm and he'd say something like, "This history stuff is great, isn't it?" When he lectured, he'd be all over the front of the classroom, and you couldn't take your eyes off of him. Then all of a sudden he'd be talking from the back of the room, and everyone's head was turned. He was like a showman as much as a teacher, and he'd go non-stop for the entire period. At the end of the class he'd say something like, "Now that was fun! See you tomorrow, historians!" You couldn't walk out of Fritz' class without a smile on your face.

2. Provide an example or examples to show the relationship between you and the subject.

   Example:

   My father had a way of making me feel very small. When he'd get mad at me, he'd just ignore me. Our family went on one trip and dad got mad at me for some reason. He didn't get mad or yell, he just quit paying me any attention. He put all of his attention for the next days on my sister, and it was like I didn't even exist. He let her sit up front with him, help pick out the motels we stayed in and the restaurants we ate in, and he put her in charge of the travel map. I felt like the lowliest person on earth, and I hated that trip. I hated my dad too, but I also craved the attention from him that I didn't get.

3. Whenever you write a general statement about your subject or your relationship with him or her, provide an example to show readers exactly what you mean.

   Examples:

   My brother is one of the strongest people I know. (Provide examples showing his strength.)

   Mrs. Hatcher took every opportunity she had to put me down. (Provide an example of one such opportunity.)

   Wilson never met a stranger. (Provide an example or examples of how he acted around people he didn't know.)

My mom was one of the most patient people ever. (Provide an example or examples of her patience.)

Clarice would help any stranger who was in need. (Provide an example of one such situation.)

Drafting Activity 2.4

For practice and to develop some potential material for your draft, provide an example for one of the qualities or characteristics of your subject that you may include in your paper. Write a sentence that reveals the particular quality, and then provide an example or examples to develop the paragraph.

Sample paragraph with examples

When I was with Rupert, there was always the danger of getting into trouble because he was a little crazy. One night we were just driving around and there were all these orange safety cones along one side of the road to keep people off the unpaved shoulder. Rupert thought it would be fun to see how many cones he could knock down, and that's what he did. Another time when I was driving, he stuck his rear out the side window and started mooning other cars. We were in a crowded parking lot one night where cars were packed together tightly, so he decided to get to our car by walking on the tops of the other cars, never touching the ground. There is no doubt that alcohol fueled Rupert's crazy antics, and it's amazing that he never got caught.

Paragraph providing example:

Drafting Activity 2.5

Write the first draft of your paper keeping the following guidelines in mind.

Drafting Guidelines

1. Write with the purpose of helping readers get to know this person like you do. Include things that typify the kind of person he or she is, and make use of your prewriting materials.

2. As you write, include your relationship with the person so that readers can understand your feelings towards him or her.

3. Include examples from life throughout your draft to show readers what the person is like, to create interest, and to reveal your relationship with him or her.

4. As you write, change paragraphs as you move to something new your draft: a new quality or characteristic of the person, a new example, a different aspect of your relationship.

5. Conclude the draft by revealing the influence the person has had on your life.

6. As mentioned earlier, writing is a recursive activity where writers continually reread sentences to help them decide what to write next. Reread what you have written regularly to keep the writing momentum going and figure out the best way to proceed.

7. Keep your readers for this paper in mind as you write: your classmates and instructor.

8. Title the draft in a simple manner that tells what the paper is about.

Sample First Draft

Coach Zinkin

Beginning my freshman year in high school, I was just ready to go through the motions and stick around until I turned 16 my sophomore year, when I could legally drop out of school. I didn't like school and wasn't good at it. It was like prison to me and I couldn't wait to get out.

One day in my P.E. class the teacher came up and asked if I had ever done any wrestling. Being a small guy, I'd been in a lot of fights to prove myself tough but I'd never wrestled. The teacher introduced himself as Coach Zinkin and suggested I drop by the wrestling room after school. "You look like you could be a pretty good wrestler," he said.

No one had ever told me I could be good at anything except ditching school, so I went to the wrestling room after school. The team was doing pre-season activities: running laps, lifting weights, getting in shape. I watched for a while and then left. It didn't look like any fun to me.

The next day Coach told me to come back again, that they were going to do some wrestling practice. I went back and watched some guys wrestle for a while, and then coach said, "Hey Juan, come on over and give it a try." He paired me up with a guy similar to my size, and he pinned me in about twenty seconds. We went at it again and this time I lasted about a minute. Coach came over and said, "Not bad for someone who's never wrestled. You've got the quickness and strength. All you need is to learn technique."

I went back the next couple days and ran and lifted weights with the team. Then after practice, Coach stayed around and helped me learn some basic wrestling holds and moves, showing me what was legal and what wasn't. I couldn't believe he was taking extra time just to help me, but it made an impression. I decided to join the wrestling team.

I was on the J.V. team my freshman year and won about half of my matches. But the hardest thing wasn't the wrestling, it was school. Coach made it clear to me and the rest of the team that ditching school or missing practice wasn't an option, and that we had to maintain at least a "C" average to stay on the team. Coach got me a tutor to help with my reading, and I stayed eligible for the year.

My sophomore year I moved up to varsity and won all of my matches the first semester. However, I had fallen behind in my school work and didn't make a "C" average that semester. I couldn't wrestle second semester and I figured it was all over. I had blown it. I'd be sixteen in a couple months and could finally get out of there.

I started ditching school again and one evening there was a knock at our apartment door. It was Coach. He introduced himself to my mom and then sat down to talk to me. "What's going on, Juan?" he asked seriously. "Don't know, Coach," I said. "I messed up and figure school and me need to part ways. I'm almost sixteen." Coach was silent for a while and then he said, "It's your decision, Juan. But realize this is the most important decision of your life. You can drop out, which will take you down one path, or you can stay in school, get your grades up, and wrestle in the fall. You know what I want you do to, and you know I'll be there for you. But it's your choice."

After Coach left, I broke down and cried. Here was this man that cared enough about me to come to my house and try to keep me from dropping out. All I had done was let him down and he wasn't giving up on me. I just knew I couldn't let him down again.

But I did. I got eligible for my junior year and had a great season. I placed first in league in my weight division, third in valley, and I made it to state. At state I got schooled by the eventual state champion, but after the match, Coach said, "That guy's a great wrestler, but all he's got on you is experience. You did great and I'm proud of you." Coach always knew how to pick me back up when I was down.

I was looking forward to my senior year. I proudly wore my letterman's jacket, I had my teammates to hang out with and had a little status for the first time in my life. But it went to my head. I wrestled great first semester but slacked off in class. I was a cool senior and everything would be fine. But it wasn't. I dropped below a "C" average and was ineligible for second semester, meaning no league, no valley, and no state. I was crushed.

The hardest thing I ever did was go to Coach. "I'm sorry Coach. I let you down," I said. Coach looked at me sharply and said, "You didn't let me down, Juan. You let yourself down. And you let your teammates down." And that's all he said. After a few moments of silence, I walked out. I'd never felt worse in my life.

I didn't see or hear from Coach, and I stayed away from the wrestling matches. Then after a few weeks there was a call over the room intercom for me to go to Coach Zinkin's office. I didn't want to go, but I went. When I went into his office, Coach was there was another man who I didn't know. "Juan," said Coach, "I want you to meet Coach Zavala, who's the wrestling coach at Sequoia College.

"Nice to meet you, Juan," said Coach Zavala. "Coach Zinkin said you weren't eligible to wrestle this semester but that you were a good kid who deserved another chance. From what I've heard, I think you could wrestle for the college team next year."

I couldn't believe what I was hearing. Here was Coach, who I had let down badly, trying to help me go to college and be on the wrestling team. "It won't be easy, Juan," said Coach. You have to graduate to be eligible to enroll in the fall at Sequoia, which means you'll have to work your tail off the rest of the semester and probably go to summer school. You're going to have to really want it, but I think you can do it." "I want it, Coach," I said without hesitation. "I want it bad."

I started going to wrestling practice after school, helping the younger guys and doing whatever Coach needed doing. I sat on the bench every match and rooted my guys on. I tried to be as much a part of the team as I could. That's the least I could do for Coach, and for myself.

Needless to say, I wouldn't be in college or writing this paper if it weren't for Coach Zinkin. I'm on the wrestling team, but I don't forget what Coach told me: "Wrestling is great, Juan, but a college education is a thousand times greater. Keep your priorities straight." And I'm trying to, taking classes to become a radiology technician and studying hard for the first time in my life. And at every college wrestling match, I always look up in the stands to see two people sitting together: my mom and Coach. The most important people in my life.

Revision

Now that you have completed your first draft, set it aside for a time before reading it to see what might be improved. After distancing yourself from your paper, you can read it more objectively and identify more clearly what you have done well and what you might do better.

Revising drafts is a part of the writing process shared by all writers. After you get your ideas on paper, you can begin to fine tune your sentence wording, add details or examples where they will strengthen the paper, retool your paragraphing, make changes that will add to the readers' interest or understanding and, if necessary, reorganize parts of the paper. The purpose of revision is to improve your paper, and you will usually find ways to do it.

In each "Revision" section, you review the elements that were covered in previous units and are introduced to new elements that help writers revise their drafts effectively. In this section, you continue to work on improving sentence wording, adding details, and improving your paragraphing, and you are introduced to a new writing feature: transitional wording.

Transitional Wording

In the most effective writing, sentences and paragraphs are tied together in ways that show the relationship among the different parts of the paper and that connect those parts to the whole. One of the most effective ways to show the relationships among sentences and paragraphs is through *transitional wording*: words and phrases that tie a writer's thoughts together and show how they are related.

Transitions can serve several functions in a paper: to show how events are related in time, how different ideas are related to one another, how one paragraph relates to another, how one sentence relates to another, or how a process moves from step to step. The use of simple, well-placed transitions such as *next, in addition, second,* or *finally* provide signposts that guide readers through a paper, indicating what comes next and its relation to what has come before.

Commonly Used Transitions

The following transitions include a variety of words and phrases writers use to connect their ideas.

1. Transitions that show the order in which ideas are presented, the steps in a process, or the events in a sequence: *first, second, next, then, now, finally.*

2. Transitions that add one idea to another: *furthermore, in addition, also, moreover, additionally, on top of that, beyond that, besides that.*

3. Transitions that introduce an example: *for instance for example, such as.*

4. Transitions that indicate a conclusion: *finally, lastly, as you can see, in conclusion, in summary.*

5. Transitions that show a contrast between ideas or events: *however, on the other hand, nevertheless, nonetheless, on the contrary, despite, in spite of, whereas.*

6. Transitions that show a cause-effect relationship - one thing occurring as the result of another: *therefore, consequently, thus, as a result, to that end, because of that.*

7. Transitions that emphasize a particular point or idea: *in fact, actually, of course, in reality, needless to say.*

8. Of the transitions, you may be least familiar with the following:

   moreover: even more importantly (similar to beyond that or on top of that)

   Example: Jules is an excellent student; *moreover*, he is a wonderful human being.

   consequently: because of that (similar to therefore or thus)

   Example: There was a power outage in the neighborhood; *consequently*, all houses were dark inside.

   nevertheless: similar to in spite of, despite that, or nonetheless

   Example: It was raining hard all morning; *nevertheless*, we still went to the soccer game.

   as you can see: based on what has been written; judging from what has come before.

   Example: Yesterday it was 95 degrees with clear skies. Today it is only 72 degrees with high winds and clouds. *As you can see*, the weather this time of year is quite variable.

9. Notice that when a transition ties two sentences together, it is preceded by a semi-colon (;), a punctuation mark which unites two related sentences. Here are some examples:

   The last subway train ran a half hour ago; *therefore*, we'll have to catch a bus downtown.

   Ike had problems on his last calculus exam; *however*, he's still doing well in the class.

   Lucinda has had a head cold for a month; *despite that*, she hasn't missed a day of work.

The following paragraphs contain a number of transitions in italics. Notice how they tie ideas within and between paragraphs together and aid the reader's understanding of the writer's living situation.

Apartment Woes

The apartment that my roommate and I rented didn't turn out to be a good deal. *First*, the walls are so thin that we hear the neighbors on both sides and above us, making it hard to study at night. *Second*, the water pressure is really low, so it takes forever to wash and rinse our hair. *On top of that*, in the morning we lose our hot water in a matter of minutes, so the second person to shower often gets cold water. We've gone to showering at night when there is less demand on the water.

    Then there is the problem with the landlord. He is supposed to fix anything that goes wrong in the apartment. *However*, when we need him, he can seldom be found. When we finally get a hold of him and tell him about the problem, he takes forever to get around to it. *As a consequence*, we've had a leaky kitchen faucet for weeks.

On the other hand, the apartment is in walking distance to school, and the rent is very reasonable. *Therefore*, we'll stick it out at least for this year. Apartments near the school aren't easy to get into, so we basically took the best one we could get. *Moreover*, anything is better than living in the dorms for a second year. Having our own apartment and the freedom that goes with it is a big improvement despite the problems.

Revision Activity 2.6

Fill in the blanks with appropriate transitional words or phrases from the list to tie the sentences and paragraphs of the following paper together. Try to use a **different** transition or transitional phrase in each blank.

Example: Nothing we tried was ridding the apartment of cockroaches; <u>therefore</u>, we had a professional exterminator come out and do the job.

The New Arena

The seating in the new on-campus arena is terrible. The 18,000 seat arena has been publicized as one of the best on the East Coast. _____, the reality does not live up to the hype.

_____, the seats are narrower than you'd expect. It is not comfortable sitting in an undersized seat, and everyone complains about it. _____, the leg space between rows of seats is not adequate. Unless you are very short, you have to scrunch up your knees to put your feet on the floor. _____, everyone sits like little toy soldiers, and it gets very uncomfortable. _____, every time someone walks in front of you, you have to stand up to let them by.

_____, the arena is an uncomfortable place to sit for two or three hours. _____, there is no solving the problem since all of the concrete rows would have to be knocked out and redone. The college wanted to cram as many seats as possible into the available space for the greatest revenue. They did this at the expense of every student or other person attending a game or concert, and _____, a lot of people are staying away. They haven't filled the arena yet. _____, they have lost the support of many longtime supporters.

Revision Activity 2.7

The following draft contains no transitional wording. Insert transitions in places that will tie sentences and paragraphs together effectively.

Example:

My computer takes forever to start working. It's relatively new, but it still takes up to ten minutes before I can get online, open my e-mail, or get into Word Perfect. I have to turn it on and then go do something else for ten or fifteen minutes before I can get onto it.

Once it starts working, it's great. I can move from one program to the next in no time, and it's the fastest computer I've owned. There must be computers that don't take forever to warm up like mine. Since it's only a year old, I'll be keeping it for quite a while, and I don't see any solution to the problem. The computer works fine, but it's slow to get going. I'll just have to live with it.

Revised (transitions in italics):

My computer takes forever to start working. It's relatively new, but it still takes up to ten minutes before I can get online, open my e-mail, or get into Word Perfect. *Consequently*, I have to turn it on and then go do something else for ten or fifteen minutes before I can get onto it.

On the other hand, once it starts working, it's great. I can move from one program to the next in no time, and it's the fastest computer I've owned. *However*, there must be computers that don't take forever to warm up like mine. Since it's only a year old, I'll be keeping it for quite a while, and I don't see any solution to the problem. The computer works fine, but it's slow to get going. *Despite* the problem, I'll just have to live with it.

Song Writer

I enjoy writing songs. I have been doing it on and off for the past three years and have written a couple dozen songs, mostly heard only by myself and my cat. I enjoy the process when I'm in the mood, and it's my one creative outlet.

When I was around ten, my dad taught me a few chords on our old piano that form the basis for most pop songs. Once I learned the chords, I discovered that with some practice and trial and error, I could play most of my favorite songs. I added new chords as I worked on more challenging melodies, and I progressed to applying the chords to melodies of my own creation.

When I'm in the mood, usually after listening to some good music, I'll go to the piano and experiment with the first notes of a melody that bang around in my head. Sometimes those first few notes lead nowhere, and other times I'm able to build on them and create a melody that I can use for a song. Composing the melody is the fun part. Writing the lyrics for the song is tough. I'm not a great lyricist, and I struggle to find an idea for the song, the best rhyming words to help tell the story, and a catchy, repeatable refrain line that most songs are anchored by. Often the words sound fake or corny, so I constantly revise for the song to have a real emotional feel. Writing lyrics is draining for me. When I finish there's a definite sense of accomplishment although I'm never completely satisfied.

I consider myself only a modest talent when it comes to song writing, and I have no illusions that I'll be the next Jewel or Taylor Swift. Like most songwriters, I dream about writing that one magical song that the world falls in love with, but the chances are one in a million. I remain content to write mainly for myself and my cat, who often sits on the piano bench when I compose. For the songs I write, a silent critic is probably the best kind.

Revision Guidelines
The following guidelines will help you revise your draft effectively.

1. Reread your draft to consider the perspective you have provided readers about the person you are writing about. Does the draft provide the clearest, most accurate portrayal of the person, that particular essence that you wish to convey to readers? What might you add or change to ensure that readers view your subject in the way that you want them to?

2. Read your draft to see what you might add to make it clearer or more interesting for readers. Are there examples you can add to help show readers the qualities and characteristics that your subject possesses or that help them see the relationship between the person and yourself? Are there details you can add that will help readers see, hear, and feel what you want them to?

3. Reread each sentence to see if its wording can be improved. Delete words and phrases that are unnecessary or repetitive, replace questionable words with more appropriate ones, reword sentences to eliminate awkward phrasing, and make vaguely worded sentences clearer. Your goal is to make every sentence as smooth, clear, and concise as you can.

4. Review your paragraphing to see whether you change paragraphs when you move to something new in your paper: a different quality of your subject, a new example, or a new aspect of your relationship. In addition, if you have any overly long paragraphs, divide them into two, and if you strung two or three short paragraphs together, combine them.

5. Read your draft to see whether you have used transitional wording to tie sentences and paragraphs together. Insert appropriate transitions in places where they would help readers understand the relationship between your thoughts and between different paragraphs.

6. Read your conclusion to make sure readers understand the impact that this person has on your life, and make any changes that would strengthen your conclusion or help readers understand the impact.

Revision Review

Before revising your draft, complete the next three review activities to practice making revisions following the guidelines presented.

Revision Activity 2.8

With a partner, read the following paragraphs and make note of places in the draft where an example or detail could be added to make the draft clearer, more interesting, or more informative.

My Niece

I love my little niece, but she is developing some habits that don't endear her to other children or adults who don't know her well. One of those habits is wanting to be in control. No matter who she is with, she is the one who has to decide what they are going to do.

She always has lots of ideas and quickly throws them out, so she often gets her way. However, when she is around older children or children her age who are also strong willed, there can be problems. As a result, some children aren't too thrilled to play with her.

Another bad habit she has developed is bragging, and she finds plenty to brag about. This can really bother other children, and they often react to her bragging negatively. Her mother is aware of the problem and working with her on it.

My niece is a pretty, affectionate child with good manners. She also has a great sense of humor. Hopefully she will grow out of her bad habits, or be broken of them, so that her good qualities will shine through.

Revision Activity 2.9

Revise the following paragraph to improve sentence wording. Reword any sentence that is overly long, repetitive, awkward, vague, or has some questionable word choices.

68

Examples:

The runner that is running in the outside lane has the advantage until the turn, when he loses that advantage.

Revised: The runner ~~that is running~~ in the outside lane has the advantage until the turn~~, when he loses that advantage~~.

Theresa didn't make out an application for the job as a student assistant to the registrar until it was too late and the application deadline had passed.

Revised: Theresa ~~didn't make out an application~~ **failed to apply** for the job ~~as a~~ **of** student assistant to the registrar ~~until it was too late and the application~~ **before** the deadline. ~~had passed.~~

The last two weeks of the summer were the hottest on record in the valley that were ever recorded in history. You could step outside in the morning to get the morning paper and be covered with beads of perspiration in a matter of a minute or so. We had fourteen days in a row of temperatures that were over 100 degrees. To make matters worse, there were power shortages in the area that were brought on by the heavy usage of air conditioning units, and many people were without air conditioning for part of the time. At least six deaths in the valley were caused by or at least their cause was devoted to heat prostration caused by lack of air conditioning. All six were senior citizens. In addition, the air was saturated with humidity at a record rate, and so what was actually 100 degrees felt more like 110 with the combination of heat and humidity. It was the most miserable two weeks of weather I had ever engaged in.

Revision:

Revision Activity 2.10

Paragraph the following first draft by marking off the beginning of each new paragraph. Change paragraphs when the writer moves to something new in the draft.

A Scary Uncle

I didn't see my Uncle Prine very often since he lived half way across the country from us. But the few times that I did see him as a young boy left a lasting impression on me. My family lived in Arizona and Uncle Prine lived in Tennessee. We drove cross country two or three times during my childhood to visit my dad's relatives in Tennessee. We saw lots of aunts and uncles and cousins, but no one stood out quite like Uncle Prine. When dad would say, "We're going to Uncle Prine and Aunt Lucy's house for a couple nights, the hairs would stand up on the back of my neck. All you had to do was look at Uncle Prine to tell that this was one crazy man. He had these wild looking blue eyes that could stare right through you, and he kept them partially hooded by eyelids that made him look like a snake ready to attack. He had a huge bulb for a nose and his nose and entire face were an angry red color all the time. His fat lips always had a smirk on them like a joke was coming and it was going to be on you. The only place I ever remember seeing Uncle Prine was sitting in a rocker on his front porch. That way he could patrol all the goings and comings from the house. And every time my sister and I would go outside to play or come back inside, I knew Uncle Prine would have something to say, his eyes lit up like firecrackers. "Boy," he'd say, "I wouldn't be goin to the back yard to play today." Being only six years old, I'd always take the bait. "Why not, Uncle Prine?" I'd ask. "Because there's alligators back there this morning, and they'd bite your feet off." I'd just stand there on the porch, half petrified, and then he'd break into this loud, awful cackle and say, "Got you good boy. You turned white as a sheet." And he'd cackle some more. Then he'd say, "Get out to that back yard. Any dummy knows there ain't no alligators in town." And I'd slink down the steps, burned again. You'd think I wouldn't have fallen for Uncle Prine's scare tactics after a while, but you'd have to see Uncle Prine and hear him to understand why I did. One time I was going into the house and there was Uncle Prine as usual sitting in his chair, just waiting for his prey. As I walked up the steps he literally leaped out of his chair, astonishingly fast for an old man, and blocked the door. "Don't go in there boy!" he shouted. "Don't go in there!" He was shaking all over and looked like he had seen ten ghosts. "What's wrong, Uncle Prine?" I asked. "The Bogeyman's in there, and if you go in, he's going to cut out your heart and eat it. That's why I'm out here." Well, that was too much for me, and I started crying. You'd think my crying would have softened him up, but not Uncle Prine. Here came that mad cackle again, and the more I cried, the louder he cackled. "Got you good that time boy. You Western boys still believe in the Bogeyman? There ain't no Bogeyman, boy. Only your Aunt Lucy in there, and she ain't no Bogeyman." Well, Uncle Prine never changed, but I did. I got older, and when I was nine, we went back again. It was the same old Uncle Prine on the porch, but I was ready for him this time, or so I thought. "How you doin', boy?" he asked me, that smirk on his mouth and gleam in his eye. "I'm doin good, Uncle Prine, I'm doin real good," I said. "That's good boy, that's real good," he said. Things were quiet for a day or so, and I could tell he was sizing me up, like he was circling his prey to figure out the best way to attack. This time though I would be ready and waiting. I went outside the next morning and Uncle Prine said,

"Boy, I wouldn't go into the back yard this morning. We got snakes back there." I thought, is that the best you can do Uncle Prine? Can't you come up with anything scarier than that? "Sure," I said to my uncle with a smile. "I'll be real careful," and went around to the back where the swings and slide were. I began swinging when all of a sudden I saw something slithering on the ground in the grass area beside the swings. I let out a scream, jumped off the swing, and ran for my life. Uncle Prine had snuck around back for a look at the fun, and I could hear his cackling as I ran for safety. Turns out he had turned a couple of harmless garter snakes loose near the swings that morning and just waited for me to call his bluff. I couldn't believe he'd go to all that trouble just to scare me, but Uncle Prine was one demented man, and when he died a couple of years later, I can't say that I was terribly sad.

Revision Activity 2.11

Revise your first draft by applying the revision guidelines presented. Then exchange drafts with a classmate, or a small group of classmates, read each other's paper, and make any suggestions that you feel will improve the paper. Then write your second draft, incorporating all of the changes that you made.

Revised excerpts from sample draft "Coach" *(final paragraphs)*

I couldn't believe ~~what I was hearing~~ **my ears.** ~~Here was Coach, who~~ I had let **Coach** down badly, **and now he was** trying to help me go to college and be on the wrestling team. "It won't be easy, Juan," said Coach. You have to graduate to be eligible to enroll in the fall at Sequoia, which means you'll have to work your tail off the rest of the semester and probably go to summer school. You're going to have to really want it, but I think you can do it." "I want it, Coach," I said without hesitation. "I want it bad." **I had never wanted anything more in my life.**

　　From that day forward, I started going to wrestling practice after school, helping the younger guys and doing whatever Coach needed doing: **rolling up the mats, spotting wrestlers during weight lifting, helping with the weigh-ins. I also** sat on the bench every match and rooted my guys on. I tried to be as much a part of the team as I could. ~~That's~~ **, which was** the least I could do for Coach and for ~~myself.~~ **my teammates.**

　　Needless to say, I wouldn't be in college ~~or writing this paper~~ if it weren't for Coach Zinkin. I'm on the **college** wrestling team **and doing well**, but I don't forget what Coach told me: "Wrestling is great, Juan, but a college education is a thousand times greater. Keep your priorities straight." ~~And~~ I'm trying to **do that**, taking classes to become a radiology technician and studying hard for the first time in my life. And at every college wrestling match, I always look up in the stands to see two people sitting together: my mom and Coach. The most important people in my life.

　　When I have the time, I go back to the high school wrestling matches to support Coach and the team. I sit down with the team, and I help Coach psych up the guys and get them ready to wrestle. When I think of what my life is like now, and what it could have been if I had dropped out of school, I feel unbelievably fortunate. Coach Zinkin changed my life forever.
(Revisions made to improve wording, smooth out sentences, add detail, and add new paragraph with which the writer wanted to conclude essay.)

Editing

Now that you have revised your paper to improve its content, wording, and paragraphing, you are ready to proofread it for errors and make any necessary corrections. The goal of the editing phase is to produce an error-free final draft to share with readers.

While editing your paper for errors is typically the final step in the writing process, it is no less important than the others. No matter how interesting or thought-provoking a paper may be, readers also judge your writing on its correctness. If a paper is filled with spelling, punctuation, or grammatical errors, readers may judge the writing rather harshly since such errors distract from the writer's ideas.

It is not surprising that readers are troubled by writing errors. They are used to reading predominantly error-free writing, whether it be textbooks, newspapers, magazines, novels, or non-fiction books. They are used to focusing on content and not being bothered by run-on sentences or misspelled words. As writers, we owe it to readers to provide them with the best writing we can. We also owe it to ourselves to write correctly to put our ideas in the best possible light.

In each "Editing" section, you review what you learned in the previous unit, are introduced to some new editing considerations, and proofread your draft for errors following the editing guidelines provided.

Sentence Fragments

In the first editing section, you proofread and edited your draft for run-on sentences: two or more sentences run together without a period. A second punctuation problem involves inserting a period before the sentence ends, creating an incomplete sentence called a sentence fragment. While sentence fragments are not as common as run-on sentences, they do create problems for some writers.

The following guidelines will help you avoid sentence fragments and correct those you find.

1. A sentence fragment is an incomplete sentence. It does not express a complete thought or idea, and it leaves readers with an unanswered question. Here are some examples of sentence fragments.

    Because you are such a hard worker. (What will happen?)
    Sitting outside on our new rocking chairs. (Who was sitting?)
    After we finish cleaning out the garage. (What will happen?)
    The woman wearing the green and white running shoes. (What about her?)

2. Most typically, fragments are created by separating one half of a sentence from the other by a period. If you remove the period, you have a complete, correctly punctuated sentence. Here are some examples, with the fragment underlined.

    The manager is going to promote you. <u>Because you are such a hard worker.</u>
    (The second half is a fragment which belongs with the first sentence.)

Corrected: The manager is going to promote you because you are such a hard worker.

<u>Before I go to the park and play softball.</u> I am going to get a lot of work done around the apartment.
(The first half is a fragment which belongs with the sentence.)

Corrected: Before I go to the park and play softball, I am going to get a lot of work done around the apartment.

Alvin really enjoys watching cooking shows. <u>Especially the ones with audience participation.</u>
(The second half is a fragment which makes no sense without the previous sentence.)

Corrected: Alvin really enjoys watching cooking shows, especially the ones with audience participation.

I enjoy doing many things in the winter. <u>Skating on the frozen pond in the park, going to hockey games, drinking hot chocolate, and warming myself by a fire.</u>
(The list of activities – skating on a frozen pond, going to hockey games, drinking hot chocolate – is not a sentence. It needs to be attached to the sentence before it.)

Corrected: I enjoy doing many things in the winter such as skating on the frozen pond in the park, going to hockey games, drinking hot chocolate, and warming myself by a fire.

3. To correct a sentence fragment, do one of the following:

   a. Attach the fragment to the sentence it belongs with by deleting the period.

   Example (fragment underlined)

   You wear the most interesting outfits. <u>While I wear the most boring.</u>

   Corrected: You wear the most interesting outfits while I wear the most boring.

   b. Add words to the fragment to make it a complete sentence. Example (fragment underlined)

   There's a lot we can do without spending money. <u>For example, window shop at the mall, hike to the top of Barker Hill, or bike across town to the pier.</u>

   Corrected: There's a lot we can do without spending money. For example, we can window shop at the mall, hike to the top of Barker Hill, or bike across town to the pier.

Editing Activity 2.12

Eliminate any sentence fragment by either deleting the period that separates the fragment from the sentence it belongs with, or by adding words to the fragment to make it a complete sentence.

Example: No one should stand around the excavation site. Until the cyclone fence is erected.

Corrected: No one should stand around the excavation site until the cyclone fence is erected.

Example: Alphonse is a formidable looking man. Tall and muscular, with a thick chest and arms.

Corrected: Alphonse is a formidable looking man. He is tall and muscular, with a thick chest and arms.

1.   The cafeteria food has improved. Since the school privatized the operation.

2.   Instead of a school-run cafeteria with your usual food. The cafeteria is now a food court with a number of different vendors selling food.

3.   Today you can get practically any kind of food you want. For example, Mexican, Chinese, Japanese, or Italian.

4.   The cafeteria also looks much different today. At least a dozen food booths around the walls of the cafeteria, with seating in the middle.

5.   The cafeteria is more crowded than ever. Especially between noon and 2:00 p.m.

6.   Although I don't eat there very often. I've always enjoyed my food when I've gone.

7.   The cafeteria has taken away a lot of lunch business from the fast food restaurants in the area. Because it has a number of fast food choices itself.

8.   The purpose of changing the cafeteria was to keep more students on campus for lunch by offering a variety of good food. Which seems to be working out well.

Editing Activity 2.13

Correct any sentence fragments in the following paragraph by deleting a period that separates the fragment from the sentence it belongs with or by adding words to the fragment to form a complete sentence.

Example

The shift key on my computer keyboard keeps sticking. Any time I hit it accidentally. When it is stuck in the down position. I can't type at all. Everything gets highlighted when I want to highlight a single word or sentence. My keyboard is old, and I think I need to replace it.

Corrected

The shift key on my computer keyboard keeps sticking any time I hit it accidentally. When it is stuck in the down position, I can't type at all. Everything gets highlighted when I want to highlight a single word or sentence. My keyboard is old, and I think I need to replace it.

Scheduling Problems

Getting the classes you need in a particular semester is difficult. Especially if are trying to schedule them around your work. If you are working, you may only have certain times you can take classes. For example, before noon, after 2:00 p.m., or just in the evening. The most difficult time to schedule classes is in the morning. Because that is the most popular time. Most students like to finish their classes by noon or early afternoon, so morning classes close fast. Late afternoon classes are the easiest to schedule since many students are working or just don't want to be in class. However, they are sometimes difficult to get into because fewer late afternoon classes are offered. If you can go only in the evening, you are lucky to get into two or, at the most, three classes. Meaning that it will take many semesters to complete your course work. Many working students take many years to complete even two years of college course work. Which also makes college more expensive.

Comma Usage

Using commas correctly is an important part of effective writing. Fortunately, there are some basic punctuation rules that govern the use of commas within sentences. In this section you are introduced to those rules and then apply them to your draft.

The main purpose for using commas is to show readers where to pause within your sentences. These pauses create a reading rhythm that helps readers follow your thoughts most clearly, and they often indicate something new to follow in the sentence. Commas are also inserted in places where their absence could change and misconstrue the meaning of a sentence for readers.

For example, read the following paragraphs, the first containing no commas and the second with commas inserted correctly into sentences.

> When you drive across the campus you run into a number of problems. First there are a number of roads that dead-end into a building or a grass area so you have to turn around. Next there are a number of one-way streets but there is no pattern to them which makes it baffling getting to where you want to go. In fact after trying to get across campus many different ways I still haven't found a way to drive from one side to the other without going out to one of two main roads adjacent to campus. I have finally come to the conclusion which I have no doubt is correct that the university doesn't want you to cross the campus using internal roads but instead they want you to use the outside roads and keep the internal roads free for students seeking parking spaces. I guess that makes sense but it would sure be nice to have at least one internal road that goes all the way across campus.

> When you drive across the campus, you run into a number of problems. First, there are a number of roads that dead-end into a building or a grass area, so you have to turn around. Next, there are a number of one-way streets, but there is no pattern to them, which makes it baffling getting to where you want to go. In fact, after trying to get across campus many different ways, I still haven't found a way to drive across campus without going out to one of two main roads adjacent to the school. I have finally come to the conclusion, which I have no doubt is correct, that the university doesn't want you to cross the campus using internal roads, but instead they want you to use the outside roads and keep the internal roads free for students seeking parking spaces. I guess that makes sense, but it would sure be nice to have at least one internal road that goes all the way across campus.

Notice how each comma in the second paragraph creates a reading pause that prepares you for the next idea in the sentence and makes it easier to follow the writer's thoughts.

Comma Usage Rules

The following general rules will help you use commas effectively in your writing.

1.   Use commas to separate three or more items joined by *and* or *or*, or to separate two or more words that *modify* (describe in some manner) the word they precede.

Examples:

Post, Kelloggs, and Sunnyside Select all had their bite-sized shredded wheat cereal on sale.
Your back pack could be in the bedroom closet, in the hall closet, or on the back porch.
The shortest, thinnest girl on the basketball court was also the fastest.
Halloween fell on a cold, windy night.

2. Use commas to separate introductory groups of words which lead to the main thought in a sentence.

    Examples:

    If you don't tie the string of the balloon to your niece's wrist, it will fly away from her.
    Trying to study for the test, Angie shut herself up in her bedroom and put on her ear plugs.
    While I was crossing the street at the intersection, a motorcycle turning to the right almost hit me.
    In the middle of the darkest night of the year, Felix walked in his sleep from his room to the next door neighbor's back door.

3. Use commas to separate groups of words at the end of a sentence which follow the main thought, relate to it in some manner, and frequently begin with *which* or an *ing* or *ed*-ending word.

    Examples:

    The favored horse for the Kentucky Derby wouldn't get in the starting gate, *rearing* up and beating at the gate with its hooves.
    One little boy at the party covered his face with birthday cake frosting, *which* didn't seem to bother anyone.
    Allison finally left the store that was having the big discount sale, *frustrated* by the length of the check-out lines.

4. Use commas to separate the two halves of a *compound sentence* (two sentences connected by a *coordinate conjunction*) by inserting a comma after the last word before the conjunction (and, but, for, so, yet, or).

    Examples:
    I'm going to the midnight concert at the campus pavilion, *but* no one else from my dorm wing is going.
    The wind blowing off of Lake Erie was extremely cold, *and* we were wearing nothing but shorts and t-shirts.
    Retail sales were up for the quarter for most major retail chains, *yet* the stock market continued its descent.

5. Place commas around a group of words beginning with *who, which,* or *whose* that provide

information that is not essential for the sentence to make sense (called a non-restrictive *relative clause*). The sentence could stand alone and make sense without the group of words.

Examples:

The Empire State Building, *which* was once the tallest building in the world, no longer is among the top five tallest buildings.
Detective Longtree, *who* works for Scotland Yards in London, has been a detective for over forty years.
The sound of a dripping faucet, *which* I hear every night in my apartment, can drive a person mad.

Note: If the group of words beginning with *who, which,* or *whose* provides essential information for the sentence to make sense (called a *restrictive relative clause*), do not insert commas. (Examples: The man *who* works in the library is my next-door neighbor. The book *which* you requested is on order in the bookstore.)

6. Use commas after introductory transitional words or phrases and before and after "interrupting" words and phrases within a sentence that require a reading pause.

    Examples:

    First, there were no cooking utensils in the cabin. *Second*, there was no silverware.
    In conclusion, I'd like to thank everyone who made today's auction a big success.
    The owner of that red Honda, *by the way*, is a Toyota salesman.
    Most of the damage, *fortunately*, was superficial and didn't harm the house's structure or foundation.

7. Often a sentence will need multiple commas due to situations where more than one comma rule applies.

    Examples:

    That particular jersey comes in red, white, or black, but the college store, unfortunately, only has the small size left.
    (Commas are used within a series of three or more items, after the last word before a coordinate conjunction in a compound sentence, and before and after an "interrupter.")

    When I decide whether to enroll in summer school, which might take a week or two, I'll let you know, but in the meantime, feel free to enroll without me.
    (Commas are used after an introductory group of words, before and after a non-restrictive "which" clause, before a coordinate conjunction in a compound sentence, and after a second introductory group of words - in the meantime - beginning the second sentence within the compound sentence.)

8. There are also situations where writers tend to use commas when they aren't needed. As a general rule, don't use commas in the following situations.

    a. In the middle of a sentence when the word connecting the two halves of the sentence is a *subordinate conjunction* (*because, while, as, if, when, since, whenever, unless*).

        Examples:

        You can return the hedge clippers *whenever* you want to.
        I don't want you to come to the tupperware party *because* you feel obligated.
        We're not going to attend the concert in the park *if* it's still raining.

    b. Preceding a coordinate conjunction (*and, but, so, for, yet, or*) that connects two words or groups of words but not two complete sentences.

        Examples:

        Julio is tired of working year after year for the college's outreach program *and* never getting a raise.
        Student assistants at the college looked into getting union representation *and* collective bargaining.
        We can carry bottled water *and* sodas into the stadium *but* not beer *or* other alcoholic beverages.

Editing Activity 2.14

Insert commas in the following sentences by applying the comma usage rules presented. Some sentences will require more than one comma, and one sentence requires no commas.

Example: When using any of the welding equipment in the shop please follow all the safety rules posted on the equipment which are for your protection.

Corrected: When using any of the welding equipment in the shop, please follow all the safety rules posted on the equipment, which are for your protection.

1. Judging by the quality of the soil and slope of the lot you will need to bring in a lot of top soil for your class landscaping project.

2. I would suggest bringing in at least enough top soil to provide a six-inch top to the current soil.

3. You can not begin digging trenches for the sprinkler system until you've brought in the top soil but you can lay out the design of your system in advance which will take some time.

4. Although the back area is rather small you will still need a number of sprinkler heads to provide coverage for the lawn the trees along the fence and the flowers and plants around the borders.

5. The area which requires the most watering is the lawn so you need a separate timing system for it and the other parts of the yard.

6. Since you may not be able to do the entire project by yourself I'll be glad to help but I know you are required to do as much as possible on your own.

7. I would suggest using rolls of sod for the lawn rather than grass seed because the lawn comes fully grown and with rolls of sod weeds aren't a problem.

8. The only thing you'll need to get from the landscaping department is a power hole digger which will make planting the trees easier and faster.

9. Putting in the sprinkler system will require measuring and cutting a lot of PVC pipe for the water lines but the pipe is light and easy to connect allowing you to work quickly.

10. I'd suggest giving yourself a full weekend to smooth out the top soil put in the sprinkler system and then lay out the sod and then I'd schedule a second weekend for all of the planting.

82

Editing Activity 2.15

Insert commas in the sentences of the following draft by applying the rules for comma usage. Some sentences will require multiple commas, and some will require none.

Example: Weather conditions in many parts of the world have become more erratic in recent years. The world has experienced warmer warms colder colds more frequent and stronger hurricanes and more tornadoes. While some weather experts attribute the changes to the natural weather cycles that have occurred throughout time others attribute the changes to man-made global warming.

Edited: Weather conditions in many parts of the world have become more erratic in recent years. The world has experienced warmer warms, colder colds, more frequent and stronger hurricanes, and more tornadoes. While some weather experts attribute the changes to the natural weather cycles that have occurred throughout time, others attribute them to man-made global warming.

The Old Dorm

The dormitory I stayed in my first year of college was an old army barracks. Many barracks buildings were converted to dorms when the college was built on the former military base many years ago and my dormitory barracks was one of the few left standing twenty years later.

The barracks consisted of an end-to-end hallway with ten small dorm rooms on each side. Each room had just enough space for two twin beds and a sink. There was no closet space anywhere so we strung a wire along one side of the room and hung our clothes. In addition since there was no space for a study desk we'd study on our beds or go to the library.

There was one bathroom for the entire dormitory with two shower stalls and two toilets. Needless to say there was often a line for the bathroom and sometimes we'd use the bathrooms in one of the newly built dorms rather than wait in line. There was also no cooling unit in any of the rooms so they got very warm in the late spring and the summer. It was also a noisy place since the thin uninsulated walls between the rooms were a conduit for sound.

Finally the dorm was in bad shape since they were planning on tearing it down soon and didn't want to put any money into it. There were holes in the walls cracked and chipped tiles on the floor and permanent mildew in the concrete shower stalls. The entire dorm had an old musty smell that always lingered and clung to your clothes. There were also holes in the walls cracks in the ceilings and cracks in the enamel sink basins. The only good thing about the dorm which was the only reason that many of us stayed was that the cost per semester was half as much as for the new dorms. As you can see no one would have lived there otherwise.

Editing Review

In Unit One, you learned to identify and correct run-on sentences and comma splices, and you learned the correct irregular verb forms for the past tense and past participle. Since it often takes more than one exposure to eliminate the most troublesome errors, there are review activities throughout the text for students who need them.

___

Editing Activity 2.16

In the following draft, correct errors with run-on sentences or comma splices by separating sentences with a period or combining them with a joining word. In addition, correct any misspelled irregular verbs.

Example: The mother cat had hid some of her babies behind the washing machine, we didn't realize how many kittens she had until we heared them crying.

Corrected: The mother cat had hidden some of her babies behind the washing machine, and we didn't realize how many kittens she had until we heard them crying.

Too Many Geese

A big drainage pond sat behind our apartment complex in the city, it filled with water during the rainy winter season. The pond attracted a variety of migrating birds which flied in before Christmas and left sometime in March.

We enjoyed the egrets, ducks, coots, and geese that came to visit, but we were also ready for them to leave in the spring. The problem was they would spend a lot of time on the back apartment lawn eating the grass seed, they leaved their droppings all over the lawn and concrete walkways. It was a real mess we couldn't walk back there without stepping on something.

Last winter while most of the birds were leaving in March, two pairs of Canadian geese hatched their babies. Rather than leave, they settled in to raise their brood, which consisted of six ducklings per couple. Apartment tenants started feeding them, which was a mistake they grew accustomed to their environment, and when the ducklings were old enough to fly, no one leaved.

Today we have fourteen large geese living year around behind our apartments, it is not a good situation. They keep the back area littered with their droppings, and they have drove off families by running at their children and squawking. They have became more and more aggressive, and now consider the back lawn area their territory. To make matters worse, a new brood of ducklings has hatched, and the numbers are going to keep growing.

The situation has got so bad that the apartment owners have brung in fish and game experts to see what can be done that was a few months ago, and nothing has happened. I seen the old movie classic "The Birds" on television, where flocks of birds start attacking people. I wonder if those geese have similar plans for us.

___

Editing Activity 2.17

Proofread your latest draft for errors by applying the following editing guidelines, and make the necessary corrections. Read your draft several times, looking for one type of error at a time. When you have corrected all errors, write the final draft of the paper.

Editing Guidelines

1. Check your sentences to make sure you haven't run any together or put a comma between sentences instead of a period. Correct run-on sentences or comma splices by separating longer sentences with periods and combining shorter, related sentences with a joining word.

2. Check your sentences to make sure there are no sentence fragments created by separating a part of a sentence from the sentence it belongs with. Correct fragments by attaching the fragment to the sentence it belongs with or by adding words to the fragment to make it a complete sentence.

3. Check your use of irregular verbs, making sure you have used the correct irregular forms and spelled them correctly.

4. Check your comma usage, making sure you have inserted commas into your sentences following the rules provided.

5. Check the spelling of any word you are uncertain of, or run the spell check on your word processing program, to eliminate any spelling errors.

Applying the Writing Process

At the end of each unit, you apply what you have learned by writing a second paper without interruptions for instruction or activities. This second writing assignment provides you an opportunity to write about another influential person in your life, some additional practice in using the writing process, and another paper to share with readers.

Writing Assignment

Choose a person to write about, someone very different from the subject of your first paper, who has had a different influence on your life. Working independently, follow a similar writing process that you used to develop your first paper. (Refer back to the drafting, revision, or editing guidelines in the unit as needed.)

- Select a person to write about
- Do some free writing, a clustering diagram, or both on your topic.
- Write a first draft.
- Revise by focusing on providing good examples, clear sentence wording, and effective paragraphing, and adding whatever will improve the draft.
- Edit the draft by correcting any errors that you find.
- Write the final paper.

Before revising, share first drafts with a classmate or two, and ask each other questions about anything that seems unclear in the draft or that you'd like to know more about. Consider your classmates' input as you revise your paper.

Readings

My Education Angel
By James E. Walton

As a city champion in the 880-yard run in Canton, Ohio, I always thought that athletics would be my ticket to college. I had wrestled varsity in high school and, sometime later, held my college's record in the mile run. In addition to my athletic ability, my grades were excellent, yet a partial scholarship to a local college was the only offer I received. So I gave up the idea of going to college.

Growing up in poverty with a stepfather who cared nothing about my siblings and me and who saw us as a burden, I knew he would not support the idea of my attending college nor would he provide any financial assistance. I'd heard it often enough. "Boy, when you turn 16 years old, there are 18 ways to get out of my house," he'd say, irritably. He was counting all of the windows along with the front and back doors.

So like my brother one year before, I graduated from high school at age 16 with no job prospects, no plan for further education and my allotted time to live at home had expired. The U.S. military offered the only hope, so I signed up for the Navy.

Two weeks prior to shipping out to Cleveland and eventually Viet Nam, I agreed to take my pastor's place in a church play performed across town at a "white" church. After the play, I was downstairs trying to arrange a ride home when a foreigner who I didn't know congratulated me on my role in the play and innocently asked, "How's school going?" "School?" I responded with some indignation. "I graduated!" "Well, why aren't you in college then?" the stranger shot back. I had no response to that impossibility.

A week later I received a phone call. "You have been on my mind," the stranger I'd met at the church said, "so I looked up your number." We talked for several minutes, then he asked to speak to my mother. As I feared, my mother mentioned to the stranger that I had signed up to join the Navy. This news spurred the caller into action. Reminding me that Seventh-day Adventists did not volunteer for the military (Seventh-day Adventists, as a matter of faith, only go to the military if drafted and only as conscientious objectors, at that), the caller tried to talk me out of going. He had no way of knowing the hateful and abusive ways of my stepfather, so I could only promise that I would try.

Even though I had not officially taken the military oath, I had given my birth certificate to a stern-faced local military recruiter and I didn't want to face him again. After some begging, my sister agreed to retrieve my birth certificate from the recruiter.

One week later, the stranger—having only met me once—called again to ask directions to my home. "I think I can get you into the college in Michigan that I attended," he told me. "I'll be at your house in about one hour. Can you be packed by then?"

I quickly tossed my few personal items in a pillow case, slung it over my shoulder, and was standing, waiting, by the time the stranger arrived. My stepfather only had discouraging words as the stranger approached our house. The Navy, he told me, was still my best option. "I won't be giving you a damn dime to go to no school," he said.

In sub-freezing temperatures and tall, drifting snow gusts, the stranger and I headed into the darkness toward a private university hundreds of miles away from Canton, Ohio in Berrien

Springs, Michigan. I had not applied to attend the university. I hadn't even taken the SAT or the ACT. Three dollars, left over from the five-dollar bill a relative had given me for graduation, was all I had to cover room, board and tuition.

On the long, treacherous drive to Michigan, I learned that the stranger's name was Dr. Joseph Nozaki, a young physician serving out his residency in a local hospital. He hadn't slept for three days and was having difficulty staying awake. We stopped the car several times and ran in the snow to stay awake. During one of our runs around the car, he lost his wallet, but we decided to continue on to the university anyway.

Many challenges awaited me: working half days, going to class half days, living on government-surplus peanut butter at times, surviving without adequate clothes in frigid Michigan winters, and being saved once by the financial intervention of Dr. Nozaki when the college threatened to suspend me for lack of funds. Somehow, scratching my way and generally depending on the kindness of strangers, I graduated from Kent State University where I'd transferred during my third year.

Unfortunately during this time, I lost all contact with Dr. Nozaki, even though I visited the alumni office of his alma mater several times for updated addresses. The letters I sent to China, to Singapore, and to Hong Kong always came back a few months later stamped "address unknown."

After teaching high school in Canton for three years, earning a doctorate, then teaching at a liberal arts college for 20 years, my family and I moved 3,000 miles away from Ohio to Fresno where I began teaching at Fresno State University. Miraculously, through a series of improbable events, I rediscovered Dr. Nozaki, who at age 79 is still a practicing surgeon. He had spent many years as a missionary on several continents before returning to his practice in Fresno. Dr. Nozaki and I had lunch together just yesterday—as we do weekly—at the church where we both are now members: Fresno Asian and Community Seventh-day Adventist Church. After 40 years I rediscovered my education angel.

Questions for Discussion

1. What obstacles did Walton have to overcome to get an education? Compare those obstacles to your own path to college.

2. Why do you think Dr. Nozaki, a complete stranger to Walton, went out of his way to help him out?

3. What qualities did Dr. Nozaki possess, and how were they revealed in the essay?

4. What do you think Walton's life may have been like had not his "education angel" intervened? What individuals in your own life have influenced, for better or worse, who you are and where you are today?

Giving Students Room to Run

by Lorna Green

In the third grade, near the end of World War II, I learned why I wanted to be a teacher.

Mrs. Wright, a woman in her late 50s (or so it seemed to an 8-year-old) taught me what every child needs to know. And I don't mean grammar or multiplication tables or how to sit quietly in our chairs, which were bolted to the floor.

Mrs. Wright was austere in appearance, wearing beige two-piece suits, sensible shoes and a white blouse with a jabot fluff held securely by an oval cameo pin. She was a gentle, supportive and knowledgeable person who was obviously born to be a teacher. Her voice never rose in anger or frustration. Her pleasant, plain face, framed by bobbed silver hair, never displayed anger or disappointment

And in the back of the room, in seat seven of row six, sat Joel, an active 7-year-old with dark unruly hair, lopsided glasses and fidgeting hands. He spoke with a decided lisp, although he did not speak to the rest of us often. Joel was in our classroom, but he was not in our "class." A mathematical genius, he was a long-time member of a national quiz show featuring children with exceptional intellectual ability. Joel's aptitude for mathematics was amazing, even to those of us who didn't know what calculus or trigonometry meant. He was taking math classes through the local high school and some college-level classes as well. But he was taking those classes while sitting in our third-grade classroom.

Today, Joel would be identified as ADHD, or perhaps even as autistic. Back then he followed a peculiar ritual. He would look at his "homework," whisper something to himself, get up, run around the perimeter of the classroom at full speed two or three times and then slide into his seat and write down the answer. With 10 to 15 problems on the page, Joel spent most of his time running around the classroom. Meanwhile, we sat quietly, participating in reading groups or individual work.

Finally, after three or four weeks, one of the children apparently had had enough, either of sitting quietly or of watching Joel whiz around the room. "Mrs. Wright," she asked, "why is it that we have to stay in our seats to do our work, and we have to mostly not talk to our friends, but Joel gets to run around and around and around and talk to himself even when he is supposed to be doing his seat work? Why? How come he gets to do that?"

Without even a pause Mrs. Wright replied, "Well, remember how we talked about how some of us learn to read very quickly, and some of us take a little longer, and some of us have very small voices and some of us have very big voices—because we are different, but we are all special. You know that Joel is very special in doing things with numbers. He is doing many things we don't even understand, things like calculus and trigonometry. Joel can do those things because his mind works very, very fast. In fact, his mind works so fast that sometimes he has to hurry so that his body can keep up with his mind. That's why he runs around the classroom when he is thinking. So he can help his body to keep up with his very fast mind." "Oh," the little girl said. "I get it—sort of like singing really fast when you are jumping rope really fast." "Yes," replied Mrs. Wright, "something like that." And everyone went back to work while Joel ran frantically around the room.

Today, a student like Joel would have an IEP, but it's unlikely he'd have a more accommodating classroom. Six decades ago, special education was in its infancy. Special needs students were often shuffled off to private schools, kept at home or shunted into separate rooms. A few unusual savants, like Joel, awkwardly made their way in general ed classrooms. Joel was different in how he worked, but we respected his differences because Mrs. Wright respected them.

I knew then that if I could make one child feel as comfortable with "specialness" as Joel was made to feel with his, and if I could help one child accept another who was "different" in any way, I would do something really wonderful. And so that is why I teach.

Questions for Discussion

1. What qualities stand out in Mrs. Wright as a teacher and person? How are they revealed in the essay?

2. The Joels of today are usually put In special classes of some sort. Do you think this is better than the "mainstreaming" of Joel sixty years ago? Why?

3. Mrs. Wright was no doubt a very special teacher. What teachers if any would you regard as special in your life and what impact did they make?

Vincent

by Gretchen Wilder

Vincent Van Gogh never made a penny from his art during his lifetime. His artistic fame came long after his death at age thirty-seven. Without the help of his younger brother Theo, Vincent would have never had an art career at all.

Before dedicating himself to art, Vincent had tried the ministry, albeit without any formal ecclesiastical training, the publishing business, and art dealing, a job his brother Theo had gotten him. Vincent never lasted long at a job because of the difficulty he had getting along with people. He was extremely argumentative, and vehemently attacked anyone verbally who disagreed with his viewpoints. His lack of social acumen no doubt led him ultimately to favor the solitary life of an artist.

Vincent lived and painted at his parent's home for a while, but the trouble he caused – constantly arguing with his father, a local parish pastor, flying into uncontrollable fits of rage, and impregnating a local girl, bringing scandal upon the family - forced his parents to expel him. On his own, he had no income to finance his art work or his lodging, at which point he turned to his brother.

Theo was a successful art dealer for one of the leading art companies in Holland. He was the opposite in personality and temperament to his brother - genial, even-tempered, a source of pride to his parents – and was gainfully employed as an art dealer his entire adult life, first in the Hague and later in Paris.

Although Vincent had a strained relationship with Theo, for the same reasons he had problems with most people, Vincent played upon the strength of their brotherly bond to entreat Theo to subsidize his art career by covering the cost of his lodging, paints, easels, canvases, and models. Theo agreed to send Vincent 150 francs a month, half of his salary, and continued to send him half his salary for the rest of Vincent's life. While he clearly appreciated the money, over time Vincent felt more and more entitled, sometimes even blaming Theo for his lack of artistic success, which was being stunted by inadequate funding!

Throughout much of Vincent's artistic career, he was not deemed even a passably good artist. His black and white pictures of orchards and fields were viewed by art critics as crudely drawn. His pictures with peasants in them, such as "The Potato Eaters," revealed a lifetime shortcoming in drawing symmetrical human figures: hands too large for their arms, torsos too short for their legs. It was not until he started experimenting with brilliant colors in paintings such as "Starry Starry Nights," "Irises," "The Café Terrace at Arles," and "Wheat Field with Crows" that he began painting the pictures that would eventually put him in the panoply of the world's greatest artists.

Vincent was one of the great tormented souls of art. There is little question that he suffered from mental illness that in part explains his tremendous mood swings and infuriating behavior. In today's diagnostic parlance, he arguably suffered from manic-depression, paranoia, and delusions of grandeur. In a manic state, he would paint in a fury of motion, lashing out at the canvas with his brush strokes, working days at a time to complete an amazing number of paintings. In his times of depression, he would experience deep guilt over his failures, his father's death, and his dependence on his younger brother.

In his darkest moods, his guilt led him to self-punishment to expiate his sins: going for days without food, sleeping in dirt-floored huts on the coldest nights, and beating himself with cudgels. His most infamous act of self-mutilation – cutting off part of his ear and slashing into his neck – occurred soon after his brother Theo had gotten married and his artist friend Gauguin had left him after an intolerably long stay at Vincent's house in Arles. Doubly abandoned by his brother and only real friend, and continually haunted by the crushing failure of his life, he resorted to a punishment most severe. Perhaps a more stable mind would not have viewed his brother's marriage or his friend's exodus as such great calamities.

Of course, the ear-cutting episode has become legendary, the torment, failure, and illness leading to it seldom dwelled upon. In fact, the ear-cutting was made legend in Vincent's time by a famous Paris art critic, Albert Aurier. In the only truly glowing review his art ever received during his life, Aurier made reference to Vincent cutting off his ear as a part of the great passion that filled the artist and his paintings, a passion unrivaled by other artists. What artist would cut off his ear for the sake of his art?

The critique by Aurier drew the Parisian public to view Vincent's art work, in part out of curiosity about the artist who cut his ear off. However, the praise and public interest garnered no sales, and as Vincent drew ever deeper into madness, suffering debilitating attacks that incapacitated him for weeks, the inevitable end of his artistry was drawing near.

A widely held myth about Vincent Van Gogh was that he took his own life at age thirty-seven. This myth has been strongly debunked by Van Gogh researchers Steven Naifeh and Gregory Smith. First of all, Vincent was shot in the stomach. Who commits suicide by shooting himself in the stomach? Second, a gun was never found where Vincent purportedly shot himself. If one commits suicide, wouldn't the gun be nearby? Third, would someone who tries to commit suicide drag himself for two miles into a village to seek help? That is exactly what Vincent did.

Vincent had never owned or shot a gun, but a young town bully, who along with his followers had badgered and tormented the little madman Vincent frequently, did have access to the only gun in the village. He may have shot Vincent on purpose or accidentally while trying to scare him. That would explain why no gun was found where Vincent was shot. That would also provide a more plausible explanation for Van Gogh's death.

Vincent Van Gogh was one of the most fascinating, brilliant, confounding, and troubled artists to ever live. His life was plagued by poverty, loneliness, dependency, mental illness, and failure. Yet he always believed that success was just off the horizon and that the faith that his brother placed in him would reap great rewards for them both. And his passion to paint, to be an esteemed artist, was always stronger than anything else that life dealt him. Suicide? Not Vincent.

Questions for Discussion

1. What did you learn about Vincent Van Gogh that you hadn't previously known? What surprised you most about his life?

2. Why do you think Theo financed his brother's art career until Vincent died despite the financial burden it placed on him?

3. In what ways did Vincent's mental illness affect every aspect of his life? Some have argued that his tormented life was a part of his being a great artist. Would you agree?

Mama

by Jess Yim Ka-mei

What does the word "mama" mean? A lady who gives birth to babies? The one who nurtures little children into great men or women? A person who owns our flesh and blood? A soft voice, sincere face, caring eyes, gentle hands, concerned personality, someone who takes care of our meals and our clothes, who helps us with our homework, guides us through our love affairs and to our marriage… is this the description of every mom? My mom seemed to be an exception.

My mom always scolded me; even the slightest mistake would be viewed as seriously as an unforgivable crime. She never helped me study for any dictations, quizzes, tests or exams, and she sent me away whenever I asked a single question. My mom never showed appreciation for any of my achievements, from a mark of 100 in a dictation to winning a prize in an art competition. To her, nothing I did seemed to be worthy of praise. She always kept me at home, didn't let me go to my classmates' birthday parties, join school camps or picnics, or participate in extra curricular activities. I felt like a wild bird confined in a cage, and I envied other girls whose lives seemed so much better than mine.

My mom never waited for me outside school, comforted me when I was sad, or brought me to the doctor when I was sick. Once when I asked her to accompany me to the doctor's, she just replied: "Kid, how old are you? Primary three already! Just tell the doctor how you feel and that's it!" I walked to the doctor's alone that day, and when he asked me where my mother was, I responded with silence.

More than once, I wished I could have another mom. I wished for a mom who would support me in every way, give me the courage to fight my fears and provide me with faith. I wished for a mom who could share my joy whenever I achieved something; share my sorrow whenever I failed; smile with me as well as cry with me. I wished for a mom who I could depend on for my whole life. No matter how bad the world treated me, she would be there to comfort me and say, "My child, have no fear, I'll be with you forever."

Only when my mom told me her story did I realize that I hadn't understood her, and from that day forward my life changed. Her own father had been a nasty man who flirted with countless women. Her mother had been a young, innocent girl who couldn't even manage to take care of herself. When my mother was born, she was loved by nobody; she was a burden to the people who were responsible for her. Her parents didn't offer a blessing nor give her a glance before giving her up, their youngest daughter. Her foster family made her work all day long, beat her whenever they were angry, and treated her as a maid while calling her daughter. When she was three, she met her real mother and was told to call her "aunt."

As she grew, she had no opportunities to attend school, spend time with friends, go to parties, enjoy childhood, or see the wonders of life. When she was eighteen, her older sister found her, but they were never to meet again. All she ever heard from her father was the message that her sister passed on: "Never approach us again." She never tried.

Without ever knowing what a loving family was like, my mother married a poor guy and gave birth to four innocent lives. Can you blame someone who had never been loved by her family for not knowing how to express her love and affection to her children?

Then suddenly, I remembered. The box of dolls my mom bought for me when I had a high fever when I was three. Her mutterings of "put more clothes on" whenever the weather turned cold. The favorite dishes she cooked for me every birthday. The cakes she always used to bring to me whenever I studied late into the night. Her visit to the boutique that I worked in last summer. The lovely shirt that I longed for and that she bought me when she went to Japan. How could she know I loved it? How could I have missed all of the times that she tried to be a good mother and showed that she cared for me in the only ways she knew?

I'm sorry, Mom. Your daughter didn't know you before. I wish I had always known your story.

Questions for Discussion

1. What is the purpose of the opening paragraph? How does it "set the stage" for what is to follow?

2. What examples does the author use to show the relationship between her mother and herself in the third and fourth paragraph? How do those examples contrast with the examples in the next-to-last paragraph?

3. What details of her mother's life before marriage affected you most strongly as a reader? Do you believe that how her mother was raised justifies how she treated her own daughter, and why?

4. How do you feel your mother's (or father's) early life may have affected how she raised you as a son or daughter? How might your upbringing affect the kind of mother or father you may be (or are)?

Unit Three
Interests

Certain kinds of writing lend themselves best to the traditional essay form that includes a thesis statement, topic sentences, and an opening, middle, and conclusion. This traditional form is used regularly in non-fiction writing, including newspaper editorials, magazine articles, journal essays, and college writing for different courses.

Thesis-centered writing is simple in design and easy for readers to follow. That is why it has been used extensively by writers in a variety of writing situations. In the opening, the writer usually introduces her topic and includes a thesis statement expressing the writer's opinion or viewpoint on the topic. In the middle or body of the paper, the writer supports the thesis statement by providing reasons or evidence revealing why she thinks or feels the way she does. In the conclusion, the writer reinforces the thesis statement in some manner and leaves readers with some final thoughts on the topic.

In this unit, you will write a thesis-centered paper. You will also use this form for much of the writing you do in the future, whether for a history, sociology, or English class, a "letter to the editor," or a letter to a local politician. Learning to write an effective thesis-centered paper is a valuable part of the writing experience.

Your writing assignment for this unit focuses on a particular interest of yours, something that you enjoy doing or that you are very committed to. Writing about an interest accomplishes three purposes. First, it allows you to write about something that you are passionate about, which often leads to the best writing. Second, it lends itself well to the thesis-centered format, the writing focus for this unit. Third, by reading about an interest of yours, readers will learn more about you and also about a topic they may know little about.

Prewriting

In each unit, the initial prewriting activities help you prepare to write the first draft of your paper. During this section, you will select a topic to write on, decide on a thesis statement for your paper, and generate some support for your thesis.

Topic Selection

No doubt you have several interests that occupy your free time. Think about things that you enjoy doing or find rewarding, that you know a lot about, and that may be somewhat different from the next person's interests. Think about interests that reveal something about you and that might even surprise readers.

Consider different interests that you find most gratifying. They may be in the area of sports, music, politics, computers, social issues, or fashion, and they might involve collecting, performing, volunteering, working, or creating.

Prewriting Activity 3.1

Select a topic for your paper following these suggestions.

1. Select an interest that you would like to write about.

2. Select a topic that readers may be interested in learning more about.

3. Select a topic about which you are knowledgeable and can write easily on.

4. If you are considering two or three interests, select the topic that may differ from your classmates' choices.

Sample topic selection

I like wearing offbeat, funky clothes and shopping at thrift stores. That's a big hobby of mine. I've enjoyed tutoring since I was in elementary school, and it has helped me make a decision about my future career. I'm also interested in the health of our planet and try to go "green." I use paper bags instead of plastic, take public transportation when I can, and always recycle. I'm not sure what I want to write about, but those are three things to think about.

Thesis Statement

Now that you have selected a topic, the next step is to consider what you want to write about it. To that end, generating a thesis statement provides a focus for your paper, something around which to develop it.

The following points clarify what a thesis statement is and its role in how you write your paper.

Thesis Statement Guidelines

1. A thesis statement expresses the main point of your paper: the primary idea that you want to convey about your subject to readers. For example, if a writer chose doll collecting as her topic, her thesis statement might be, "While collecting dolls may seem like child's play to some, it is an interesting hobby for women of all ages."

2. A thesis statement generally reveals the writer's opinion or viewpoint on the topic: what she believes or how she feels about it. For example, on the topic of "politicians," if a writer's thesis is, "Politicians learn to say nothing in a lot of different ways," the writer's opinion of politicians is quite clear.

3. The thesis statement is usually found in the opening so that readers know what the paper is about. For example, on the topic of bird watching, the thesis statement, "Bird watching is the most exciting hobby imaginable," lets readers know that they will discover the excitement of bird watching from the writer's perspective.

4. A paper is written in support of its thesis, which is called thesis development. For example, following the thesis statement on doll collecting, the writer would relate to readers everything interesting about doll collecting. Following the thesis statement on bird watching, the writer would explain and show to readers the excitement of bird watching.

5. A thesis statement should express what a writer believes about his subject. If the thesis expresses the writer's true feelings about a topic, it will lead to the most interesting and authentic writing.

6. Papers by different writers on the same topic may have quite different thesis statements. For example, on the topic of interior design, one writer's thesis statement may be, "Interior design provides a creative outlet like nothing else," while another writer's thesis may be, "Interior design is all about geometry: combinations of shapes blending together in interesting forms." Clearly, these two thesis statements would lead to very different papers.

Prewriting Activity 3.2

Underline the thesis statement in the following opening paragraphs of different papers: the one sentence that best expresses the writer's viewpoint on the topic.

Last summer I registered on-line for the fall semester for the first time. Previously I had always gone on campus for the traditional registration in the gymnasium, waiting in line after line to try and get the classes I wanted. What a difference on-line registration made, as I sat comfortably in my room in front of the computer instead of standing in line at school. It was still frustrating when a class I wanted would show up on the monitor as "closed," but not nearly as frustrating as driving to campus to find out the same thing. On the whole, on-line registration is much better than the traditional way, and I'd recommend it to anyone.

Before going to college, I always shopped for groceries at the regular supermarkets, not worrying much about the price of one thing or another. However, when I came to college and began cooking for myself and buying my own groceries, I became very price conscious. I soon found that there are alternatives to shopping at the big-name stores. As I discovered, you can save a lot of money shopping at discount supermarkets, and you don't have to sacrifice quality. That was one of the best things I learned my freshman year.

I like all kinds of music, from the 1950's to today's. I listen to different radio stations that play oldies, classic rock, alternative, and hip hop, and I'll flip from station to station to find a song I really like. However, one day a friend of mine told me to go on-line to "You tube" and plug in the name of the artist and song I wanted to hear. I tried it, and I not only heard the song but saw a video. To hear the music that you want when you want to hear it, "You tube" is the best place to go. It couldn't be easier to use.

Today I'm sitting in the cafeteria watching every person that walks in or out. I station myself with a friend at a table with a good view of the door, and there we sit, eating a little and looking a lot. When there's a lot of traffic, our lunch stretches out quite a while. I don't know if you'd call it a hobby, but people-watching ranks as one of my favorite activities. That may sound weird to some, but to me and my friends, it's good fun. There are a lot of interesting people in the world.

Living inland my whole life, with hot summer and cold winter weather, I wasn't prepared for the weather on the coast where I'm going to school. There were no more 100 degree summer days or 20 degree winter nights. Every day the weather seemed about the same: the low 70's with mild breezes. Some seasons were a little cooler than others, but they fluctuated by just a few degrees, not the forty or fifty I was used to. Having lived on the coast for over a year, I realize that coastal weather has some real advantages.

Prewriting Activity 3.3

For practice generating thesis statements, write a potential thesis statement for any four of the following topics that expresses your viewpoint on the topic and that you could support in a paper.

Examples

Topic: Punk rock bands
Thesis: To really understand the whole punk rock scene, you have to attend live performances.

Topic: Classic cars
Thesis: Cars of the 1950's and 60's have more style than today's copycat automobiles.

1. Topic: Country music
    Thesis statement: _____
    _____

2. Topic: Rap music
    Thesis statement: _____
    _____

3. Topic: Fast food restaurants
    Thesis statement: _____
    _____

4. Topic: Cafeteria food
    Thesis statement: _____
    _____

5. Topic: iPads
    Thesis statement: _____
    _____

6. Topic: Texting
    Thesis statement: _____
    _____

7. Topic: Working while going to school
    Thesis statement: _____
    _____

8. Topic: Professional football
    Thesis statement: _____
    _____

Prewriting Activity 3.4
Generate a thesis statement for your topic that expresses the main idea that you want to develop in your paper. Create a thesis that reflects your viewpoint on the topic and that you could support in a paper.

Sample thesis statement
Topic: being a vegetarian

Thesis statement: Becoming a vegetarian was one of the best choices I've made.

Making a List

During prewriting, writers often make a list of ideas on their topic that they may include in their draft. For your upcoming paper, you could make a list of points that support your thesis statement and develop them in separate paragraphs in your draft.

For example, the writer whose topic was "being a vegetarian" listed the following points in support of her thesis.

Thesis statement: Becoming a vegetarian was one of the best choices I've made.

Supporting points: I eat healthier food.
I feel better.
I've lost weight.
I am committed to not eating animals.

While listing some supporting points doesn't restrict you to those ideas or obligate you to use them, it does get you thinking about your topic, provides some beginning ideas from which to develop paragraphs, and puts some ideas on paper that you can reorganize to present most effectively in a paper.

Prewriting Activity 3.5
Make a list of four or five points in support of your thesis statement.

Sample supporting points
Thesis statement: Working with the elderly is very rewarding.

Supporting points: They have great stories to tell.
They are very appreciative of any help.
They are honest and tell you what they think.
Cheering them up makes me feel better.

Thesis Statement:

Supporting points:

1.

2.

3.

4.

5.

_____

First Drafts

Now that you have done considerable prewriting work for your paper, you are ready to write your first draft. The drafting considerations in this section include the three parts of a thesis-centered paper -opening, middle, and conclusion -and the use of topic sentences.

The purpose of having an opening, middle, and conclusion is to make the paper as readable as possible. Readers first want to know what a paper is about, which they discover in the opening. Next, they want to know what you have to say about the topic, which they discover in the middle paragraphs. Finally, they want to understand why you wrote the paper, which they usually discover in the conclusion.

Opening, Middle, and Concluding Paragraphs

While opening, middle, and concluding paragraphs vary in nature depending on the kind of writing you are doing, they generally have one thing in common: each is distinct from the others. Readers have a clear sense of when they are moving from the opening, which introduces the topic, to the middle, where the topic is developed, to the ending, which wraps up the paper.

The following are the basic elements that characterize each of the three parts of a paper.

Opening or Introductory Paragraph(s)

1. The opening introduces the topic to readers and provides the writer's viewpoint on the topic, which is revealed in the thesis statement.

2. The opening captures the readers' interest and also reveals the writer's interest in the topic.

3. The thesis statement usually comes at or near the end of the opening and prepares readers for what lies ahead in the middle paragraphs.

4. The opening gives readers a reason for reading further, by emphasizing, for example, how serious or interesting the topic is or why readers should know more about it.

5. While openings are typically one paragraph long, they may include two or three paragraphs, with the thesis statement often in the last paragraph.

Middle Paragraphs

1. The middle paragraphs develop and support the main idea expressed in the thesis statement.

2. The middle paragraphs provide the reasons that the writer believes as he does about the topic.

3. In support of the topic sentence, the middle paragraphs may do several things: explain more about the topic, provide points of support for the thesis, or provide examples to further develop those points.

4. Middle paragraphs often begin with a *topic sentence*: an opening sentence that tells what the paragraph is about. The rest of the sentences in the paragraph develop that idea. The purpose of the topic sentence is to let readers know what a paragraph is about, to highlight a supporting point for the thesis statement, and to ensure that a paragraph is developed around one central idea.

For example, if the thesis statement for a paper is, "I enjoy playing the keyboard for relaxation," the supporting points in the middle paragraphs might include the following: forget about problems, be creative, play favorite songs, play to my mood. In the paper, these four points could be expressed in the following topic sentences, each of which would begin a separate paragraph.

a.   Playing the keyboard helps me forget all my problems for a while.

b.   I also enjoy trying out new melodies on the keyboard

c.   Playing the keyboard, I can enjoy hearing my favorite songs over and over.

d.   Whatever mood I'm in, I play music that fits that mood.

The following paragraphs show how the middle paragraphs were developed from the four topic sentences in a., b., c., and d.

Playing the keyboard helps me forget my problems for a while. I forget my job, my homework, and my crazy schedule by thinking about nothing but the music I am creating. When I'm playing the keyboard, there's nothing else on my mind and I have an hour of pure enjoyment and relaxation, free from any worries. To know that I always have that outlet when I need it is very comforting.

I also enjoy trying out new melodies on the keyboard. I'll start with a part of a melody in my head and try it out on the keyboard. Then I'll add to it or change it as I try out different series of notes. Sometimes I'll realize that I'm starting to play a melody of a song that I've heard, so I go in a different direction. Sometimes I end up with something that isn't too bad, and other times I end with nothing I like. But it is fun to try and create something new rather than always playing someone else's songs. I'm smart enough to keep my melodies to myself.

Playing the keyboard, I can enjoy playing my favorite songs over and over. For a while, I was really into the Adele songs and I would play a song like "Someone Like You" over and over because I liked it so much. I did the same thing with songs like Train's "Soul Sister," Miley's "Wrecking Ball," and Beyonce's "Single Ladies." There are certain songs that just grab me and I love playing them again and again.

Finally, whatever mood I'm in, I play music that fits that mood. For example, if I feel upbeat and happy, I might play something by Train or Bruno Mars. If I'm in a romantic mood, I might play some classic ballad like "Wicked Game" or something by Journey. If I'm in an introspective mood, I might play something from Green Day like "Boulevard of Broken Dreams." If I feel like moving, I'll try something by Beyonce or Rihanna. Whatever my mood, there's some music to fit it, and I always feel better after playing the keyboard.

Concluding Paragraph

1.   The concluding paragraph brings the paper to an end in a way that reinforces the thesis statement.

2. The concluding paragraph may do any number of things: summarize the main supporting points in the paper, restate the thesis in different words, provide a final powerful point or example to support the writer's viewpoint on the topic, explain the writer's purpose for writing about this particular topic, influence the readers' attitude towards the topic, project what the future mayhold regarding the topic, or leave readers with a final powerful thought to take with them.

3. The concluding paragraph should be more than just a summary or restatement of what has come before. It should go beyond what has been presented, leaving readers with something new to think about.

4. Being the last thing that is read, the conclusion should make an impact on readers, leaving them with something to ponder, laugh about, be concerned with, or learn more about.

Sample Draft

The following draft provides an example of a paper with an opening that includes a thesis statement, middle paragraphs beginning with topic sentences, and a conclusion that reinforces the thesis statement and projects into the future. The thesis statement is italicized, and the topic sentences in the middle paragraphs are underlined.

Politics

A lot of people my age aren't interested in politics, but I am. I come from a politically active family, and my dad has worked locally on a number of campaigns. While many college students feel disconnected from politics and have no interested in who gets elected to what, I feel that the decisions that politicians make today can affect the future of my generation. *Younger voters have a stake in the political process, and I know from experience that we can make a difference.*

As a child, I spent a lot of evenings in campaign offices, eating pizza and watching TV while dad was doing phone banking. I also walked precincts with him, leaving campaign flyers on people's doorsteps. I didn't really know what I was doing, but I enjoyed being with my dad and getting his praise for helping out. I also got to attend some victory parties, which meant lots of food and colored balloons. <u>I didn't know it at the time, but these experiences paved the way for my becoming politically active.</u>

<u>There is nothing glamorous about working in political campaigns.</u> The things you have to do to win a campaign are very basic: stuff thousands of envelopes, make hundreds of phone calls, walk precincts to reach the voters, man a voter registration table, put up candidate's signs around town. Most campaign work is rather tedious, and many times I'd rather be doing something else. That's why you have to believe in what you're doing and the candidate or candidates you are working for. If you become a political volunteer for the glamour of the campaign, you won't last.

<u>Of course, it's the ultimate pay-off that brings the excitement.</u> When your candidate wins the election, there is no better feeling in the world. You know that all of the hard work that you and many others put in helped to make the difference. When you share in the victory party with your candidate and all the supporters, it's a time of sheer jubilation. In later days, that rush is replaced with a feeling of satisfaction. All of the hard work becomes a faint memory. Before long you're ready for the next campaign.

<u>While the political highs are thrilling, the political lows are devastating.</u> It's hard to describe the feeling of utter despondency and sadness when you are on the losing end of a long campaign. One of the feelings that always gnaws at me is guilt. What could I have done that I didn't do? Why did I go to the concert one night and skip the phone banking? However, instead of wallowing in self-pity, I just recommit myself to working harder the next time. To work in politics, you have to be an optimist.

When it comes to politics, I feel out of touch with most of my fellow students. However, as a voting bloc, I know that the 18-to-21 year olds have a lot of power. So I sit at the voter registration tables on campus, I recruit members to join our political club, I write political pieces for the school paper, and I try to get people to help on a campaign. More students are starting to see the connection between political decisions and the availability of student aid or college loans, the cost of tuition, the price of gas, and the health of our environment. As politics is a big part of my life, I think it's also going to get bigger for a lot of students. I'm going to do what I can to help make that a reality.

Notice in the opening paragraph how the writer introduces her topic, explains her interest in it, and concludes with her topic sentence. In the next paragraph she tells how she became involved, and in the three subsequent middle paragraphs, she relates what it is like to be a political volunteer. Finally, she concludes the paper by telling readers more about her political involvement and how she hopes it spreads to many college students. By the end of the paper, we clearly understand the writer's passion for politics and her knowledge of the political process.

Drafting Activity 3.6

Read the following essay. With a classmate, identify the opening, middle, and concluding paragraphs, the thesis statement in the opening, and the topic sentences in the middle paragraphs. Then analyze the content in each part of the essay and what the writer accomplishes in the opening, middle, and conclusion.

Passion for Football

Every Sunday during football season, you'll always find me in the same place most of the time: sitting in front of the television. I'm there again every Monday night, and sometimes on Thursdays. Those are the times when NFL football is on television, and I seldom miss a game. Every year I can't wait for fall to roll around so I can enjoy my favorite pastime: watching professional football.

While I like watching all levels of football, professional football is by far the best. The players are the best in the world, and the speed of the game is amazing. I like everything about the game, especially the long bomb, the big hits, the breakaway running plays, and the acrobatic catches. Professional football players are some of the best athletes around, and when they play together as a team, it is beautiful to watch.

While I'll watch any pro game, I do have my favorite teams that I prefer watching. I like the Colts because of their high-powered offense and the Steelers because of their toughness and in-your-face defense. I like the Patriots because they always perform at a high level. When any of these teams are playing, I always have a team to cheer for. The rest of the times I just sit back and enjoy the game.

I particularly like it when two games are on at a time, which usually happens on Sunday mornings. Then I can switch back and forth between games and watch two at a time. If I time it right, I can catch almost every play of both games since seldom do both games have a play occurring at the same time. Sometimes there will even be three games on at once, and I'm flipping that remote all over the place.

I watch a game differently from a lot of guys I know. I'm not like some of them who love to go to the sports bar and root for their team along with a hundred other screaming maniacs. I'm not into all that emotional stuff and high-fiving. I don't even care if no one is watching the game in the house but me. Sometimes a friend will be over to watch with me, but I'm just as happy sitting there by myself. I watch the games just to enjoy the great athletes and great plays, so that makes me different from a lot of fans.

Although some people tell me to get a life, they don't understand that watching pro football is a big part of my life. They don't really understand how much I enjoy what I'm doing, and I don't waste my time telling them. If there's anything better to do than watching Peyton Manning throw a perfect strike into the end zone through three defenders, or Marshawn Lynch breaking through the line and juking the linebackers, or Michael Crabtree leaping high to snare a pass with one hand, or T.J. McDonald flying across the field and smashing into a startled running back, I haven't seen it. It's like watching great artists at work.

Football season is almost over for the year, but the Colts are in the Super Bowl, so I'll have one last Super Sunday to enjoy. Then my life changes for the worse. I have nothing to do that replaces the enjoyment I get from watching NFL football, and watching a baseball game on a spring Sunday afternoon is boring with a capital B. I go through football withdrawal for a couple months, then switch gears and start getting out of the house on weekends and doing things I don't do during football season, like going to the gym.

By mid-summer, the upcoming football season is in the news again, and I read every article I can. In a way, I start preparing for the new season like the players do, by checking the playing schedule, seeing how the draft picks and free agency trades are working out, analyzing the coaching changes, and gearing up for hundreds of hours of games. By the start of the season, I've got my game face on and am hunkered down in the living room with fresh batteries in my remote. Let the games begin.

Drafting Guidelines

Keep the following guidelines in mind when you write your first draft.

1. Write an opening, middle, and conclusion for your draft. Include your thesis sentence in the opening, and begin each middle paragraph with a topic sentence that expresses the main idea for the paragraph.

2. Include some of your list ideas from prewriting to help develop your paper, using them to generate topic sentences for your middle paragraphs.

3. If you are writing on a topic your reading audience may know little about, include some explanation in the beginning of your middle paragraphs.

4. As you write, reread your sentences to help you decide what to write next.

5. Your writing purpose is to help your readers understand why you feel the way you do about your topic. Keep that goal in mind as you write.

6. Your purpose in writing the first draft is to get your ideas on paper without concern for wording perfection or whether you make an occasional error.

Drafting Activity 3.7
Write the first draft of your paper keeping the drafting guidelines in mind.

Sample First Draft

Tutor

In fourth grade when the bell rang for recess, my classmates couldn't get outside fast enough to play ball or run around the playground. Not particularly good at games or sports and a slow runner, I was less enthusiastic, often watching the fun from a distance or hunting ladybugs and rolly pollys with a couple friends. Then I found out about an activity that changed my recess time dramatically.

Knowing my dislike for the rigors of the playground, my teacher told me that students could earn service points towards the Block R award by tutoring kindergarten students. She said I could do it during some recess periods. I told her I'd like to give it a try and the next recess, three of us reported to the kindergarten building.

I sat with students individually and helped them with their numbers, letters, and small art projects. I enjoyed it, and the students seemed to respond well to me. The kindergarten teacher said I was doing a good job, and before long I was spending practically every twenty-minute recess in the kindergarten room. It was a part of the day I always looked forward to.

Looking back, it wasn't too surprising that I took to tutoring. From the time I was very young, I liked playing school with my younger sister and grandparents, and I was always the teacher. Tutoring kindergarten students seemed a natural extension of my play. I earned enough service points that year that along with my grades and other activities, I earned my Block R plaque, a great accomplishment for me. I also enjoyed my "students" shouting out to me across campus or waving to me in the cafeteria. I had many little friends.

I continued my tutoring for the remainder of elementary school, working with first graders as a fifth grader and with second graders as a sixth grader. Admittedly some of my classmates let me know that they thought it a little strange that I preferred tutoring to recess, but no one made fun of me. I was also getting a lot of positive feedback from teachers, and some teachers would request me specifically to work in their classrooms. I also continued racking up the Block R service points, but by this time I would have kept tutoring without them. I remember one teacher saying, "Imelda, you are a born teacher," an observation I would never forget.

In middle school there was no tutoring program similar to elementary school, and I found fewer opportunities to work. Once a week middle school students could volunteer to tutor at the elementary school for an hour, and I did that, but it was far from the regular tutoring routine I had in elementary school, and I missed that. However, once I got into high school, I had a plan.

I felt confident in my tutoring abilities by this time, particularly in reading, writing, and math, the three areas that students most needed help. Reading was my first love and something of a specialty for me, and I spent a lot of time learning about reading instruction, including phonics, sight word memorization, and contextual clues. Since I wasn't doing any after-school activity at the time, I asked my mom about me starting an after-school tutoring business. I could earn a little money and continue doing what I enjoyed. She said to give it a try although we were both skeptical that I'd get any students to tutor.

I advertised in the local paper for tutoring elementary age students in reading, writing, and math, and I got a few phone calls. I would meet with the mothers of prospective students at my house, with my mom present, and tell them my qualifications and years of experience. The students would be coming to me since my mom didn't want me going all over town to different people's houses. I started out with just a couple students, but the business grew as I continued to advertise and word of mouth began spreading that students and parents were happy with the results. Soon I was tutoring three-four days a week, sometimes taking two students at a time with similar skill levels.

I continued my tutoring business through my junior year of high school and then experienced my first burn-out. I had been tutoring kids since the fourth grade and I felt I needed a break. My enthusiasm for the work was dropping, and the tutoring sessions were becoming more like drudgery. I wanted to relax and enjoy my senior year, spend more time with my friends, and have no after-school obligations. So I put tutoring out of my mind, thinking perhaps that it had run its course for me.

I learned that you sometimes have to get away from something that you have done for a long time before you realize how much it meant to you. I had a full year to recharge my battery, and by the time I started college, tutoring seemed like a good idea again. However, I wanted to try something different this time, and the college provided the opportunity. The college hired peer tutors to work with students who were working below college level to help bring them up to grade level. Prospective tutors were interviewed and also did mock tutoring sessions. I decided to specialize in reading instruction, my greatest love and aptitude, and during the mock sessions, showed off the considerable teaching skills I had developed over the years. The head of tutorial instruction was impressed, and I was hired.

Over the past two years, I have gotten as much tutoring work as I wanted and made a number of friends. I realized that I instilled some of my passion for reading with my students as well as helping them develop their skills, and I often left books with them that I thought they might like. Although I had expected for some time that my future career lay somewhere in the area of teaching, my college tutoring brought a clearer focus to what I wanted to do.

I enjoyed tutoring my peers, but I knew that my first love was working with elementary age children, and I knew that I had a good rapport with them. I also realized that while I loved working with students one-on-one or in small groups, that working with a class of thirty students might not be my strong suit. Finally, I knew that teaching reading was what I loved the most and did the best, and it was something I could imagine doing the rest of my life.

After doing some research, I learned that most school districts had one or more reading specialists who went from school to school working with individual students or small groups on a pull-out basis. In addition, they helped to develop and coordinate reading programs in the district, conduct reading staff development, and assess student progress in reading. I couldn't think of a job that I would enjoy more or was better suited for.

After I get my liberal studies degree in two years, I will apply to a reading specialist credential program at a nearby college whose program has a good reputation. To have that direction in my life gives me a very good feeling, particularly as I see classmates who have no idea what they want to do or major in. Who knows. If I had been more athletically inclined and enjoyed recess like most students, I may have never gotten into tutoring, which sent my life in the direction it's going. And I still hearken back in the fifth grade to one teacher's comment, "Imelda, you are a born teacher." Maybe I am.

Revision

Now that you have written the first draft of your paper, you are ready to make any changes you feel will make it more interesting, informative, complete, or better written. Writing the first draft is a major step towards completing your paper, but there is still work to be done.

Often writers feel a sense of completion after finishing a first draft, and aren't anxious to jump in and start revising it. That is a good reason to set your draft aside for a few hours or even overnight. Then when you take a fresh look at it, you may feel more motivated to improve the paper. You will also find yourself less enchanted with what you wrote and realize that some changes are probably in order.

Think of your writing process as creating a sculpture. In the first draft, you have chiseled out the rough form of your sculpture, and viewers can clearly see your intended figure: a child with a cat in her lap. In the second draft, you use a finer chisel and more refined sculpting skills to turn the roughly formed figure into a finely featured work of art. Neither writer nor artist can create a finished product in a single step

In the "Revision" sections, you are introduced to new elements of revision and also apply what you learned in previous units to help revise your draft. In this section, the new revision consideration is organizing your paper.

Organization

An important element of an effectively written paper is its organization: the order in which its content is presented to readers. In a well-organized paper, ideas are presented in an order that best conveys the writer's ideas. There is a logic to the organization, and the ideas in one paragraph follow naturally from the previous paragraph and lead sensibly into the next one.

While different types of writing favor particular organizational schemes, there is one organizational constant in most writing. Writers begin with an opening that introduces their topic, continue with a middle that develops what they have to say about the topic, and end with a conclusion that "wraps up" the paper for readers, providing a sense of completion. This basic organizational scheme has stood the test of time, providing writers with the most efficient structure for communicating with readers. Within this basic framework, however, there are other organizational decisions you make with any paper that you write. The following guidelines will help you make the best choices as you determine the most effective way to present your ideas.

Organizing Guidelines

1. Narrative papers that tell a story usually have the most straightforward organization. The story is told in chronological order, with events presented in the order that they occurred. This is the organizational scheme you used in your first paper in Unit One.

2. Papers often contain a number of points or ideas that support the thesis statement of a paper. These points should be presented in their most effective order, usually one of the following:

   a. Start with the most important point and conclude with the least important.

   b. Start with the least important point and conclude with the most important.

---

c.   Start and conclude with the two most important points and sandwich the other points between them.

d.   Group related points together in sequential paragraphs.

The order in which you present your points will depend on what you believe is the most effective and logical presentation of ideas, based on what you want to accomplish in the paper.

3.   Certain types of papers lend themselves to a particular organizational scheme. For example, in a problem/solution paper, which you will write in a later unit, a typical organizational pattern includes introducing the problem, presenting its causes, explaining its effects, and providing possible solutions.

4.   Often in a paper, you will use the middle paragraphs to do different things: explain more about the topic, provide examples supporting your thesis statement, present reasons why you feel as you do about the topic, or present other information related to the thesis statement. In such cases, you would order your ideas based on these considerations:

a.   What is the most logical, natural order for the ideas to be presented in?

b.   What is the most effective order for readers to follow your thoughts?

c.   What order would best accomplish your writing purpose?

For example, if readers need to learn more about your topic, it is best to provide that information before getting into the supporting points for your thesis statement.

5.   While you might decide on a rough organizational scheme during your prewriting planning, you often need to get your thoughts on paper before discovering the best way to organize them. On rereading a first draft, a particular paragraph or sentence may appear out of place, so you move it to a location where it fits better.

It is important to check the organization of your paper during the revision process to see how effectively you have ordered your ideas. Sometimes moving a paragraph or two to a different location can significantly improve a paper, and using a word processing program, moving paragraphs or sentences is a simple task.

Revision Activity 3.8

For the following two topics, number the supporting points in the order you would present them in a paper. Be prepared to explain the order you choose.

Topic: Rugby

Thesis statement: Rugby is a great sport that most Americans know little about.

Supporting Points: Requires great stamina and running ability
Extremely fast, tough sport
Tremendous individual skills of top players
Originated in Europe
Basic rules of the game
Exciting to watch

Topic: Elementary school teacher

Thesis statement: Being an elementary school teacher is a challenging job.

Supporting Points: Discipline problems to deal with
Long hours
Teaching non-English speaking children
Responsible for children testing at grade level
Helping children who have bad home lives
Endless paper work to fill out from district and state

Revision Activity 3.9
Read the following first draft and reorder the paragraphs in a more effective way by numbering the paragraphs in the order you would recommend.

Escaping the Gang
I am one of nine children, the son of Mexican immigrants. My family moved around a lot when I was young. Once after we went to back to Mexico, our family split up. My dad stayed in Mexico where he was working and my mother moved the rest of us to Los Angeles. My father was going to join us later. I never saw him again.

I am one of the lucky ones. I escaped from gang life, I'm not in prison, and I'm still alive. Every day I see young kids hanging out on the street and I know where their lives are heading. That's why I spend time at the youth center on weekends talking to kids and playing with them. I know the lure of gang life and also how gangs ruin lives. If I can help one kid stay out of gangs, maybe I've saved a life.

We eventually moved to a small two-bedroom apartment, the first of many that we lived in. There were a lot of other poor kids like me around, and they became my friends. We began hanging out in the streets, sometimes very late. I had a lot of anger in me, especially towards my father, and I vented it by getting into fights. Some of the guys that befriended me were gang members. When you're young, you don't judge people who are nice to you, and I had someone to back me up and to pass the time with. My mom was busy trying to keep nine children clothed and fed.

When you are young, you really don't know what a gang is about. Once you are older, things change. People start shooting at you. You can't go certain places because you'll get jumped. And when you get hit by members of another gang, you have to retaliate. My homeboys and I would go on patrol searching for rival gang members. We'd smoke weed to get up our courage, and then we'd see a couple guys and jump out of the car and fight, hitting them with bats and "jacking" their stuff.

By the time I was in fifth grade I had begun to steal, breaking into homes with my homeboys and grabbing video games or any cash we could find. By the time I was a freshman, I was "jumped" into my gang, getting pounded for several minutes by some gang members. I fought back and got in some punches, just to show I wasn't going down like a punk. I passed the test.

I got kicked out of high school for being a trouble maker and went to continuation. Luckily, there were some teachers there who didn't give up on me. I got my high school diploma. However, once I got out of school, I had more time to hang out with my homeboys. We broke into homes, and when we weren't stealing, we smoked marijuana and drank beer. We'd steal booze from a liquor store and trade it on the street for some weed. We'd spend most of the day getting drunk and high.

My life fell apart after my homeboys and I robbed a clothing store. Someone got our license number, and soon police were rounding up my friends. I left the area and stayed on the run for a few weeks. Finally, I turned myself in because I missed my girlfriend. I was convicted of grand theft and sent to county jail with other gang members. Being in jail got my attention. I wondered whether I'd end up rotting in prison ten years from now. I didn't want that, and I decided to drop out of the gang.

I told an officer I was dropping out, and I was moved to another center to "protect" me. I made it through, and once I got out, I was put in touch with Jorge, a former gang member who was director of New Hope. I got in a program where I learned to manage my anger, fill out a job resume, and stay clean. After I got through the program, Jorge lined me up with a job. He also probably saved my life.

Today I look at my time in jail as a blessing because I had the opportunity to see what I was doing wrong. I'll be on probation for three years and I can't mess up. My old friends still want to hang out, but I've got too much going for me to lose it.

When I talk to the young guys, I tell them straight up what it's like. I tell them the temptations are great, but they need to be strong and stay away from the street life. I tell them to respect their moms and to care about school so they don't ruin their lives. Some of them listen to me; some of them don't. I keep trying because I know they want to have a future like everyone. They just don't know how to get there.

When I see young kids on the street, I feel for them. I know how poor they are and how lonely it can get. I also know that being around older guys seems exciting. They are your role models, and when they give you attention, it's a big deal. You don't imagine what it's like once you start stealing, gang banging, and getting shot at.

Most importantly, I take an interest in them. I talk to them and listen to them. I spend time with them so they know that I care. Maybe I'm a role model for some of them, and if I had had someone like me in my life when I was growing up, things might have been different. I hope it is for them.

Revision Guidelines

The following guidelines will help you revise your draft effectively.

1. Reread your draft to determine whether readers will understand clearly what the topic means to you: i.e., the enjoyment, sense of satisfaction, excitement, or sense of accomplishment it may bring. Revise your draft in ways that help readers understand your passion for the topic.

2. Check your opening paragraph to make sure you have clearly introduced your topic, created some interest for readers, and included your thesis statement. What might you add or change to make your opening even more interesting for readers?

3. Check your middle paragraphs to make sure that each paragraph begins with a topic sentence expressing its main idea, and that each paragraph relates to and supports the thesis statement in some manner. Also check the organization of your paragraphs, and decide whether any paragraphs or any sentences within a paragraph could be moved to a more effective location.

4. Check your concluding paragraph to make sure that it provides readers with a sense of completion, relates to your thesis statement, and adds something for readers beyond what you have already written. What can you add or change in the conclusion to make it one of the strongest parts of your paper?

5. Read each paragraph to see if there is anything you can add -an example, a reason in support of your thesis, a specific detail or description, an explanation -to make the paper more interesting, informative, or complete.

6. Check your use of transitional wording to tie sentences and paragraphs together. Add any transitions (e.g. first, second, also, in addition, finally, therefore, however, etc.) that will help readers understand your ideas and how they are connected.

7. Check your paragraphing to make sure you have changed paragraphs when you move to something new: a different part of the paper, a new supportive point, a different example, a different time, place, or event. Divide overly long paragraphs into two, and combine very short paragraphs containing related material.

8. Check the wording of each sentence, and revise sentences to make them clearer, smoother, and more concise by eliminating unnecessary words or phrases and rewording awkward or unclear sentences.

9. Reread your draft a last time with your readers' response in mind. What final changes might you make to heighten their interest in your topic or further their understanding?

Revision Activity 3.10

With a classmate, or a small group of classmates, read the following first draft and apply the revision guidelines. Make note of changes that you would recommend the writer make in her next draft.

Crazy for Windmills

Driving along a country road or through a suburban neighborhood, I'm often looking for something that most people seldom notice. I never noticed them either until my young niece started pointing them out to me one day. She loved finding new windmills, and I'd help her look for them after picking her up at school. Now even when she's not in the car, I catch myself looking for windmills.

What you probably don't realize until you look is that there are windmills everywhere. You will find them in country pastures, beside barns, on hillsides, in back yards and front yards, and even on the tops of buildings. You will also find that windmills come in all different shapes and sizes.

I became more interested in windmills as I learned more about them. They've been around for hundreds of years in various parts of the world, and many of the better known ones dot the landscapes in Holland, Norway, Russia, and Greece. They have served various purposes over the years, including grinding grain into flour, pumping water from wells, and creating electricity, all using the power created by the wind turning their blades and the shaft connected to them.

The windmills in the United States and in Europe are very different in looks as well as function. I find them both attractive but favor the European mills. Interestingly, you can find European style windmills in the US, most of them ornamental but a few of them functional. I have yet to see an American styled windmill in Europe based on hundreds of pictures of windmills I've seen on the Internet.

I've even started collecting windmills. I have a charm bracelet with small windmill trinkets on it, and relatives will add to the collection on my birthday. I bought a table light windmill from a collectable store whose blades turn when you turn on the light. I also have a couple small American windmill replicas sitting in my room that I put together from kits.

Outside our house I have some decorative back-yard windmills. One is silver and red and stands about seven feet tall. Another is a wooden replica of a Dutch windmill that is about four feet tall. The last one is a black five-foot American windmill that I can see from my bedroom window.

With my niece's help, I even wrote a small children's book for her which she illustrated with drawings of windmills. It was a story about a girl who loved windmills and an old windmill she named Old Windy that was going to be torn down for a housing development. The story has a happy ending, and my niece had a good time illustrating it and taking it to school to share with her class. She is quite an artist for her age and is even taking some art instruction from a local teacher/artist who holds art classes after school.

One great thing about being a windmill hound is that a long trip is never boring. My niece went with me and our family on a two hundred mile trip across the state recently. My niece and I spent almost the entire trip looking for and finding windmills, and we found over thirty on our way. We get excited over any windmill we find, but we particularly like the big ones, and if they are spinning, that's a bonus. On this particular trip, we saw what has to be one of the tallest American windmills anywhere.

One of the highlights of our windmill experiences was when I took her to a place called

Windmill World on the outskirts of a small town about an hour from where we live. The old man who owns Windmill World builds windmills for farms and ranches across the country, and he has over fifty windmills on this property. For a windmill fanatic, seeing fifty windmills in one place is as good as it gets. We spent over an hour looking at the windmills and talking to the man, who was thrilled to find people who loved windmills as much as he does. In the end he gave each of us a windmill kit to build a two-foot ornamental American windmill. That was the perfect ending to a great outing.

I can't separate my enthusiasm for windmills from my niece's because we are in this thing together. We have gone on-line and found a couple of windmill museums in the US, one in Oklahoma and one in Texas. Our goal in the near future is to visit both museums on one trip. We may be the only two people in the country with such a goal.

Revision Activity 3.11

Revise your draft by applying the revision guidelines presented. Then exchange drafts with a classmate and suggest any further revisions that you feel would improve each other's paper. Finally, write the second draft of your paper, including all improvements you have made in content, wording, and organization.

Revised excerpts from sample draft "Tutor" *(First five paragraphs)*

In fourth grade when the bell rang for recess, my classmates couldn't **wait to** get outside ~~fast enough~~ to play ball or run around the playground. Not particularly good at games ~~or sports~~ and a slow runner, I was less enthusiastic, often **just** watching the fun ~~from a distance~~ or hunting ladybugs ~~and rolly pollys~~ with a couple friends. Then I ~~found out about~~ **discovered** an activity that changed my recess time dramatically.

Knowing my dislike for ~~the rigors of~~ the playground, my teacher told me that students could earn service points towards the Block R award by tutoring kindergarten students. ~~She said I could do it~~ during ~~some~~ recess periods. I told her I'd like to ~~give it a try~~ **try it** and the next recess, three of us reported to the kindergarten building.

I sat with students individually and helped them with their numbers, letters, and ~~small~~ art projects. I enjoyed it, and the students ~~seemed to~~ responded well ~~to me~~. The kindergarten teacher said I was doing a good job, and before long I was spending ~~practically~~ **almost** every ~~twenty-minute~~ recess in the kindergarten room. It was ~~a part of the day~~ **something** I always looked forward to.

Looking back, it wasn't too surprising that I ~~took to~~ **enjoyed** tutoring. ~~From the time I was very~~ **At a** young **age**, I liked playing school with my ~~younger~~ sister and grandparents **who babysat me**, and I was always the teacher. Tutoring kindergarten students ~~seemed a natural extension of my play~~ **natural to me**. I earned enough service points that year ~~that along with my grades and other activities, I~~ **to get** my Block R plaque, a great accomplishment for me. I also enjoyed my **kindergarten** "students" shouting ~~out~~ to me across campus or waving ~~to me~~ in the cafeteria. ~~I had many little friends.~~ **It made me feel good.**

I continued ~~my~~ tutoring ~~for the remainder of elementary school~~ **in fifth and six grade,** working with ~~first graders as a fifth grader and with second graders as a sixth grader~~ **first graders and second graders.** ~~Admittedly~~ Some ~~of my~~ classmates let me know that they thought

116

it ~~a little~~ strange that I preferred tutoring to recess, but no one made fun of me. I was also getting ~~a lot of~~ positive feedback from teachers, ~~and~~ some ~~teachers~~ **who** would request me ~~specifically~~ to work in their classrooms. I also continued racking up the Block R service points, but by ~~this time~~ **then** I would have kept tutoring without them. I remember one teacher saying, "Imelda, you are a born teacher," ~~an observation~~ **something** I would never forget.

(Revisions made to improve wording, eliminate unnecessary words and phrases, smooth out awkward sentences, and add detail and feelings.)

Editing

In the final phase of the writing process, you rid your paper of any errors that could distract readers from its content. Error detection and correction come at the end of the writing process because there is little point in editing a paper for errors while you are still working on its content and wording. You proofread your paper after all revisions have been made so that you are working with the final product.

In each "Editing" section, you are introduced to new elements of punctuation, grammar usage, or spelling that give writers problems, and you review what you have learned in previous units in order to apply all of your editing knowledge to your latest draft. In this section, you are introduced to subject-verb agreement, and you review what you have learned about run-on sentences and comma splices, sentence fragments, irregular verbs, and comma usage.

Subject-Verb Agreement

An important element of correct grammar usage is subject-verb agreement: making sure that you use the correct present tense verb form, depending on whether the subject is singular or plural. When you use the correct verb form, the verb agrees with its subject.

Subject-verb agreement is not difficult for most writers when the subject and verb are beside each other in a sentence. However, when they are separated by a group of words, or when their order is inverted, with the verb coming first, writers can have problems. This section will be devoted primarily to the more problematic constructions.

For example, in the sentence "That smell nauseates me," it is obvious that the verb form "nauseates," ending is s, agrees with the subject "smell." If the s were left off of "nauseates," the sentence, "That smell nauseate me," would sound wrong to most writers. However, in the sentence, "That smell from the sewer farm beside the housing projects nauseate me," the verb form "nauseate" may not sound as bad, although it is still incorrect. The separation of a subject and verb in a sentence often makes it more difficult to "hear" the correct verb form.

Subject-Verb Agreement Rules

The following basic rules and guidelines will help you avoid subject-verb agreement problems in your writing.

1. **The *subject* of a sentence is what the sentence is about: the main person, place, thing, or idea on which the sentence is centered.**

   Examples (subject underlined):

   Your <u>aunt</u> from Wisconsin is a very friendly person.
   The <u>separation</u> of subject and verb in a sentence makes selecting the correct verb form more difficult.
   In the end, a person's <u>wealth</u> is a poor indicator of happiness.

2. **The *verb* in a sentence expresses an action or a state of being. It tells what the subject is doing (action) or the condition of the person or thing (state of being).**

Examples (verb italicized, subject underlined)

The <u>separation</u> of subject and verb *creates* agreement problems for some writers.
The <u>mouse</u> constantly *darts* out of the closet and down the hallway.
Your <u>aunt</u> from Wisconsin *is* tired from her long flight.

3. **Subject-verb agreement involves present tense verbs: verbs that express something that is happening or existing in the present.** The following agreement rules apply to present tense verbs.

    a. If the subject of the sentence is singular (one person, one place, one idea), the present tense verb ends in "s."

        Examples (subject underlined, verb italicized):

        My baby <u>niece</u> *enjoys* banging on the piano.
        The <u>Empire State Building</u> *is* no longer the tallest building in the world.
        My <u>roommate</u> *works* in a delicatessen on weekends.

    b. If the subject of the sentence is plural -two or more persons, places, or ideas - the present tense verb does not end in s. (Exception: verbs already ending in s like dress, press, or guess.)

        Examples:

        My baby <u>nieces</u> *enjoy* banging on the piano.
        The <u>Empire State Building and Sears Tower</u> *are* no longer the two tallest buildings in the world.
        My <u>roommates</u> *work* in a delicatessen on weekends.

    c. The subject pronouns you and I are treated as plural when applying the agreement rule.

        Examples:

        <u>I</u> *like* early morning classes.
        <u>You</u> *enjoy* evening classes.

4. **When there is a group of words separating the subject and verb, ignore these words when determining subject-verb agreement.** (An exception is explained in 6.a.)

    Examples:

    The <u>boys</u> in the back of the room seldom *participate* in discussion.
    The <u>women</u> working in the cold storage plant on "N" Street *belong* to the retail employees' union.

The <u>woman</u> who works in several different store departments *is* seventy years old.
Only <u>one</u> of the men *works* the night shift year around.

5. **When a sentence begins with *There* + a *to be* verb (is, are, was, were), the subject comes after the verb, so find the subject to determine the correct verb form.** (Note: The verbs *was* and *were* are the only past tense verbs to which the subject-verb agreement rules apply. *Was* is used with singular subjects, and *were* is used with plural subjects.)

    Examples:

    There *is* a full <u>moon</u> tonight.
    There *are* very few <u>stars</u> in the sky tonight.
    There *were* several <u>students</u> absent on the day of the concert.

6. **Four other subject-verb agreement situations warrant your attention.**

    a. If the subject *most, more, some, a lot,* or *all* is followed by a *prepositional phrase* (most of the cake, more of the men, some of the rules, a lot of money, all of the lobsters), the last word in the prepositional phrase determines the correct verb form.

        Examples:

        <u>Most</u> of the spectators *sit* under the covered bleachers. (Since "spectators" is plural, the verb "sit" does not end in s.)
        <u>All</u> of the cake *needs* to be eaten before tomorrow. (Since "cake" is singular, the verb "needs" ends in s.)

    b. In some sentences, two or more verbs go with the subject. In such cases, each verb must agree with the subject.

        Examples:

        My <u>cat</u> always *mews* under my bedroom window in the morning and then *scratches* on the window screen to awaken me.
        The eastbound <u>train</u> that *runs* from Hanford to Bakersfield *is* often late.

    c. In some sentences, there are two or more pairs of subjects and verbs. In such cases, each present tense verb agrees with its subject.

        Examples:

        The <u>moon</u> *is* yellowish-white when <u>it</u> *rises* above the horizon, but <u>it</u> *turns* a pale orange as <u>it</u> *moves* higher.
        While <u>Josh</u> *vacuums* the hallway carpet, <u>you</u> *mop* the bathroom floor.

d.   If a relative pronoun such as *that, who,* or *which* precedes the verb, the verb must agree with the subject that the relative pronoun refers to.

Examples

The <u>men</u> who *pour* foundations for the houses being built in the neighborhood *work* very long hours.

The one garage sale <u>item</u> that *attracts* me the most *is* the reading lamp.

Editing Activity 3.12

Underline the subjects and circle the verbs in the following sentences, and be prepared to explain why each verb ends or doesn't end in s.

Example: Joan and I *walk* to school in the fall, but we usually *drive* in the winter when the weather *gets* colder. (subjects underlined, verbs in italics)

1.   The sudden sound of a car alarm in a parking garage always startles me.

2.   One of the reasons that I go to movies frequently is that I enjoy getting out of the house on weekends.

3.   There are several large bins behind the apartment building that we dump our trash in.

4.   Students who do the most reading often possess the best vocabularies.

5.   Concert attendees in the back of the arena have the least expensive seats.

6.   The aroma of barbecued hamburgers lingers in our back yard.

7.   The lottery for student basketball tickets is at 9:00 a.m. tomorrow in the cafeteria, but few students seem to know about it, and those students that know appear rather indifferent.

8.   A lot of students really like the cafeteria's donuts because by the time I get there in the morning, the donuts are all gone.

9.   The colorful ornaments that you put on the Christmas tree give it a festive look.

10. The head of my golf club loosens every time I hit the ball near the bottom of the club, so I try to hit the ball in the center.

122

Editing Activity 3.13

Underline the subject or subjects in each sentence, and then underline the correct verb forms in parentheses.

Example: Julian and Lucy (<u>try</u>, tries) hard when <u>they</u> (<u>play</u>, plays) doubles in tennis but seldom (<u>win</u>, wins).

1.   One of your friends (enjoy, enjoys) teasing me about my collection of rubber bands.

2.   There (appear, appears) to be several large pigeons nesting in the eaves of the science building.

3.   The sounds coming from the upstairs apartment (indicate, indicates) that someone (are, is) in trouble.

4.   Most of the wedding cake (were, was) eaten, but few of the anchovy appetizers (were, was) touched.

5.   My best guess from analyzing the early election returns (are, is) that all of the incumbent board members on the voting ballot (are, is) likely to win.

6.   Maxine and Sue (realize, realizes) that their friend Nagumi, who frequently (attend, attends) campus functions with them but (go, goes) to another school, (like, likes) her school very much, and despite their pleas for her to switch colleges, (plan, plans) to stay where she (are, is).

7.   In the back of the classroom by the double doors (sit, sits) a guy who (sleep, sleeps) through most of the class and sometimes even (snore, snores).

8.   Most of the people who (attend, attends) presidential debates (mill, mills) about outside the auditorium after the debate and (discuss, discusses) the candidates' performances.

9.   The debate over whether the recent global warming (are, is) man-made or part of the natural weather cycle (appear, appears) to favor the side who (believe, believes) that man and his creations (are, is) responsible.

10.   Most meteors from distant space that (fall, falls) towards earth (burn, burns) up in the atmosphere long before they (get, gets) close to our planet.

Editing Activity 3.14

Proofread the following draft for any subject-verb agreement errors, and make the necessary corrections.

Example: The plans for the new performing art center is impressive, but there is no timetable in place for its construction.

Corrected: The plans for the new performing art center are impressive, but there is no timetable in place for its construction.

The foul smells emanating from the garbage bin beside the apartment spreads across the complex and leaves everyone feeling nauseous. No person in the apartments are to blame, but everyone suffers from the effect.

The problem is that garbage collection for the apartments occur on a two-week cycle. You can imagine the combination of unpleasant odors that come from dirty diapers, rotting food, and souring milk products that sits in the garbage bin for two weeks. Each day the odor gets worse, and by the end of the week, the smell is beginning to creep inside the apartments. Besides that, by the end of the second week, the garbage bin are overflowing, and garbage is dragged around by dogs.

The answer to our garbage problems are, of course, a weekly garbage collection schedule by the city. For some reason the city does a weekly collection at individual houses in the area but collect at the apartment complexes every other week. That seems unfair to all of the apartment residents and make little sense when you consider that the garbage trucks are in the neighborhood every week.

Editing Review Activity 3.15

Before editing your latest draft for errors, proofread and edit the following draft by correcting any errors involving run-on sentences or comma splices, sentence fragments, irregular verbs, or comma usage.

Example: The once beautiful river was now a dry river bed with the smell of dead fish fouling the air, the dam builded above the river had cut off the river's flow filling a reservoir with water to be used for farm irrigation.

Corrected: The once beautiful river was now a dry river bed with the smell of dead fish fouling the air. The dam built above the river had cut off the river's flow, filling a reservoir with water to be used for farm irrigation.

Parking Woes

Parking at the college was getting worse every semester. As more and more students enrolled. To park in one of the main lots for an 8:00 a.m. class, you had to get to the school by at least 7:30 which was hard for a lot of students. If your first class was at 9:00 a.m. your only chance of finding an on-campus parking space was if someone from an 8:00 a.m. class left the lot, which didn't happen frequently.

If you couldn't park on campus you had to park on one of the streets adjacent to the campus that allowed parking, or you had to park in the large dirt lot across from campus which also filled with cars by early morning. A lot of students had to park more than a mile away and walk to campus, and for them getting to class on time was difficult, teachers complained about late students but it wasn't their fault.

The other option that a surprising number of students taked was to park illegally on campus they would park in "teacher only" lots which often had available spaces in "administration only" parking lots in ten-minute parking green zones and in loading zones. Sometimes the students would get away with it and sometimes they'd get ticketed. It was a game of chance, for some students it was an expensive game.

Finally the college done something to ease the terrible parking crunch they built a five-story parking garage behind the Event's Center at a significant cost but it was the only thing they could do. Now almost all students can park on campus. And have no more than a five minute walk to class. The number of students who are late to class has gone down markedly and everyone seems more relaxed including the teachers and administrators.

Editing Guidelines

When you proofread your paper for errors, read it several times, looking for a particular type of error each time. If you try to find all types of errors in one reading, you may overlook some. The more proficient you become at proofreading, and the fewer errors you make, the easier it becomes to identify and correct your errors in fewer readings.

The following guidelines will help you proofread and edit your papers effectively.

1. Check your sentences to make sure you haven't run any together or put a comma between sentences instead of a period. Correct run-on sentences or comma splices by separating longer sentences with periods and combining shorter, related sentences with a joining word.

2. Check your draft for any sentence fragments: incomplete sentences with a period after them. To correct fragments, attach them to the complete sentence they belong with, or add words to make them complete.

3. Check your use of irregular verbs, making sure you have used the correct irregular forms and spelled them correctly.

4. Check your comma usage, making sure you have inserted commas into your sentences following the rules presented in the text.

5. Check the spelling of any word you are uncertain of, or run the spell check on your word processing program, to eliminate any spelling errors.

6. Check all present tense verbs to make sure that they agree with their subjects, following the rules presented in this section.

Editing Activity 3.16
Proofread your draft following the guidelines presented and make the necessary corrections. Next, exchange papers with a classmate, proofread each other's drafts, and point out any undiscovered errors. Then write the final draft of your paper to share with classmates.

Applying the Writing Process

At the end of each unit, you write a second paper, applying what you have learned to this point in the text. The purpose of this assignment is to allow you to work independently through the writing process, to write without interruptions for instruction or activities, and to gain more experience writing thesis-centered papers.

Writing Assignment
For your first paper in this unit, you wrote about a topic that you had a keen interest in, something that you enjoyed doing. For this paper, you are going to do just the opposite: write

about something that you don't enjoy. While we can learn about writers from knowing what they like, we can also learn from their dislikes.

For your topic for this paper, choose something that you don't enjoy, whether it be giving a speech in front of an audience, sitting through a soccer game, taking early morning classes, working on weekends, listening to presidential debates, or going to the dentist. Choose a topic that has enough substance to write a paper on, and one that your classmates might find interesting or relate to.

Working independently, follow a similar writing process that you used to develop your first paper. (Refer back to the drafting, revision, or editing guidelines in the unit as needed.)

- Select topic to write on.
- Decide on a thesis statement for your essay.
- Make a list of supporting points.
- Write a first draft.
- Revise by focusing on providing strong supportive points, clear sentence wording, and effective paragraphing, and adding whatever will improve the draft.
- Edit the draft by correcting any errors that you find.
- Write the final paper.

Before revising, share first drafts with a classmate or two, and ask each other questions about anything that seems unclear in the draft or that you'd like to know more about. Consider your classmates' input as you revise your paper.

Readings

Helping the Homeless
by Malcolm Feeley

I help the homeless. I give money to non-profit organizations that help street people. I volunteer at shelters and soup kitchens. I pass out cards to homeless people that list local shelters. I donate food, clothing, and toys for homeless children. On occasion I take a homeless person to an AA meeting or a drug rehab center. I don't help the homeless out of any noble or altruistic sentiment. I don't help them out of guilt. I help the homeless for one reason: they are my brothers and sisters. And yours.

I was homeless for over five years. I am an alcoholic, and I lost my job and family when drinking took over my life. I lost interest in everything but my next bottle, and before long I was on the streets living from drink to drink. Unless you are an alcoholic, it is hard to understand how a person could lose everything just to pursue the pathetic goal of staying drunk. I hit rock bottom on the streets and stayed there for five years.

Life on the streets is tough for everyone. I slept on sidewalks, under bridges, in parks, in abandoned cars, and in shelters. I panhandled for money to buy booze and rummaged through dumpsters and garbage cans behind restaurants for food and recycled cans and bottles. I was beaten up by thugs or someone who wanted my bottle more than me, and I was arrested several times for loitering. I was often sick and in and out of free medical clinics. Cold and hunger were constant companions along with uncontrollable tremors when I went too long between drinks. I figured I'd be dead in a few years.

I made a few friends on the streets, and we hung out together, sleeping in a park until we'd get kicked out, then moving under a bridge, and then back to another park. We shared bottles and food when someone didn't have anything, and we watched each other's back. We also shared our pasts -other lives once lived and how we got where we were. You can't judge a person by their life circumstance, and I met some good people on the streets: decent, honest, and yes, hardworking. I also met some bad people, as there are in all walks of life, who preyed upon their homeless brothers and sisters.

Who are the homeless people? Many are drug addicts or alcoholics like me who didn't get or seek out treatment for their disease as their lives spiraled downward. Other homeless, through no fault of their own, have lost their jobs and can't pay rent. Many are war veterans who returned with emotional or physical problems that prevented them from holding jobs or fitting back into society. Many abandoned or abused women end up on the streets, sometimes with children in tow. They often turn to prostitution to survive and drugs to escape.

People you see muttering to themselves or sitting lifelessly on a sidewalk often suffer from mental illness such as schizophrenia, bipolar disorder, or depression that goes untreated year after year. Younger people who run away from home or who believe living on the streets is an adventure are among the transient homeless who come, eventually leave, and are replaced by an endless flood of alienated youth. Many people who have lost their jobs eventually find other work and vanish from the streets. The older homeless are a more entrenched group, often living out their lives on the street.

People seldom see the homeless as individuals, and they are generally viewed as the dregs

128

of society, unworthy of human contact. These filthy, bedraggled human flotsam and jetsam have committed the cardinal sin of our society: financial failure. Become a street person for one day, sitting on a sidewalk, and you will see in the faces of passersbys what every homeless person sees: disgust, scorn, hatred, curiosity reserved for freaks. Of course, there are always the exceptions who treat you like a human being, but most of society would rather cross the street to avoid the slightest contact. And homeless people, who already blame themselves for their plight, often perceive themselves as they are perceived by society, adding to the guilt and self-loathing many already carry.

I was one of the lucky ones. I was staying in a shelter during one bitterly cold winter week and began talking with a volunteer. He was an alcoholic who had been sober for five years. He invited me to an AA meeting and said he'd come by the next day to pick me up. I'd been invited before, but I'd never wanted to give up the only thing I lived for. This time, however, I felt particularly vulnerable, maybe because I was feeling ill or because of the frigid cold or the fatigue in my bones from five years on the street. When he came to pick me up the next day, I didn't run.

After five years of drunkenness, getting sober wasn't easy and I fell off the wagon more than once. However, the volunteer named Jim never gave up on me, so I was accountable to someone who cared about me. I had a dream that kept me going -to someday be reunited with my family -and although it was an improbable dream, it was something to hold onto. Jim finally got me into a half-way house that had the structure I needed and a part-time job with a soft drink distributing company. Eventually as I got physically and mentally stronger, I was able to work full-time and move into my own apartment. They speak of the lure of the streets calling the homeless back to their carefree, independent life, but I never heard it. That was the last place I wanted to go, and there is nothing carefree about living on the streets.

Jim helped me find out where my family was living, but their lives, naturally, had moved forward. My wife had remarried and my two teenage children were in a stable family situation with a good step-father. My ex-wife had no interest in seeing me again, and I didn't blame her. However, she let me meet with my kids in a restaurant while she and their step-dad waited next door. Just to see my kids brought a flood of emotion I couldn't restrain. I couldn't begin to tell them how sorry I was for everything I had done. I hugged both of them when I left, and it was the best feeling I had had in years. Just to be a small part of their lives is my dream come true.

I don't remember the moment when I decided to start helping the homeless, but I know they had never left my mind from the time I left the streets. They were the only family I knew for over five years, and I couldn't abandon them. So I do what I can do, never enough and with no delusion that I am making a big difference. But if I can help get one person off the streets from time to time, or make life a little more tolerable for others who may always be homeless, the gift I receive is greater than the one I give.

There are thousands of people like myself who help the homeless, but there are never enough. The homeless need our help, and there are things that we can all do. The next time you pass by a homeless person, look him or her in the eye, smile, and say, "How are you doing today?" In other words, acknowledge their humanity. I know how much that can mean.

Questions for Discussion

1.   What is the thesis of the essay? How is the thesis developed as the essay unfolds?

2. What is the purpose of the paragraphs in which the author relates his own experiences on the street?

3. What impact does the author having been homeless himself have on the reader?

4. What did you learn from the essay about homeless people that you didn't know, and how may it affect your attitude towards them?

My Personal Experience with Schizophrenia
by Kurt Snyder

I have paranoid schizophrenia. I developed schizophrenia gradually over a period of nine years, with the most severe symptoms appearing when I was twenty–eight years old. For most of those years, my family, friends, and colleagues were unaware that I was experiencing any mental problems.

My illness, as is true with all mental illnesses, started in the privacy of my own mind. My thoughts slowly wandered away from the normal range–I began to think less and less about daily life and more about a fantasy created in my mind. I cannot think of anything physical or psychological that could have triggered a change in my mental state. I had wonderful, supportive parents, relatives, and friends, and I had a wonderful childhood.

Somewhere between the ages of nineteen and twenty–one, I was exposed to the mathematical idea of fractals. I began to think obsessively about fractals and infinity. I thought I was going to discover some incredible and fabulous mathematical principle that would transform the way we view the universe. This delusion occupied my thoughts all day long, every day. I couldn't concentrate on my regular university studies, and my academic career eventually ended in failure. Still, I thought I was going to become famous. I was a genius just waiting to be discovered by the world. Soon everyone would know who I was because I was going to solve the riddle of the universe. I was having grandiose ideation.

I thought about fractals and infinity for many years. I always told myself I was on the verge of discovery, but I simply had to think a little bit harder about it. I just wasn't thinking hard enough. The reality is that the problems I was trying to solve were far beyond my mental abilities, but I didn't recognize this fact. Even though I had no evidence to substantiate my self–image, I knew in my heart that I was just like Einstein, and that someday I would get a flash of inspiration. I didn't recognize the truth–that I am not a genius. I kept most of my mathematical ideas to myself and spoke to very few people about them. I was paranoid that someone else would solve the riddle first if I provided the right clues.

At about the age of twenty–two, I had my first significant paranoid episodes. The first episode happened when I was on vacation with my girlfriend, my brother, and his wife in the mountains. We had rented a cabin together. For some reason, I started to think about images from horror movies where an insane man breaks into the house and kills everyone. I actually started to believe this was going to happen to us. I created a fantasy in my mind that we were very vulnerable and helpless, and that someone was going to kill us. It did not occur to me that this scenario was unlikely. The more I thought about it, the more I believed it was going to happen. I remember that I tried to reinforce the doors of the cabin with chairs. Everyone else seemed bewildered by my behavior. Eventually, however, I calmed down and went to bed.

Later that year, I had two more minor paranoid episodes. The first one happened when I hurt my leg and had to go to the university clinic. I was again feeling very vulnerable. I began to imagine that the nurse might try to hurt me in some way. I thought she might try to infect me with the AIDS virus by injecting me with a tainted needle. Of course, this idea was completely irrational, but I thought somehow that it could be true. A few weeks later, I became paranoid again–I thought the police were following me. But this idea only lasted a few hours. It would be several more years before any other symptoms of paranoia returned.

At about the age of twenty–four, I started to become preoccupied with the idea that people were watching me. I wondered about this several times a day. This idea began occurring to me more and more frequently, and the feeling that I was being watched became more intense. By the age of twenty–six, the thought that I might be under observation was occurring to me more than a hundred times a day. I became severely self–conscious in public places. I also became very sensitive to security cameras. They made me think I was being watched all the time. Oftentimes I thought the security cameras were watching me exclusively. At the age of twenty–seven, I took a job at a high–security facility where there were cameras in every room, every hallway, and all over the exterior of the building. I did not anticipate how this environment would affect me. During my first day on the job there, I could not escape the feeling that I was being constantly watched. The idea took on a life of its own. THEY were watching me. THEY could see everything I was doing. Long after I left the building to go home, I wondered if THEY were still watching me — somehow. Soon, THEY, whoever THEY were, were now watching me — all the time.

As one becomes more insane, rational thought fades away, but it happens gradually. In the midst of irrational thought, there still exists some rational thinking. I knew that no single individual could be watching me all the time, so I thought, "It must be a group of them. THEY are watching me, collectively."

The idea that THEY were watching me was irrational but persistent. The idea of who exactly THEY were, and why THEY were watching me, was an idea that evolved. My concept of THEM grew and began to color every experience I had. After a few months, everything that happened to me was somehow related to THEM, or was caused by THEM. When I started experiencing problems with my home computer, I blamed THEM. When I got a parking ticket, it was THEIR influence with the police that got me in trouble. Every thought I had was somehow associated with THEM. THEY were observing me, 24 hours a day.

At the age of twenty–eight, I suddenly started to become psychotic. I am using the word psychotic to mean that my understanding and perception of the real world diverged sharply from reality. I could no longer work. At one point, I wondered whether my whole existence and everything I experienced was manufactured by a virtual reality machine and whether my whole life was spent in a laboratory run by some type of alien creatures. This initial psychotic episode lasted for a few days. Then the most bizarre thoughts seemed to dissipate. However, the delusions involving THEM were persistent and continued for the next year, through two more psychotic episodes.

In my second psychotic episode, I experienced for the first time auditory and visual hallucinations. Only three months after that, I had another psychotic episode where I experienced another visual hallucination. At the time, these hallucinations seemed real to me, absolutely real. I could not distinguish them from reality. They came from some part of my brain that had never been activated before.

During each psychotic episode, my family tried to get me medical help. Medications were prescribed, but I refused to take them. I didn't believe anything was wrong with me. I thought I was just having an unusual experience. I didn't want to take anything that altered my brain–those pills were for crazy people!

After several months I finally decided to take the medication (Geodon), but my decision was based in part on a delusion. Thankfully, I took the medication regularly. Approximately two months after I started taking Geodon, I developed a severe case of depression. This depression lasted for at least one month, perhaps two. I wanted to die rather than continue to experience this feeling. I remained in bed for most of every day. My doctor prescribed an antidepressant, and my situation improved.

It took a long time for me to admit to myself that I had been mentally ill, and that I needed to take some type of psychiatric medication for the rest of my life. At first I wanted to hide this fact from other people, but eventually I accepted the fact that I couldn't have done anything differently, and I couldn't blame myself for being sick.

I continued to take Geodon for two years. My progress was very gradual, but I noticed a steady reduction in positive symptoms for that entire period. Eventually I was able to go back to work. At the end of my second year of taking Geodon, I began to experience severe akisthesia. This unusual type of anxiety is the worst emotional feeling I have ever experienced in my entire life, even more disturbing than the severe depression I had felt. I wanted to escape from existence. My doctor switched my medication to Zyprexa, and the akisthesia gradually diminished.

I have now been taking Zyprexa for three years, and it seems to be working beautifully, except for the extra twenty pounds of fat I'm carrying around. However, I wouldn't change it for anything. I have continued to notice steady improvement in my condition over the last three years, both for positive and negative symptoms. I now believe that I have fully recovered from schizophrenia, and I realize that my recovery is owed entirely to medication. I now experience no delusions, no paranoia, and I do not have bizarre thoughts. To get better, I did not perform any mental gymnastics (such as meditation or positive thinking), nor did I pursue any type of psychoanalysis. I simply took the medication, and I improved. Most people I know would never suspect that I ever had a mental illness, and many people are surprised when I tell them I have schizophrenia. I plan on having a normal existence for the rest of my life.

I hope that my story can help others who suffer from schizophrenia, who have gone through some of what I went through without the help needed, and who, with that help, can find the right medication to put them on a path to a normal life. I have devoted my website *SchizoWorld* to helping people who may suffer from schizophrenia, and I hope to continue doing my small part in educating people about the illness. My message is simple: that anyone suffering with schizophrenic symptoms should seek out professional psychiatric help, that medication is a necessary component of getting well, and that a normal, productive life is possible. I am living proof.

Questions for Discussion

1. What if anything did you learn about schizophrenia from the essay? Based on the essay, in what ways does untreated schizophrenia debilitate a person?

2. Why do you think that the author remained untreated for so many years? Do you think this may be common among people with schizophrenia?

3. Do you know of people who have suffered from mental illness? How did they and those around them cope with the condition?

Working on the Ranch

by Paul Kaser

"Is this really what I want as a hobby?" I asked myself when the ranch foreman first told me to shovel out Bandit's stall, spread fresh bedding, refill the grain bin and water trough, then move on to the next stall to repeat the process. This seemed more like a tiresome job without pay than a pleasant pastime. Why had I listened to that "friend" who thought this gig would be such a great avocation for me?

An avocation, commonly called a hobby, is an activity you take up outside and beyond your regular job. It's supposed to provide time away from the nine to five routine and a chance to relax, to enjoy new experiences, and to improve skills in a field of interest to you. The right hobby is supposed to offer physical and psychological rewards.

After that first day, I asked myself if volunteering at this non-profit therapy ranch would ever provide any of these benefits to me. I could understand how someone whose hobby was fixing up old cars felt justified when his repaired and polished old classic won a trophy at the car show. Likewise it was clear why the fly fishing hobbyist felt pride when one of her hand-tied flies brought in a trophy rainbow. However, it wasn't clear what all this stall cleaning would get me. Nobody was ever awarded a trophy for mucking out a horse stall.

I soon learned I had misjudged the whole thing. It certainly provided time away from my regular job. I started by doing chores at the ranch one day a week for two or three hours. I soon found myself going out to the ranch more and more often and spending as much time working there as I could spare. Why?

At times it's hard, hot, smelly work caring for horses like Bandit and the others. They demand a lot from their human keepers. Still, it's somehow relaxing to serve these big animals whose job it is to give disabled kids a chance to brush and pet them, talk to them, and maybe even ride them. I learned that being able to help these kids find a new pride and courage in themselves makes all the hard work worthwhile.

Horse therapy has proven beneficial for many children who have emotional, physical, or behavior problems, or who have autism or Asperger's syndrome. Children learn new skills, improve their motor abilities, build their self-confidence, and learn to be responsible. For some, forming a close relationship with a horse is much easier than connecting with other humans. For others, caring for and riding their horse is one thing in their lives that they can look forward to. To play even a small role in helping the ranch provide this wonderful therapy began to mean more and more to me.

As for new experiences, my work at the ranch certainly provided those. I had ridden horses in the past but never had to spend time cleaning up after them, grooming them, and taking care of their tack (saddle, bridles, etc.). Someone once said, "When you've got a horse, you've got a thousand pound friend." That is a warning to be cautious, no matter how convinced you are he or she is your friend.

But as big and brawny as these animals are, they are surprisingly vulnerable to injury and disease. In my continuing work at the ranch, I was learning to spot signs of stress in horses and to help treat them when they were sick or injured. Helping an animal in discomfort is one of the great rewards of this hobby.

I also had to learn how to watch and listen for what they are communicating to each other and to their riders. That skill helped me in training retired "cow ponies" like Bandit to become gentle, tolerant therapy horses.

All of the horses I have helped train passed the gentleness test except for the misnamed Curly, who should have been called Dynamite. Taking exception to my being on his back, the first time I mounted Curly, he promptly reared up and unceremoniously tossed me into a sticker patch. As I looked up, I could swear Curly was snickering at me. After pulling about a hundred stickers out of my backside, I had to put a pillow on my saddle for a couple weeks. Needless to say, Curly flunked out as a therapy horse but still remains on the ranch. The ranch owner Guy has a soft spot for troubled horses as well as troubled kids.

Everything I learned increased my appreciation of what goes into running a horse ranch, especially a therapy horse ranch. It soon became obvious to me that this hobby was providing a lot more for me than just a way to kill some off-duty time. The physical and psychological benefits were beyond anything I had imagined.

Of course the greatest reward comes from seeing the benefits to the children for whom we offer this service. One example was an eight year old girl, Gracie, who had lost a leg in an accident when she was one. The first time she came to the ranch, she fell in love with the horses. We had a saddle modified so she could ride Bandit around the training corral. Just walking the horse around and around in a circle wasn't enough for her. She showed remarkable poise, balance, and natural understanding of the movements of the horse.

Gracie definitely had the can-do spirit, and she told us her dream was to ride in the entry parade for the professional rodeo held in our town. This seemed a far off goal to us, but by that spring she was handling the horse so well that she was able to ride proudly and competently in the big parade. Judging by the applause, she was the rodeo crowd's favorite. It certainly was the greatest moment of her young life, and one of the great ones for those of us working at the ranch.

After two years of enjoying this hobby, I have improved my own riding skills to the point where I have participated in horseback riding competitions myself. I no longer complain about heading out to the stalls to do the less glamorous work of horse-keeping. Bandit gives me a friendly whinny when my chores are done and he's ready for me to lead him out to meet, entertain, and encourage more kids. Once a professional quarterhorse, he has retired from his old job of driving and sorting cattle, but, like me, he too has found a good avocation.

Questions for Discussion

1. What details does the author provide to show the somewhat unpleasant work that is a part of his hobby? How would such work appeal to you?

2. What benefits does the author get from his hobby that far outweigh the drudgery of the work? What do you feel he finds the most rewarding and why?

3. There are horse therapy ranches throughout the country. Why do you think that horses are perhaps the best "therapy" animals for children with problems or handicaps? What do they provide the children that other animals may not?

Explaining the Unexplainable
by Jeff Belanger

This past January, Dr. Hans Holzer turned 85 years old. He laughs when you mention retirement. "I retire every day," he says with the hint of an Austrian accent. "Every night at midnight." After penning 138 books as well as several plays, musicals, films, and documentaries and hosting a television show, the only thing that slows him down today is a mishap from an operation on his leg three years ago. What does it slow him down from? "Swing dancing," he said. I laughed. Then I realized he wasn't kidding. "Not just swing dancing, *any* kind of dancing!"

Supernaturally speaking, Dr. Holzer has seen and heard it all. He's worked with psychic legends like Sybil Leek, he's investigated some of the most prominent haunted locations around the world, and he's come as close as a living person can to touching the "other side of life" – a term he's quick to point out that he invented.

In 1938, 18-year-old Holzer saw a very big war coming to his region. He figured being that close to Nazi Germany while a World War was brewing wasn't healthy, so he and his brother came to New York. He's lived in New York City ever since.

"What was your first paranormal experience?" I asked.

"It's not a question of whether I had experiences," he said. "My interest has nothing to do with personal experiences. In other words, you don't have to be an investigator to experience things first-hand."

"I've read you don't like the term 'supernatural'," I said.

"I use the term because it is the one that people use," Holzer said. "But nothing in my scientific view does not have an explanation. The question is, sooner we get it or later we get it, but there has to be an explanation. You can't say nobody knows. I don't accept that. And the paranormal is part of our experience – we just don't always understand it as such."

Eventually, we did get to speak about some of Holzer's personal experiences. "My first visual experience was when I lived in New York City with my father in a penthouse apartment on Riverside Drive. I was asleep in bed, and I woke up and there was my mother dressed in a white nightgown, pushing my head back onto the pillow. My head had slipped off the pillow. At that time I was subject to migraines. Had I not had my head back on the pillow, I probably would've had one, and there would've been dizziness and I would've been out of business for a day. I said, 'Oh, hello, Mama.' And she disappeared."

We talked about the difference between a ghost or a spirit – how a ghost is a residual entity, like a psychic imprint left in an area that some people can pick up, whereas a spirit is intelligent and interactive. Holzer also mentioned a third category I hadn't heard about before: the "stay behinds."

"'Stay behinds are relatively common," he said. "Somebody dies, and then they're really surprised that all of a sudden they're not dead. They're alive like they were. They don't understand it because they weren't prepared for it. So they go back to what they knew most – their chair, their room, and they just sit there. Next, they want to let people know that they're still 'alive.' So they'll do little things like moving things, appear to relatives, pushing objects, poltergeist phenomena, and so on."

I asked him what we can expect to find waiting for us on the other side. His reply came without hesitation, and very matter-of-fact. "We all pass out of the physical body and we are now on the other side of life. It's a world just like this one – it has only two differences: there's no sense of time, and if you're ill when you die you're now no longer ill. But other than that, you'll find houses, trees, gardens, and your relatives, friends, and so on. It looks like a very real world. Maybe a little nicer, but still a normal, real world. And you are just the way you were before. Maybe a little bit younger-looking if you wish, but you're still in a very real world."

"You'll notice that the other side of life is a bureaucracy just like this one. You can't just call Uncle Frank [who's still living]. You have to get permission from a group of people who call themselves guides – spirit guides. They will say, 'Why do you want to make contact? What's your purpose?' And if they approve of it, they'll say, 'Okay, find yourself a medium somewhere, speak with them, and they will make contact for you.' Or if you're that strong, you can try to make contact yourself."

"And if you don't like where you are after a while -- you may have a consciousness that you've been there a certain period and feel that you would rather be back on the other side with friends and loved ones. You'll say, 'I'd like to get reborn again.' These are the words I got from them, they're not my invention. They [the spirits] said you have to go to a line, and you have to register with the clerk. 'Clerk' is the word they used. So you get in line and register with the clerk that you want to go back. The clerk says, 'Okay, I'll let you know when I find an appropriate couple for you that will advance your development.' They have no real sense of time, so they just stand there, and eventually the clerk will say, 'I've got a couple for you.'"

"There is a well and they [the spirit about to go back] must walk through that well. They call it 'The Well of Forgetfulness.' They are sprayed with this water – not 100%, it never quite covers everything. That's why people have memories, dejá vu experiences, and recurrent dreams. And then they are a baby again."

"What I have learned in my investigations is that there are seven levels of consciousness on the other side of life that are concentric with our world. It's not up or down, it's just concentric. We can't see it because it moves at a different rate of speed than we move."

"The idea is reincarnation. This concept has been a part of many religions and belief systems for millennia." Holzer continued with his ideas on how our physical and spirit bodies connect. "There's three levels when you are born. You are born with a physical outer body, a duplicate inner body, and at the very moment of birth – that's very important – the moment the child is supposed to see the light [during childbirth], that is when the soul or the spirit is inserted from the pool of available spirits from the other side. Therefore all this nonsense about abortion killing a child is pure lies, pure nonsense. The fetus, until the spirit of the child is inserted, is a physical part of the mother. It does not have any life – it's not a separate entity."

Holzer said he worked with several mediums to compile this information on how things work in the afterlife. Holzer believes a good medium is the most critical element to a good supernatural investigation. He believes the medium is the person who can speak for those on the other side and deliver clear messages.

"That's putting a lot of faith in a person who is hopefully not a charlatan, but could be," I said.

"That's why you don't ask questions of a psychic," he said. "You just sit there and listen. I'll give you an example. Philip Solomon, a British trancemedium, once called me out of the blue because I had written a rather harsh piece in a magazine. It was about psychics who didn't deliver – not fakers – but incompetent psychics. So we talked on the phone and became friendly, and then he suddenly said, 'Your uncle Henry is here.' It became clear that he was talking about somebody who really is my uncle Henry. Weeks went on, and from time to time he would call me and give me messages from my parents and from Henry, which I found valid. Months went by, and he [Philip Solomon] said, 'Yes, Uncle Henry is here again.' So I said, 'If it's my uncle Henry, what does he want me to know?' And Philip said, 'Just a moment.' And then he came back and said, 'Your uncle Henry says the dog's name was Rigo.' Who the hell would know that? But it *was* Rigo."

"That's what I call evidence. There was no way that he could have known that my uncle's dog's name was Rigo. No way he could have known that – that was years and years ago. The only explanation of that particular case was that this was my uncle Henry. That was his way of proving himself. That's the kind of evidence I demand. It cannot be explained away."

"Have you ever been afraid during an investigation?" I asked.

"Fear is the absence of information," he said. "Fear is created by not understanding something. You bring on the fear. There is no object to fear. I've never been afraid during an investigation. I shouldn't be in this business if I was. There's nothing out there that isn't one way or the other human. Hollywood notwithstanding, there are no monsters out there. There is no other supernatural race, no devils, no fellows in red underwear. It doesn't exist."

"What have you learned about yourself during all of these years of investigations?" I asked.

"First of all, the other side, being a bureaucracy and being a well-ordered world, invests in people's abilities. When the other side decides some individuals have very good minds and good hearts, then they are given talents with the proviso that they will use those talents for the betterment of the world and mankind. If you don't, they won't like it. So they make it very plain: you have a gift. Use it. I found out early enough that they had something in mind for me. I accepted that it's an assignment."

"How do you want to be remembered?" I asked.

"As a man who told the truth. I won't have a tombstone. Cemeteries are real estate wastes, and I don't believe in funerals of any kind. The sooner you burn the body the better. It's just a shell.

"What will you be doing on your 100th birthday?"

"Looking forward to my 101st," he said. "I do what I'm meant to do. A man who takes himself too seriously, others won't take seriously, so I'm very careful about that. I want to be factual and to be useful – and I try to help anybody who wants help."

Questions for Discussion

1. Do you believe, like Dr. Holzer, that study of the paranormal is a science? Why?

2. Dr. Holzer claimed that a medium conversed with Holzer's dead uncle and provided information that he could only have gotten from the uncle. Do you believe his claim? Why?

3. Dr. Holzer has very specific information about what the "afterlife" is like, information he gleaned from his investigations and various mediums. What do you think of his depiction of an afterlife? Do you agree that an afterlife exists?

Unit Four
Beliefs and Values

One of the higher purposes to which writers apply their skills is to share their beliefs and values with readers. Through their writings, we discover what issues they feel are important, what they believe in, and what values guide those beliefs.

For example, if a writer values the health of children, she may be concerned about the issue of obesity in children. She may feel it is important that they eat nutritious foods and avoid less healthy, fattening foods. To that end, she may write an essay expressing the belief that eating at fast food restaurants is not good for children, and that the best way for them to get nutritious meals is through home cooking. What she values - the welfare of children - guides her concern for their eating habits.

In this unit, you will write about an issue of importance to you based on your personal beliefs and values. You will decide what issue to write about and what you believe about the issue. In addition, you will decide who your reading audience will be and your purpose in writing to them.

The purpose of this assignment is to expose you to a different type of writing. In the first three units, you wrote about your life - memorable experiences, influential people, and particular interests - with the primary purpose of informing your audience and engaging their interest. In this unit, rather than writing about yourself, you write about an issue that may affect you as well as others, and you move beyond informing your reading audience to influencing how they think and feel about something important.

Although the writing for this unit provides a different challenge, it can still be rooted in your personal experience. When you consider possible writing topics, think of issues with which you have some experience that have perhaps affected your life in some way, or consider the experience of friends or relatives. For example, the writer of the sample essay in this unit based his belief in the value of "illegal" Mexican immigrants to America by citing the experiences of his grandfather and grandmother. Using your own experiences or the experiences of others to support your beliefs will provide a transition between this unit's writing and your writings from experience in the first three units.

Prewriting

In preparing to write the first draft of your issue-oriented paper, you will first spend some time deciding on a writing topic, using the *brainstorming* technique to generate potential topics. Next, you will decide how you feel about the issue, and express that viewpoint in a thesis statement that you will support in your paper. Finally, you will make a list of some of the reasons that you believe as you do, and also consider why some people may feel differently.

Topic Selection

For your upcoming paper, you will choose an issue that you feel is important and that people may have differing opinions on. In deciding upon a topic, consider the following:

1. What is a particular issue that interests you and that also may interest other people?

2. What is a particular issue that you know something about and have an opinion on? *Since this is not a research paper, choose a topic that you are familiar with, perhaps something that affects you personally or that is an issue at your school, in your community, or among your friends. Consider topics with which you have had some personal experience or know of other people's experiences.*

3. What is a particular issue that people have different opinions on? For this paper, you are selecting a topic that everyone doesn't feel the same way about.

4. You may write about an issue from any area or field: sports, music, college, family, food, health, children's issues, television, etc.

Brainstorming

Needless to say, there are many issues in different fields that could be subjects for your paper. One way to consider a number of possible writing topics is to brainstorm on the topics: writing down any issue that comes to mind without evaluating it. When you brainstorm, you try to get as many ideas on paper as possible.

The purpose of this brainstorming session is to generate and consider different topic choices with the goal of deciding upon the best topic for your paper. The freewheeling nature of brainstorming helps you come up with ideas you may not have thought of otherwise, perhaps leading to a topic you hadn't considered.

Prewriting Activity 4.1

Brainstorm as many issues as you can think of within different fields. Write down any issue that comes to mind without evaluating it.

Sample Brainstorming:

Cost of textbooks	Revitalizing our downtown -worth it?
Parking on campus	Reality TV
Should campus security carry guns?	All the testing in elementary grades

Public vs. private schools	Gangs and violence
Outsourcing American jobs	Dress codes for high schools?
Free song downloading	Juveniles tried as adults?
Playoff for college football?	Torn up streets in town

As you can see, some of the "brainstormed" topics are too general to write an effective essay on, such as "reality TV," "outsourcing American jobs," or "gangs and violence." However, from these general topics may come ideas for more specific writing topics:

Some of America's best singing talent is found on reality TV shows.
Outsourcing American jobs can have a profound effect on college graduates.
Gang violence and drug dealing go hand in hand.

As you evaluate your list of brainstormed topics, see if there are any general topic areas which you could narrow down to specific writing topics for an essay.

Prewriting Activity 4.2

From your brainstormed list and other topics you may be considering, choose an issue for your upcoming paper, keeping in mind the four suggestions for topic selection. You may want to steer clear of issues such as abortion, gun control, capital punishment, or gay marriage that are quite complex for a single essay and have been written on so often that fresh ideas are rare. Since this is not a "research" paper, make sure to select a topic that you know enough about to write knowledgeably.

Topic for essay:

Thesis Statement

As you recall from the previous unit, your thesis statement expresses the viewpoint on your topic that you want to develop and support in the paper. The thesis statement accomplishes a number of purposes: letting readers know what your paper is about, providing direction for you as the writer, giving your paper a focus that influences everything you write, and sharing with readers what you believe in and value.

For the thesis statement for your upcoming paper, consider how you feel about the topic. For example, if your issue were the parking situation on campus, you may believe any of the following: that there is adequate on-campus parking for students; that there is not adequate parking for students unless they get to school early to find it; that there is only a parking issue because students who live near the campus are too lazy to walk or ride a bike; or that the parking issue is so serious that students are opting to go to other local schools as a result.

As another example, let's say you are writing about a proposed downtown lake that is being considered by the city council as a way to attract people and revitalize the area. You may be in favor of the project, you may be opposed to the project, or you may feel that while building a lake doesn't sound feasible, a different kind of downtown water feature might accomplish the same purpose. The most important consideration is that you decide on a thesis statement that most accurately expresses your belief on the issue, one that you can enthusiastically and convincingly support in a paper.

Prewriting Activity 4.3

Decide on a thesis statement for your upcoming paper. Generate a statement that clearly expresses your viewpoint on the topic and that you can support and develop in a paper.

Sample thesis statements

| Topic: | Creating a lake in the downtown area |
| Thesis: | Creating a lake downtown would be a big step towards revitalizing the area. |

| Topic: | Serving beer at the on-campus pizza restaurant |
| Thesis: | Serving beer on campus would not be in the interest of students or faculty. |

| Topic: | Campus police carrying handguns |
| Thesis: | In today's world, campus police should be armed with handguns. |

| Topic: | Proposed new gambling casino |
| Thesis: | The last thing this county needs is another gambling casino. |

Tentative thesis statement:

Thesis Support

Some writers initially believe that if they have a good thesis, the paper will take care of itself. Unfortunately, that is not the case. Some readers may disagree with your thesis and have an opposing viewpoint. Others may be disinterested in your topic and your thesis. Still others may take a "wait and see" attitude, deciding how they feel about your viewpoint after reading your paper and learning more about the topic.

How well a writer supports her thesis determines the effectiveness of a paper and its impact on readers. A good assumption to make is that every reader will need to be convinced that the writer's viewpoint is valid and sensible. Before beginning a draft, a writer should have the mind-set, "My readers don't agree with me yet. How can I write this paper so that they will agree with me by the end?"

Thesis Support Guidelines

You can support your thesis in a variety of ways.

1. By explaining the issue clearly so readers understand it.

2. By providing and developing strong reasons in support of your viewpoints. To develop your reasons, you may include you own personal experiences and/or the experiences of others.

3. By anticipating some readers' arguments against your thesis and addressing them in your paper.

4. By showing readers how they may be affected by the issue and how it is in their best interests to agree with your viewpoint.

5. By using comparisons to support your thesis. For example, the writer who was against serving beer at a pizza restaurant on campus compared the negative experiences of other colleges that had tried it. The writer who supported campus police carrying handguns compared how unarmed campus police responded to a knife-wielding assailant on campus to how armed police could have handled the situation.

Considering these five points, let's say that the issue for your paper is the proposed tuition increase at your college. You might proceed with a draft as follows:

Topic: Increase in college tuition proposed by the Board of Trustees

Thesis: The proposed increase will be a great burden on many students.

1. **Show financial difference between current and proposed tuition.**

    This would show the Board of Trustees the exact financial effect on students each year.

2. **Generate some supportive points for your thesis to develop in essay.**

    Many students can't afford a tuition increase (include personal experience).
    Students are still struggling with tuition increase of three years ago.
    School could lose money due to declining enrollment from tuition increase.
    Increase isn't justified based on the school's current needs.
    Similar colleges are not raising tuition on their students.

3. **Provide an alternative to tuition increase:**

    Fund raising activities.
    Sale of unused college-owned acreage.
    Savings with a number of cost-cutting suggestions.

4. **Appeal to Trustees' obligation to all students' education:**

The college should keep an "open door" to all students.
Increase would fall hardest on minority students and students with families.
Trustees were elected by public to make education available to all.

In this paper, then, you would have done the following:

Helped readers understand the tuition issue and financial impact.
Presented and developed a number of points in support of your viewpoint.
Addressed the concern that led to the proposed increase: need for money.
Involved the readers (trustees) by emphasizing their obligation to students.

Making a List

Making a list of supporting points for your thesis helps you consider why you believe the way you do, determine whether you have some good supportive reasons, see where the strengths of your upcoming paper may lie, and develop some material for your paper. You might even find that you can't think of many supporting ideas, and that you may be better off writing about something else.

Prewriting Activity 4.4

Make a list of supporting points for your thesis statement which you may develop in your first draft. List any point that you feel may be relevant.

Sample list

Topic: Illegal Immigration
Thesis: America has benefitted greatly from the economic contribution that illegal immigrants have made and continue to make.

List of points: My grandparents' story
                U.S. agricultural success built on back of illegal immigrants
                Contribute to the economy as consumers
                Form the backbone of many rural American towns
                Commit few crimes compared to Americans
                Successors of earlier immigrants become mainstream Americans

List of possible supporting points:

1.

2.

3.

4.

5.

144

Opposing Viewpoints

Some readers will initially not agree with your thesis, and they will have their own reasons for believing otherwise. Recognizing and addressing arguments supporting their opposing viewpoint may make readers reconsider. Refuting opposing arguments may have a greater effect on readers than presenting your own support.

For example, let's say you support the creation of a downtown lake to attract people and help revitalize the area. However, you are also aware of the opposition's arguments: that a lake project is too expensive and taxpayers will foot the bill, and that since no other plans have worked to revitalize the downtown, a lake probably won't help either. If you raise those arguments in your paper and then reveal their flaws to readers, you may win some people over who had based their opinion on those arguments.

Prewriting Activity 4.5

Come up with two or three arguments in opposition to your thesis and consider how you might counter them in your draft.

Sample arguments

Topic: Illegal Immigration
Thesis: America has benefitted greatly from the economic contribution that illegal immigrants have made and continue to make.

Opposing arguments:

1.   Illegals take jobs from Americans.
2.   Illegals are an economic drain on the country.
3.   Illegals have a high crime rate.

Counters:

1.   Illegal aliens have always done the jobs that Americans won't do.
2.   Illegal aliens contribute much more to the economy than they cost the country in services.
3.   Illegal aliens have a low crime rate compared to their American counterparts.

Possible opposing arguments:

1.

2.

3.

Possible counters:

1.

2.

3.

First Drafts

As mentioned previously, writing about issues is different in some ways from the writing you have done in earlier units. Rather than writing primarily to inform, as you did in previous papers, you are now not only writing to engage your readers' interest but also to influence their beliefs and behavior. The writing challenge has clearly been stepped up, and the writing considerations have become more complex, an important step in continuing to develop your writing skills.

Audience and Purpose

Two primary concerns with issue-oriented writing are your reading audience and your purpose: whom you are writing for and why. For example, if you support the creation of a downtown lake in your city, you may have at least four different audiences that you may want to reach at some point: the city council members who will decide the fate of the lake project, the residents who are opposed to the lake, the residents who are indifferent or uninformed, and the residents who like yourself favor the idea. All four audiences may have an impact on whether the lake is ever built, and you might target each group for your writing.

Your purpose for writing, however, and what you write to each audience may differ depending on their attitude towards the project. For example, your purpose in writing to the council members would be to support those who favor the project and to change the minds of those who don't. Your purpose in writing to residents in opposition would be to change them into supporters or at least neutralize their influence with the council. Your purpose in writing to neutral citizens would be to inform them on the issue and get them to support the project. Your purpose in writing to residents who favor the project would be to get them to support it actively and influence the council directly.

Reading Audience

When you consider your reading audience for your upcoming paper, ask yourself the following:

1. What people would be most interested in the issue?

2. What people might have an impact on the outcome of the issue?

3. What people would support your viewpoint, who would probably oppose it, and who would probably be neutral or indifferent?

Drafting Activity 4.6

Considering the preceding four questions, decide on the primary reading audience for your paper: the people that you feel should definitely read your paper. It may be your classmates, a particular group of classmates, college students in general, the school board, the college president, instructors at the school, all adults residing in the area, a certain state legislator, all music lovers, men in particular, women in particular, wild animal lovers, and so on.

146

Sample audience:
Primary audience for paper on illegal immigrants: The general public, whose viewpoint will help determine the direction the country takes with immigration "reform."

Writing Purpose

Going hand in hand with your reading audience is your writing purpose: what you hope to accomplish by writing to this audience. Once you determine your purpose, you can consider the best ways to accomplish that purpose, which will influence both the content and the tone of the paper. Your *tone* is the attitude that you convey through your writing, whether it be angry, courteous, sarcastic, humorous, enthusiastic, negative, attacking, concerned, and so on. The tone that you set in your paper, which may change in places depending on your purpose, may have as much of an impact on readers as what you have to say.

Let's say that you strongly oppose the new earlier class drop date the college is considering. Regarding your writing purpose, here is how you might proceed with three different audiences:

Thesis: The new earlier drop date would hurt students by forcing them to decide whether to drop a class prematurely.

Audience #1: Instructors

Purpose: To get instructors to come out publicly against the proposed drop date.

Tone: Friendly, serious (Since the drop date change wasn't the instructors' idea, many will not support it, so the tone should show that you and the instructors are in agreement.)

Audience #2: Board of Trustsees

Purpose: To get the Board to reject the proposed drop date change.

Tone: Respectful, firm, serious (You don't want to alienate the decision-makers, so a respectful yet firm, serious tone may produce the best results.)

Audience #3: Students

Purpose: To get students to attend a board meeting en masse and speak out against the proposed drop date change.

Tone: Angry, emotional (Students are on your side, so getting them riled up and ready to take action may be important. You can express the anger over the anti-student drop-date change that you suppressed with the board and instructors.

To decide on your writing purpose for the upcoming paper, consider the following:

1. What do you hope to accomplish by writing to this audience?

2. What is the most that you can realistically expect to achieve?

3. What is the best tone for the paper in order to accomplish your purpose?

4. How do you think you can best accomplish your purpose through your writing?

Drafting Activity 4.7
For the following topic, consider how the content and tone of a letter might differ when written to the each of the audiences below. Then write a short letter to each audience that reveals those differences.

Topic: Improving the quality of food in the college cafeteria

Audiences: The board of trustees for the college
            Students who you want to support your cause
            The cafeteria manager

Drafting Activity 4.8
Decide on your writing purpose for your upcoming paper and the best tone for accomplishing that purpose.

Sample writing purpose
Topic: Illegal Immigration

Purpose: To get readers to see illegal immigrants in a positive light.

Tone: Serious, committed

Topic:

Purpose:

Tone:

Drafting Activity 4.9

Read the following first draft and with a classmate and analyze it by answering the following questions.

1.   What is accomplished in the opening paragraph? What is the thesis statement?

2.   What is the purpose of the author relating the story of his grandfather? What is he trying to accomplish?

3.   What are the main supporting points for the thesis, and how are they developed?

4.   What are the opposing arguments that are raised and how are they countered in the draft?

5.   What is accomplished in the final two paragraphs? What is the writer's primary purpose in communicating with his reading audience?

6.   What is the tone of the paper - the attitude the writer displays - and how appropriate is it?

Sample First Draft *(reading audience - general public)*

Illegal Immigration

When I read about immigration "reform" recommendations like sending all illegal Mexican immigrants back to Mexico or not allowing children of illegal immigrants to attend public school or receive medical care, I think of my grandfather. He is one of these illegal immigrants that some people claim are ruining America: taking our jobs, living off our benefits, and committing crimes. In fact, America has benefitted greatly from the economic contribution that illegal immigrants have made and continue to make.

My *abuelo* came to America as a young man from the Mexican state of Jalisco. He came from a large, poor family and like millions of Mexicans, came to America for a better life. Later, he was joined by a brother and two sisters, but to his deep regret, he never saw his parents again although he sent them money for as long as they lived.

Had my *abuelo* had the option of entering the U.S. legally, he certainly would have done so because crossing the border illegally was risky and dangerous. However, U.S. quotas for Mexican immigrants didn't begin to cover the number of Mexicans wishing to immigrate, so my *abuelo's* options were to scratch out a life of poverty in Mexico or come to America illegally. It is not hard to understand why he, like so many Mexicans, chose the latter.

Once in America, my *abuelo* found work on the West Coast as a migrant farm laborer, moving at different times of year from the strawberry and garlic fields of Salinas and Gilroy to the grape fields of the Central Valley to the apple orchards of Washington. The work was back-breaking and the life was hard, but my *abuelo* followed the crops for ten years. In a grape field near Selma one year he met a young female worker who would become my *abuela*. They had three children, including my father Gilbert, who traveled with them as my *abuela* cut back on her work to be with the children.

My *abuelo* was a good worker and a smart man, and to his and his family's good fortune, he was given year-around work at a farm outside of Dinuba in the Central Valley. He began by pruning vines and trees in the winter, fertilizing and thinning crops in the spring, and picking grapes, peaches, and plums in the summer and early fall. He went on to do irrigating, tractoring, and machine repair work, and within a couple years he was helping to manage the farm and oversee the migrant workers. He rented a house on the farm property with two bedrooms and an indoor bathroom, luxurious lodgings to a family used to living in labor camps.

Living in one place, my dad, his sister and brother were enrolled at a Dinuba elementary school, where they began getting an education for the first time. My *abuelo* realized that education was the key to escaping a life of manual labor, and he and my *abuela* made sure that their children were in school every day and did their lessons. Given the opportunities my *abuelos* never had, the U.S. citizenship they never received, the command of English they never gained, and none of the hardships they endured, my father flourished in America, doing well in school, graduating from college, and becoming a high school counselor. Thanks to my father and mother, who works as an administrative assistant in the county schools' office, I along with my sister and brother grew up in a middle class environment with a nice house and a beautiful life, all which we took for granted.

I am currently in college, my older brother is attending law school, and my sister recently graduated with a degree in physical therapy. Our futures are very bright, and we learned to work hard from our parents, who learned from their parents, who were all illegal immigrants. Most young Mexican-American adults my age in the Valley have similar family histories, with either their grandparents or great-grandparents coming to the U.S. from Mexico illegally. They, like my *abuelos*, worked hard, sacrificed greatly, lived poorly, took nothing from the government, and scrimped and saved so that their children and their children's children would have a better life. They worked hard for low wages and helped build one of the vastest and most successful agricultural industries in the world, which today's illegal immigrants continue to do.

Recognizing the tremendous work ethic and willingness of Mexican immigrants to work for lower wages, U.S. employers also hire today's illegal immigrants in all manners of labor including housing construction, gardening, house and hotel cleaning, and a variety of mechanical work. And these immigrants will continue to follow a pattern established long ago by people like my *abuelos*: get married, raise families, send their children to school, and spawn future generations of solid, hard-working U.S. citizens.

Every objective account I've read of illegal immigrants in the U.S. bear out these facts: they contribute much more to the economy than they take from it in educational and health services; they are not welfare recipients; they don't take jobs from Americans, doing the back-breaking work that Americans won't do; they commit significantly fewer crimes proportionately than American citizens do, doing nothing that would cast a light on themselves and their status; they make food products and housing cheaper for Americans by keeping agricultural and building overhead low; and they make life easier for the middle class by mowing their lawns and cleaning their houses. And like all American immigrants past, they beget future generations of U.S. citizens who have continued to make this country greater since its existence.

Is there then an illegal immigrant "problem" in the U.S.? Certainly not in the way that it is cast by right-wing politicians. First, of course, illegal immigration is a two-way street. Illegal immigrants have not only been welcome but are recruited by employers throughout the U.S.

150

who rely on their employment. If there were no jobs available, there would be little immigration, but employers and the American public profit greatly from the influx of illegal aliens. The first step, then, in any attempt at "reform" would be to grant citizenship to all immigrants who have lived and worked in this country for a given time, say at least five years. They have earned their citizenship by the great good they have provided our country. I do not believe that a realistic part of the "solution" is to punish employers who hire illegal aliens. First, too many American industries rely on the hard work and low salaries that illegal aliens provide. No flood of Americans is going to rush in to fill the void for the kinds of work and wages that are available.

Will there come a time when the flow of illegal immigrants surpasses America's need for low-salaried employees? I can't say, but one thing is certain: when the job availability dries up, so will the flow of illegal immigrants. People emigrate for a better life and for jobs that aren't available in their country. If those jobs aren't available in America, the incentive for immigration drops dramatically. In the meantime, current illegal aliens who are long-term U.S. residents should be granted citizenship, and every illegal alien in the country should be treated with dignity and respect. My *abuelo* and *abuela* certainly deserved that, and America is a better country because of them and immigrants like them. So right-wing politicians should quit scapegoating illegal aliens for the recessionary problems that they had no role in creating and turn their attention to real problems like the deficit and the outsourcing of American jobs. When it comes to the economy, illegal aliens have always been a part of the solution, not the problem.

Drafting Activity 4.10
Write the first draft of your paper keeping the following guidelines in mind.

Drafting Guidelines

1. In your opening paragraph, introduce your topic, create reader interest, and include your thesis statement at or near the end of the paragraph.

2. Develop the support for your thesis statement in your middle paragraphs, including some or all of the points from your prewriting list. To develop your supportive points, you might include your personal experience, the experience of others, and any relevant comparisons.

3. Towards the end of the middle paragraphs, introduce and counter one or two opposing arguments to your viewpoint.

4. Conclude your paper in a manner that reinforces your thesis statement and makes your purpose clear, whether it be to move readers to action or to reconsider their viewpoint on the topic.

5. Keep your reading audience and purpose in mind as you write, and try to maintain the best tone to accomplish your purpose.

6. Don't limit yourself to just the ideas that you developed during prewriting. Often new ideas will come to mind, triggered by what you have written. Keep your mind open to new thoughts.

Revision

A critical part of the writing process is revising your drafts. All writers share the task, and it is an invaluable part of producing your best writing. Many writers feel that revision is the most important part of the process, and the oft-heard phrase "writing is revision" reflects that belief.

When writing your first draft, your main concern is getting your ideas on paper without a lot of thought to your wording or organization, or the effect your writing may have on readers. When you begin to revise, you shift your focus to evaluating how well you have expressed your ideas and the impact your writing may have on readers. Your focus has shifted from getting your ideas on paper to expressing those ideas in the most effective way.

In this section, you revise your draft based on revision considerations from previous units and new considerations that apply to your issue-oriented paper. You learn the importance providing evidence to convince readers of the value of your supporting points.

Providing Evidence

When readers read and evaluate an issue-oriented paper, they seldom agree with everything the writer says without question. They may have a different viewpoint on the topic or little or no opinion, reading to decide whether they might embrace the writer's viewpoint. In either case, they may be reading with a degree of skepticism, waiting to be convinced rather than accepting the writer's thesis.

Let's say, for example, that you are writing about the drop-date change at your school that was mentioned previously in the unit. You are writing to the board of trustees for your college, and you have good reasons to believe that moving the drop date forward is a bad idea. However, the board members may be a skeptical lot since they are considering changing the drop date. They are going to take some convincing.

One supportive reason you include is that changing the drop date will result in more students receiving a "F" grade for dropping late. What evidence can you provide to influence board members?

Supportive point: Changing the drop date will result in more students receiving an "F" grade.

Evidence: Currently, most students drop between the 6th and 8th week without penalty, but if the drop date were changed to the 4th week, these students would have all received "F's." *(Information received from the Admission's Office.)*

Students at a nearby college hated the drop date change at their school and the college later moved it back. *(Information received from students at the college.)*

A second supportive point you include is that an earlier drop date doesn't give students enough time to evaluate their progress. What evidence can you provide to influence board members?

Supportive point: With a 4th-week drop date, students don't have enough time to evaluate their progress.

Evidence: In my experience in a number of different classes, few tests were given or papers evaluated in the first four weeks, so I had little to go on regarding my progress. *(Information based on personal experience.)*

Class syllabi of a number of instructors reveals very few tests occurring during first four weeks in a semester, giving students little to evaluate their progress. *(Information received from students' syllabi in several different classes.*

The evidence that you provide in support of your thesis statement is very important. For example, you might write that "Students are almost unanimously opposed to the proposed change in the drop date." Skeptics may not believe that statement by itself, but when you provide evidence - a student newspaper survey that found 98% of the student respondents opposed - those skeptics may be more convinced.

Guidelines for Providing Evidence

The following guidelines will help you provide evidence effectively in your papers.

1. Provide evidence to support any statement that you make in defense of your thesis. The following are examples of such statements.

   People are friendlier during the Christmas season that at any other time. (How do you know? What evidence can you provide?)

   If global warming continues, many coastal cities will be underwater within fifty years. (What proof do you have? Who says so?)

   The best way to prepare for a test is to study an hour a day for a week before the test. (What evidence do you have? How do you know that?)

   The more experience you have revising your drafts, the easier it becomes. (How do you know that? What evidence do you have?)

2. Provide evidence that would most effectively show that your supportive points are valid.

   Supporting Point: Chocolate ice cream is by far the favorite of most Americans.

   Evidence: Based on a survey of employees in ice cream parlors, on a survey of college students, and on a survey of supermarket employees.

   Supporting Point: Biology 101 is one of the most difficult science classes at the college.

   Evidence : Based on personal experience, on the experience of other college students, and on the high drop-out rate.

Supporting Point: Cherry tomatoes are very easy to grow.

Evidence: Based on personal experience, on the experience of neighbors, and on the opinion of horticulture instructors.

Supporting Point: The Windmill Inn has excellent barbecued ribs.

Evidence: Based on personal experience, on the popularity of the menu item, on the comments of friends, and on comparisons with other restaurants.

3. Use any types of available evidence that would help convince readers of the validity of a claim: personal experience, the experience of others, examples, surveys, expert opinion, credible statistics, or relevant comparisons.

Revision Activity 4.11

Read the following paragraphs that support the thesis statements provided. With a classmate, identify the supportive point in each paragraph, the types of evidence used to support the point, and the effectiveness of the evidence provided.

Topic: Extinction of Dinosaurs

Thesis: The extinction of the dinosaurs was caused by an asteroid crashing into earth.

Scientists have discovered a high concentration of iridium, a metal rare to earth but common in asteroids, in the sedimentary layer of rock laid down during the last era of the dinosaurs. In addition, a 150-kilometer crater was discovered near the Yucatan Peninsula in Mexico, evidence of a huge falling mass that struck the earth. Such a collision, scientists theorize, created a dust-filled atmosphere that blocked out sunlight, dropped temperatures drastically, and killed off over 70% of all plant and animal life, including the dinosaurs. Only such a cataclysmic event could destroy the creatures that had dominated the earth for hundreds of millions of years.

Topic: Cars for the future

Thesis: The auto technology is available to end our dependence on oil.

While Toyota has taken a major step in producing gas-saving hybrid vehicles, a bigger innovation is quietly taking place. A small company in North Carolina can add a second plug-in battery to the Toyota Prius car battery system. You can drive thirty-five miles on the newly installed battery before Prius' battery/gasoline system kicks in, and then plug it in overnight for another thirty-five miles. For most people, a thirty-five mile range will cover most of the daily driving they do, which would virtually eliminate gas usage. Car rental companies are lining up their fleets for conversion, and the genie is out of the bottle. The future is near.

Revision Activity 4.12

The following paragraphs contain some unsubstantiated supporting points that the writer needs to support to convince readers of their validity. With a classmate, identify the unsubstantiated points that readers might question and the kinds of evidence the writer might use to substantiate them.

College Library

The school library is probably the most underused building at the college. Many times I've been in the library during the day and only a handful of students were in the huge building. At night it's even worse, and it feels eery, almost like you're in an abandoned building. One night I counted a total of five students in the building.

One problem is that students don't like studying in the library. In addition, the library's strict rules don't help the situation. The location of the library is also a problem. It is situated far from the center of campus where most classes are held. It sits on the northern end of campus near the technical and industrial buildings, a half-mile walk from most classrooms. The new student center near the middle of campus is a comfortable place to sit and study or read a magazine, so most students go there rather than trek a half mile across campus.

Finally, with most students having Internet access, there is little need for the library anymore. Perhaps technology is beginning to make traditional libraries obsolete.

Revision Activity 4.13

Revise the first draft of your paper by applying the following guidelines.

Revision Guidelines

1. Reread your paper and reevaluate your thesis and support. On careful analysis, have you taken a position on the issue that you feel is the most valid and defensible? At this point, you are not obligated to retain your current thesis if on reexamination and reflection, you are persuaded that a different or altered position is more valid or makes more sense. If that is the case, revise your thesis and support to reflect your change of mind.

2. Check your opening paragraph to make sure you have clearly introduced your topic, created some interest for readers, and included your thesis statement. Is there anything you can add or change to make your opening more effective?

3. Check your middle paragraphs to make sure that each paragraph relates to and supports your thesis statement, that you have used topic sentences to express the main idea of each paragraph, and that you have presented your supporting points in the best order.

   In addition, make sure that you have provided effective evidence to support each supportive point you have provided. Finally, make sure you have included one or two opposing arguments near the end and countered them effectively.

4. Check your concluding paragraph to make sure that it provides readers with a sense of completion, relates to your thesis statement, and adds something new for readers.

5. Read each paragraph to see if there is anything you can add - an example, a supporting point, a specific detail, new evidence - to make the paper more informative or convincing.

6. Check your use of transitional wording to tie sentences and paragraphs together. Add any transitions (e.g. first, second, also, in addition, finally, therefore, however, etc.) that will help readers understand your ideas and how they are related.

7. Check your paragraphing to make sure you have begun a new paragraph when you move to something new in your paper: a different part, a different reason, a new example, further evidence. Divide overly long paragraphs, and combine very short, related paragraphs.

8. Check the wording of each sentence, and revise sentences to make them clearer, smoother, and more concise by eliminating unnecessary words or phrases, rewording awkward or unclear sentences, and replacing questionable word choices.

9. Read your paper to make sure that your purpose is clear to readers and that you did everything possible to accomplish that purpose.

Revision Excerpts from "Illegal Immigration" draft *(first three paragraphs)*

When I read about **politicians'** immigration "reform" recommendations like sending all ~~illegal~~ **undocumented** ~~Mexican~~ immigrants back to Mexico or not allowing **their** children ~~of illegal immigrants~~ to attend public school or receive medical care, I think of my grandfather. He is one of these "illegal immigrants" that some people claim are ruining America: taking our jobs, living off our benefits, and committing crimes. In fact, America has benefitted greatly from the economic **and cultural** contributions that illegal immigrants have made and continue to make.

My *abuelo* came to America as a young man from the Mexican state of Jalisco. He came from a large, poor family and like millions of Mexicans, ~~came~~ **emigrated** to America for a better life. Later, he was joined by a brother and two sisters, but to his deep regret, he never saw his parents again, **one of the greatest sacrifices that millions of immigrants have made.** ~~although he sent them money for as long as they lived.~~ **However, he continued sending them money for the rest of their lives.**

Had my *abuelo* had the option of entering the U.S. legally, he certainly would have done so because crossing the border illegally was risky and dangerous. **He tells stories of hiding in bushes from border-patrol helicopters, of being captured, sent back, and trying again, and of greedy "coyotes" who took his last cent for helping him cross.**

However, U.S. quotas for Mexican immigrants didn't begin to cover the number of Mexicans wishing to emigrate, so my *abuelo's* options were to scratch out a life of poverty in Mexico or come to America illegally. It is not hard to understand why he, like so many Mexicans, chose the latter. **How many Americans, if the situation were reversed, would not do the same?**
(Revisions made to improve wording, to add detail, to provide new, relevant information, and to split one paragraph into two when the paragraph was expanded.)

Editing

You are nearing completion of your issue-oriented paper, with little left but to clean up any errors and make a last-minute revision or two as you proofread your draft. It is important to apply the same thorough, meticulous approach you used to evaluate the wording and content of your paper to proofreading your draft for errors. An error-free final paper is certainly an attainable goal.

In this section, you review the punctuation and grammar elements covered in previous units and are introduced to two new grammar elements: subject pronouns and pronoun-antecedent agreement. Then you apply what you have learned to editing your latest draft for errors.

Pronoun Usage

Pronouns are among the most frequently used parts of speech. We use them to replace words rather than repeat the same words over and over in our writing. For example, if pronouns didn't exist, a sentence might read like this:

Jason brought Jason's dog with Jason to the restaurant, and Jason ate breakfast while Jason's dog waited outside for Jason.

Of course, such a sentence sounds ridiculous because we are used to the repeated word "Jason" being replaced by pronouns:

Jason brought *his* dog with *him* to the restaurant, and *he* ate breakfast while *his* dog waited outside for *him*.

Most of the time, writers use pronouns correctly because the correct forms sound right. However, when errors do occur, they usually involve subject pronouns or pronoun-antecedent agreement, where the pronoun must agree in gender and number with the word it replaces. You will learn how to avoid such errors in this section.

Subject Pronouns

Subject pronouns are only a problem when the subject is compound: two or more subjects joined by *and* or *or*. When there is only one subject, the correct subject pronoun form sounds right: I like to study late at night. He likes to study in the morning. They prefer studying together. We would never write, "Me likes to study late at night," or "Them prefer studying together."

However, when the subject pronoun is compound, the incorrect form doesn't sound as bad to some writers. For example, while you would never write, "Me like to go to outdoor concerts," some writers might write, "Alicia, Munro, and *me* like to go to outdoor concerts," rather than "Alicia, Munro, and *I* like to go to outdoor concerts."
To use the correct subject pronoun forms with compound subjects, follow these rules and suggestions.

1. A subject pronoun is a pronoun used as the subject of a sentence: *I* am tired of this heat.

2. Always use the correct subject pronoun forms in your writing: *I, he, she, it, you, they, we.*

3. Never use the following object pronouns as subject pronouns: *me, him, her, them. us*.

4. When the subject of a sentence is compound - two or more subjects joined by *and* or *or* - you use the same correct subject pronoun forms: *I, he, she, it, you, they, we*.

5. To always use the correct pronoun with a compound subject, mentally cross out the other subject(s) and decide which form sounds best by itself.

Examples:

Breanna, Jordan, and (we, us) went to the county fair on Sunday. (Would you say "*We* went" or "*Us* went?" The correct pronoun - *we* - is obvious when you separate it from the other subjects.)

Matt, Fletcher, Monroe, and (he, him) enjoy eating breakfast in the cafeteria. (Would you say "*He* enjoys" or "*Him* enjoys?" The correct pronoun - *he* - is obvious when you separate it from the other subjects.)

Editing Activity 4.14

Underline the correct subject pronoun form in each of the following sentences.

Example: Matt and (her, <u>she</u>) have been friends since childhood.

1. The Gomez brothers and (us, we) enjoy sitting in the end zone seats at the football game.

2. Gloria and (she, her) have roomed together for three semesters.

3. Julius, Raymond, Phyllis, Jorge, and (them, they) all tried out for the school debate team.

4. Your grandmother and (him, he) graduated from the same high school sixty years ago.

5. (She, her) and (him, he) have very different opinions on whether Miriam and (me, I) should attend the anti-war rally on campus.

6. (They, them) and (us, we) always park in the same area of the dormitory parking lot.

7. Britanny and (her, she) don't look like sisters.

8. Your uncle and (him, he) gave me their tickets to Thursday's art gallery exhibition.

9. The other tourists in our group and (us, we) got on the wrong subway line and ended up in East Manhattan when we wanted to go to downtown.

10. Whenever you and (them, they) want to play backgammon again, just let me know.

Pronoun-Antecedent Agreement

The purpose of pronouns is to replace words that would otherwise be repeated needlessly. For example, the sentence, "John brought John's art portfolio with John to class," sounds odd. Therefore, we use pronouns to make the sentence sound normal: John brought *his* art portfolio with *him* to class.

Since a pronoun replaces another word, it needs to agree with that word - called its *antecedent* - in number and gender. For example, in the previous paragraph, the pronouns *his* and *him* replace the word *John* and agree with their antecedent because like John, they are singular in number and masculine in gender.

The following rules will ensure that your pronouns agree with their antecedents.

1. The following pronouns are grouped according to their number and gender.

   Singular masculine: *he, him, his, himself*
   Singular feminine: *she, her, hers herself*
   Singular neutral: *it, its, itself*
   Plural: *they, them, their, theirs, themselves*
   Plural including self: *we, us, our, ours, ourselves*

   (Note: The first-person singular pronouns *I, me, my, mine* and the second-person singular/plural pronouns *you, your, yours, yourself* do not replace other words and don't create pronoun -antecedent agreement problems.)

2. A pronoun always agrees with its *antecedent* - the word it replaces - in number and gender. Number refers to singular or plural, and gender refers to masculine, feminine, or neutral. For example, the antecedent Maria is singular and feminine, so any pronouns that replace the word Maria must also be singular and feminine: *she, her, hers, herself.*

   Examples: (Antecedent is underlined and pronoun(s) are italicized.)

   <u>Sabrina</u> brought *her* mother to college movie night. (The singular, feminine pronoun *her* agrees with its singular, feminine antecedent "Sabrina.")

   Those maple <u>trees</u> lose *their* leaves early in September. (The plural pronoun *their* agrees with its plural antecedent "trees.")

   The <u>moon</u> loses much of *its* luster as *it* descends towards the horizon. (The neutral pronouns *its* and *it* agree with the singular, neutral antecedent "moon.")

   <u>Vanessa and I</u> ruined *our* concert <u>tickets</u> when *we* put *them* through the washing machine. (The plural pronouns *our* and *we* agree with their plural antecedent "Vanessa and I," and the plural pronoun *them* agrees with its plural antecedent "tickets.")

A <u>pronoun</u> should agree in number and gender with *its* antecedent. (The singular, neutral pronoun *its* agrees with its singular, neutral antecedent "pronoun.")

3. If an antecedent may be either singular masculine or feminine (e.g. *person, student, employee*), use the pronouns *he* or *she*, *his* or *her*, or *himself* or *herself* to replace it.

Examples:

If a <u>person</u> believes in *himself* or *herself*, *he* or *she* can weather bad times.

A <u>student</u> who does *his* or *her* best has nothing to be ashamed of.

Note: In essay writing, when continued use of *he* or *she* and *himself* or *herself* seems awkward, you can alternate between the masculine and feminine singular forms as is done throughout the text, or change singular antecedents to plural ("<u>Students</u> do *their* best ..." instead of "A <u>student</u> does *his* or *her* best . . .").

4. An indefinite pronoun - *one, everyone, anyone, everybody, anybody, someone, somebody, nobody* - is always singular, so any pronoun that replaces it must also be singular.

Examples:

<u>Everyone</u> on the girls' volleyball team played *her* heart out tonight.

<u>One</u> of the rose bushes lost *its* blossoms because of the frost.

<u>Everybody</u> should bring *his* or *her* umbrella along on the hike.

Editing Activity 4.15
Fill in the blanks in each sentence with pronouns that agree with their antecedents. Underline the antecedent(s) in each sentence.

Examples: <u>Audrey and I</u> seldom see *our* roommates on weekends.
The mother <u>cat</u> hid *her* newborn kittens behind the washing machine.

1. One of the barns in the area lost _____ tin roof when a tornado blew through the valley.

2. New students need to have _____ photos taken for _____ student ID cards.

3. Regina and I brought _____ sleeping bags with _____ when _____ lined up at 5:00 a.m. to get tickets to the Shakira concert at the campus arena.

4. Fred treated _____ to a double cheeseburger after _____ survived five weeks on a meatless diet.

5. Everyone needs to park _____ car in the south parking lot since _____ is the only lot on campus not being repaved today.

6. The weather will be mild for the rest of the week, and _____ should remain pleasant for most of the month.

7. Ralph and Freda bought _____ computer at a discount warehouse, and now that _____ is having problems, _____ have no warranty to cover the cost of fixing _____.

8. Amanda and Trevor don't realize how large _____ Newfoundland puppy will get, but _____ will find out for_____ in the next six months.

9. One out of every five residents living along the river had to evacuate _____ home as the water rose from the heavy storm.

10. Azaleas will start losing _____ blossoms if _____ don't get enough water, but _____ leaves will start turning yellow if _____ get too much water.

Editing Review

In the previous units, you have edited your drafts for errors involving run-on sentences and comma splices, sentence fragments, irregular verb forms, comma usage, and subject-verb agreement. Writers prone to such errors usually don't eliminate them overnight. For that reason, it is important to continue working on them, which the review activities allow you to do.

Editing Activity 4.16

Proofread the following paragraphs for errors involving run-on sentences or comma splices, sentence fragments, irregular verb forms, comma usage, and subject-verb agreement, and correct all errors.

Example

I get very sleepy during my biology lab after lunch, I can barely stay awake. Sometimes my lab partners who is also my roommates has to nudge me. When I start drifting off. I yawn the entire period and I have trouble keeping my mind on the lab experiment we are doing.

Corrected

I get very sleepy during my biology lab after lunch, *and* I can barely stay awake. Sometimes my lab partners, who *are* also my roommates, *have* to nudge me when I start drifting off. I yawn the entire period, and I have trouble keeping my mind on the lab experiment.

House Calls

In England today doctors actually still make house calls which is unheard of in America.

For example in London if you have a very bad stomach ache you call a doctor. From a list

of physicians that make house calls in your area. Within half an hour a doctor will be at your

doorstep, he will treat you at home unless your condition requires hospitalization.

In America the house call are a thing of the past it happens very rarely and only in the

smallest towns. Americans who experience sudden onsets of pain sits endless hours in emergency

waiting rooms with other patients. Any person who has went through the experience know how

unpleasant it is, compare that experience to having a doctor assist you in the privacy of your

home.

Such comparisons with other health care systems have drove many Americans to question our health care practices. London is just as big as New York City so why can't American doctors make house calls? It seems that in England the doctor-patient relationship is different than in America. In England the doctor goes where he must to serve the patient, in America, the patient goes where he must to see the doctor. In England, the doctor is saw more as a public servant who serve the people, in America, the doctor is saw more as an elite person who see the people when he is available.

Editing Activity 4.17
Proofread your latest draft for errors by applying the following "Editing Guidelines," and make the necessary corrections.

Editing Guidelines

1. Check your sentences to make sure you haven't run any sentences together or put a comma between sentences instead of a period. Correct run-on sentences or comma splices by separating longer sentence with periods and combining shorter, related sentences with a joining word.

2. Check your draft for any sentence fragments: incomplete sentences with a period after them. To correct fragments, attach them to the sentence they belong with, or add words to make them complete.

3. Check your use of irregular verbs, making sure you have used the correct irregular forms and spelled them correctly.

4. Check your comma usage, making sure you have inserted commas into your sentences following the rules from Unit Two, and that you haven't inserted commas where they aren't required.

5. Check the spelling of any word you are uncertain of, or run the spell check on your word processing program, to eliminate any spelling errors.

6. Check your verbs in each sentence to make sure that they agree with their subjects.

7. Check your pronouns in each sentence to make sure they agree with their antecedents, and make sure you have used the correct subject pronoun forms.

Editing Activity 4.18

Exchange papers with a classmate, proofread each other's drafts for errors, and make any necessary corrections. Then write the final draft of your paper to share with readers.

Applying the Writing Process

To conclude the unit, you write a second issue-oriented paper, applying what you have learned to this point in the text. The purpose of this assignment is to give you more practice writing issue-oriented papers, to give you freedom to write more independently, and to help you internalize what you are learning to apply to future writing.

Writing Assignment

Select a second issue to write on that interests you and that people have different viewpoints on. Select a topic that you are knowledgeable about and that you would like to share with readers. Your issue may come from any field: sports, education, politics, fashion, music, health, family, your particular college or community, and so on.

Working independently, follow a similar writing process that you used to develop your first paper. (Refer back to the drafting, revision, or editing guidelines in the unit as needed.)

- Select an issue to write about.

- Decide on a thesis, list some supportive points, and consider evidence you may use to support those points.

- Write a first draft.

- Revise by focusing on providing strong supportive points and compelling evidence, by refuting opposing arguments, by using clear sentence wording and effective paragraphing, and by adding whatever will improve the draft.

- Edit the draft by correcting any errors that you find.

- Write the final paper.

Before revising, share first drafts with a classmate or two, and ask each other questions about anything that seems unclear in the draft or that you'd like to know more about. Consider your classmates' input as you revise your paper.

Readings

Is College Worth It?
by Alicia Frey

Go to college, get your degree, and get that good-paying job. That has been the common wisdom for decades for anyone who wants to secure a piece of the America Dream. But does it still apply today? Many young people are questioning the value of a college education, wondering if the time and money spent are worth it. Is a college education the best chance for success that it once was?

Naysayers and skeptics point to a multitude of factors that have eroded faith in the college pathway to success: a down job market for college graduates, increasing numbers of good jobs outsourced to other countries, skyrocketing college costs and years of student loan repayments, the need for a "higher" degree to get hired in many professions, and the outrageous success of some college drop-out entrepreneurs, proof that you don't need that sheepskin.

It is easy to see why some young people aren't particularly keen on beginning a long college trek that may lead to nowhere certain, and the falling numbers of male college students nationwide indicate that many young men are opting out. However, while a college degree may have lost some of its luster, the options to attending college are even less attractive.

What kinds of jobs are available for high school graduates? In the days of America's industrial heyday, there were many decent-paying, unionized blue-color jobs for high-school grads. But the industries that provided those jobs – e.g. manufacturing, steel, textiles, automobile – have either shrunk or disappeared, and millions of jobs along with them. Most of today's high school grads face the prospect of hourly wage jobs and little job security, whether as clerks, salespeople, nursing home aides, manicurists, auto mechanics, maintenance workers, waiters, or cooks. The prospects for high school drop-outs are, of course, even grimmer.

Studies invariably show that college graduates make significantly more money than high school graduates. A 2012 Census Bureau report estimates the lifetime earnings of American workers by educational level, calculated from 2011 statistics in its American Community Survey. The report predicts $1.371 million in lifetime earnings for a high school graduate with no higher education compared with $2.422 million for a four-year bachelor's degree graduate. This gives a college graduate a lifetime earnings advantage of more than $1 million. In addition, holders of two-year college associate degrees also earn significantly more in lifetime earnings than high school grads. It is clear that the longer one stays in school, based on the degree obtained, the more money that he or she will make.

Of course, money isn't everything, and many people for whom money is the Holy Grail are always searching for that elusive happiness. It is the lack of money that is the problem: not enough money to live in a safe neighborhood, to buy a reliable car, to afford health insurance, to ever buy a house, to save enough to weather a catastrophe, to escape poverty. Having enough money helps to keep the budget balanced, to stay out of credit card debt, to raise healthy, happy children, to have health care, to save for the future, to live with peace of mind. A job, and the salary, obtained by a college degree gives you the best chance of enjoying a living wage and everything positive that comes with it.

It is not surprising, yet worth noting, that college graduates are also more likely to marry than high school graduates and more like to stay married. Greater financial security is no doubt the main reason. College graduates are also more likely to be healthier, to live longer, and to travel more frequently. The children of college graduates are more likely to get better grades in school and to graduate from college themselves, enjoying the advantages that college-educated parents can provide. Getting a college degree can provide dividends not only for the degree holder but for generations of his or her family to come.

Of course, many first-generation college students from working-class backgrounds excel wonderfully, and their growing numbers are a positive sign, but students of college-educated parents have fewer obstacles to overcome. They receive more financial help for college from their parents, and on average, don't have to work as much while attending school and, consequently, can often take more units per semester and graduate more quickly.

But what of that bleak job market for college graduates? It may not be as great as it was ten or fifteen years ago, but all of the professional jobs available – doctor, lawyer, engineer, teacher, researcher, computer programmer, CPA, architect, administrator, agronomist, geologist, registered nurse – go only to college graduates. Future graduates may have to evaluate the job market carefully before choosing a major, be a bit patient before getting the job they want, and have to move out of their desired area of residence, but that is nothing new. A college education has never been a guarantee of a good job, but it's far closer to a guarantee than any alternative.

Of course, college isn't for everyone, and there are alternate paths to success for some young people. But even two years of college to get licensed or certified in, for example, automotive tech, radiology, fire science, forestry, office management, dental assisting, aeronautics, welding, or health information technology opens doors to jobs that would not be available to high school graduates. And compared to four-year schools, a community college education is still a bargain.

There are also the less tangible advantages of getting a college education. College graduates tend to read more, to be more knowledgeable of the world, to have a greater appreciation of the fine arts, to be more tech savvy, and to be more politically engaged. With the knowledge gained and thinking skills honed in college, they are best prepared to understand and navigate the ever-more complex world in which we live. None of this makes them any better than the next person, but it gives them advantages that can lead to a richer, fuller life.

Is a college education still worth getting? When considering the alternatives, it is perhaps more worth getting today than ever before. And given our ever-more diverse population and the growing numbers of Americans living below the poverty level, it is essential for America's future that the doors of our colleges remain wide open for everyone. Financial hardship should block no one's entry to college.

Questions for Discussion

1. What evidence does the essay present to support the value of a college education? What evidence do you find the most compelling?

2. Why do you think that the enrollment of men in colleges throughout the nation has been in decline? What might be some of the reasons, and how might that trend be reversed?

3. Do you agree with the essay regarding the value of a college education? Discuss your own college aspirations and career goals.

What a Wall Can't Stop
by Richard Rodriguez

To placate the nativist flank of his Republican Party, former President Bush promised to brick up the sky. But that will not prevent the coming marriage of Mexico and the United States. South and north of the line, we are becoming a hemispheric people -- truly American -- in no small part because of illegal immigrants.

As the son of Mexican immigrants legally in the United States, I have long wondered about the future of Mexico, a nation that every night for nearly a century has lost hundreds of its most hopeful youths to its neighbor and rival, the North.

I think historians will come to recognize the illegal immigrant as the great prophetic figure within the Americas. The illegal immigrant Americanized us all by a simple and frugal migration; by sojourning in the North; and by sending the dream of the North (a money-gram) back into Mexico.

From the early 20th century, the migrant worker commuted between here and there, hot and cold, high and low, past and future, rich and poor, Spanish and English, life and death. The legend of the North spread throughout the Americas. Today Peruvians and Bolivians know when there are apple-picking jobs in the Yakima Valley; when the godawful fisheries in Alaska will begin to hire; when a dishwashing job in a Bronx restaurant is coming open.

By the late 20th century, the rumor of the North had ascended to the middle and the upper class in Mexico. They, too, followed the peasant's lead. In Mexico City, a capital of abundant but vulnerable wealth, the rich have learned the prudence of a second home in La Jolla.

The Americanization of Mexico is as inevitable as the Mexicanization of the United States, though the cross-pollination will never be equal because the United States is the more potent transgressor.

Americans take our imperial influence for granted. We assume, do we not, the desirability of Wal-Mart? Shouldn't we build Wal-Mart in Mexico? Of course we should. Where shall we build Wal-Mart in Mexico? How about right there -- where it will appear in the photograph of the Pyramid of the Sun.

Commentators did not seem to know what they were watching when millions of brown people recently marched along U.S. streets. This was obviously a "demonstration," but a demonstration of what? I believe it was a reunion -- of family, of hemisphere. Children and parents walked as one family. Brothers born there, sisters born here, walked as one hemisphere.

A great many Americans are alarmed by how much of Mexico is within the United States -- the tongue, the tacos, the soccer balls, the street gangs, the Spanish Catholic Masses, the workforce swarming into New Orleans in the wake of Hurricane Katrina. The extent of the Mexicanization of U.S. culture renders any notion of a fortified border irrelevant.

Twenty-five years ago, Joel Garreau wrote "The Nine Nations of North America," in which he described a nation he called "MexAmerica" -- a puzzle to both Washington and Mexico City -- encompassing much of the U.S. Southwest and Northern Mexico as well as Baja California. A quarter-century later, one is struck by how prescient Garreau was but also how modest his forecast was. MexAmerica now includes vast sections of Chicago and blocks along Main Street in Kansas, as well as the Baptist Church in North Carolina.

In the other direction, MexAmerica includes not just the Mexican border towns that have become drug supply centers for U.S. addiction but also Jalisco, Colima, Michoacan and points south.

Mexico, the poorer country, does not have the luxury of an appalled demeanor when the Atlanta couple transforms a beachfront property into a saltwater Tara or when senior citizens from Ohio park their retirement village in Baja.

And watch closely -- I implore you -- watch the eyes of Mexican busboys and waiters as they observe U.S. college students conducting wet T-shirt competitions on the beaches of Cancun. Do not believe, America, that you are alone in your reservations concerning this marriage.

Questions for Discussion

1. What does Rodriguez mean by the "Mexicanization" of America? What examples does he provide? Do you agree with him that any notion of a fortified border is "irrevelant?"

2. Likewise, Rodriguez sees the "Americanization" of Mexico. What examples does he provide? How does the "Mexicanization" of America differ sharply from the "Americanization" of Mexico?

3. The Latino population is by far the fastest growing in the U.S., with California nearly 40% Latino. What impact will this growth have on the culture, the economy, and U.S. politics?

The Intelligence of Beasts
by Colin Woodard

If you've ever doubted that elephants are contemplative, Joshua M. Plotnik has some video you should watch. Plotnik, a postdoctoral fellow in experimental psychology at the University of Cambridge, wanted to see if Asian elephants could pass a classic cooperation test designed for chimpanzees. The elephants already knew how to use a rope to pull a food-bearing table within reach. But what if the only way to move the table was two elephants pulling on separate ropes simultaneously?

On one video, one elephant ambles up to the rope and waits patiently, trunk and tail gently swinging, for its counterpart to arrive, half a minute later. Then, without hesitation, they grasp their respective ropes in synchronicity, pulling the food to themselves. In another segment, a young female simply stands on her rope, which—the way the mechanism is set up—forces her colleague to do all the work for the both of them. In 60 trials, all six pairs of elephants waited for their partners, with an average success rate of over 93 percent, suggesting that they easily understood cooperation.

"We were very excited by the results," Plotnik says into his cellphone as he walks home, after midnight, through the streets of Chiang Mai, Thailand, not far from his research sites. "Their behavior was comparable to that of the chimpanzees. We're getting further into understanding how intelligent they are."

For much of the last century, research on animal cognition focused almost exclusively on primates, on account of their relatively close evolutionary kinship with humans. But in recent years, many researchers wishing to understand how higher intelligence evolved have taken a different approach, looking to apparently intelligent species that are only distantly related to ourselves, like elephants, dolphins, or ravens. In the process, many cognitive traits once thought to be exclusive to humans—including some that are considered definitive of human uniqueness—have been found in far-flung provinces of the animal kingdom.

"In understanding evolution, human cognition is like the elephant's trunk: It's a very unusual thing, and it really stands out," says Evan L. MacLean, a doctoral student in evolutionary anthropology at Duke University, which is coordinating a collaborative project to compare 30 species, as varied as dogs and octopuses. "The best source of evidence we have are the closest relatives—chimps and bonobos—but we've been missing a ton of very interesting variation by just looking at primates."

Nine-week-old puppies have been shown to be very good at recognizing human gestures and interpreting them for their own benefit, while adult dogs provide and request information, predict social events, and perhaps even speculate on what their masters are thinking—for example, finding hidden food by picking up on subtle human cues. Dolphins recognize themselves in mirrors, while the New Caledonian crow fashions tools with which to capture grubs. The common raven has demonstrated the ability to test actions in its mind, solving complicated puzzles to obtain food on the first try.

"There used to be this chimpocentrism in the field, with research narrowly concentrated on primates," says Ádám Miklósi, a professor of ethology at Budapest's Eötvös Loránd University and an expert on canine cognition. "It's really great to see research in other species expand exponentially, because we really need the breadth and depth of species to be able to say anything meaningful about animal cognition."

While there are many reasons to study the thinking ability of animals—devising better conservation strategies, opening new pathways in artificial intelligence—the great evolutionary question driving many researchers is this: Under what evolutionary pressures do different types of cognitive abilities tend to develop? If several entirely unrelated species turn out to have a given intellectual ability—mirror recognition in humans, dolphins, and elephants, for instance— are there common denominators in the conditions they confront (membership in complex social groups, for example) that might explain the development? Can the study of such examples of convergent evolution help us understand how and why higher intelligence arises in nature? Researchers have taken only the first steps toward finding definitive answers to both of those questions.

Elephants are fascinating subjects in this regard. They have enormous brains, bigger than those of humans. Like many other animals thought to possess unusual intelligence, they live in complex societies in which individuals cooperate and interact to solve problems. They're also unrelated to humans. Whereas we and chimpanzees had a common ancestor about five million years ago, with elephants (and their relations, the aardvark and manatee), it was 100 million years ago, a relationship even more distant than the ones we have with dolphins and whales.

"If you find an elephant and a human sharing an ability that most other primates don't have, you can be pretty sure" it's an example of convergent evolution at work, says Richard W. Byrne, a professor of psychology at the University of St. Andrews, in Scotland, who has studied cognition in both primates and elephants. "If you can see shared circumstances in which these animals use this ability, that can help show what its biological function is."

Researchers like Byrne are finding that elephants have all sorts of intriguing cognitive abilities comparable to—and sometimes exceeding—our own. They recognize their reflections in mirrors. They act empathically toward fellow elephants in distress and offer them assistance. They mourn and even bury their dead. As Plotnik has shown, they're not flummoxed by cooperative problem solving. And both Asian and African elephants make tools for a variety of purposes, from flyswatters to backscratchers.

Byrne's fieldwork has taken place in Kenya's Amboseli National Park, site of a long-term, multidisciplinary study of elephants, in its 39th year. (That research is described in an edited collection, *The Amboseli Elephants: A Long-Term Perspective on a Long-Lived Mammal*, published this spring by the University of Chicago Press.) In recent years, Byrne and his colleagues have conducted field experiments that show two additional mental abilities not seen in any other animal.

In one experiment, elephants were presented garments worn by two different human ethnic groups: the Masai (who sometimes spear elephants) and the Kamba (an agrarian people who rarely interact with elephants). Whether given access to smells of previously worn clothing or to visual inspection of unworn clothing, the elephants responded with greater fear or aggression toward the Masai clothing. This led Byrne and his colleagues to conclude that elephants are able to categorize another species, humans, into subclasses. "We don't know any other animals that categorize dangers in this way, but that may be because they haven't been tested," he says.

In the second experiment, the researchers wanted to test if elephants understand "person permanence" and "invisible displacement"—that is, if they are aware that absent individuals exist and if they contemplate the movements and activities of those individuals in absentia, an ability that human beings develop in infancy. Knowing that the members of the extended elephant family they were working with sniffed one another's urine deposits, the researchers began moving the deposits around. "The nice thing was to see their surprised reaction when they encountered a sample from an individual who was actually a half-kilometer or more behind them, a much greater reaction than if the sample was from someone who was actually ahead of them," Byrne explains.

The results suggested that each elephant was keeping track of the location and expected movements of everyone else in its foraging group—17 individuals, in this case—a remarkable display of working-memory capacity.

"They don't use their eyes in the bright Amboseli sun, but they're still able to keep track of 17 individuals in an environment that they cannot scan," Byrne notes. "Think of a parent with 17 kids roaming around a department store; I think we would find it extremely challenging to keep track in our minds of where everyone is. This is an ability that appears to be rather more than humans can do."

Miklósi, who is using cognition work with dogs to program robots that will, doglike, anticipate, serve, and respond to human needs, suspects that scientists will discover many more instances in which animals are found to have mental powers that humans lack. "So far, no matter how much you read in the literature, there is this notion that humans are always the best at everything," he says. "If the tests were not so anthropocentric, we would probably lose a lot more often."

Some other researchers agree that animal-cognition research will inevitably challenge human presumptuousness. "From ancient times, it's always been us versus the rest of the animal world, and it wasn't really considered that animals were thinking creatures," says Diana Reiss, a professor of cognitive psychology at Hunter College of the City University of New York, who studies elephants and dolphins. "The big message is that we're not the pinnacle of the tree, the only creatures who are thinking complexly. We share the upper branches of the tree with many species, each so beautifully evolved for their own environmental niche and social structures."

But other scientists take a more skeptical view. They include David Premack, a professor emeritus of psychology at the University of Pennsylvania and the father of the influential "theory of mind," which refers to the ability to infer the mental states of others. "I have a prejudice that's not common among people who study animals, who tend to do so primarily to show similarities between the animal and the human," he explains. "That's a noble cause, but I feel it's easily abused, as when they leap from similarity to equivalence."

Humans and certain animals might similarly recognize that a large rock is more likely to break a branch than a small one, but Premack says there's no evidence that this understanding of a physical action is equivalent to causal reasoning. That is, if an animal comes across a large rock lying beside a crushed plant, it won't infer, as a human might, that the rock crushed the plant, he argues.

Microscopic study of the human brain, he notes, has revealed neural structures and forms of connectivity not found in any other animal. And cognitive research has not been able to keep pace with those developments. "Things that the naked eye can see—that the human is a very different entity than the nonhuman—is very much corroborated under the microscope," he says. "If you can't see we're special, you have to be permanently drunk."

Byrne agrees that it would be foolish to jump from similarity to equivalence, but he says comparative-cognition researchers are by no means trying to show that animals are "little humans in disguise." "None of the interpretations we make of our experiments require one to treat superficial resemblance as deep equivalence," he says.

As for his own research interests, Byrne would like to explore what creatures in other, unstudied corners of the animal kingdom might be thinking. Most species thought to be especially intelligent are social creatures, but what about large-brained nonsocial species? "I don't know anybody who's looking at bears. They have very large brains—I wonder why," he says. "If someone offered me a long-term study of grizzlies, I'd take it."

Discussion Starters

1. Why has the study of intelligence in animals other than primates been lacking historically? How do recent findings change our thinking about the intelligence of some non-primates?

2. How might the treatment of animals change given our understanding of their intelligence? What current practices regarding animal captivity should be examined?

3. What does the intelligence found in completely unrelated species – e.g. elephants, birds, dogs – infer about animal intelligence? What does it infer about evolution across the species?

How Black is Black Enough?

by Leonard Pitts Jr.

I suddenly find myself concerned about my blackness. It had never occurred to me to worry about it before. Then came the incident on ESPN's "First Take" program that initially got commentator Rob Parker suspended and then, last week, fired outright. It seems Parker, who is black, analyzed what he saw as the insufficient blackness of Robert Griffin III, rookie quarterback for the Washington, D.C., football team that is named for a racial slur.

Having returned their team to relevance for the first time since the Clinton era, RG3, as he is known, can do no wrong in the eyes of Slurs fans. But Parker, saying that the young man's fiancee is (gasp!) white and that he himself is rumored to be — cover the children's ears — a Republican, found him lacking in the area of authentic blackness. "My question," he said, "which is just a straight, honest question: is he a brother, or is he a cornball brother? He's not really … OK, he's black, he kind of does the thing, but he's not really down with the cause. He's not one of us. He's kind of black, but he's not really like the guy you really want to hang out with..."

That explosion you hear is the sound of my mind, blown. I'm left second-guessing my own blackness. I mean, I listen to Bruce Springsteen, for crying out loud! There's even a Dixie Chicks album on my iPod. And I read books sometimes, man — even when no one's making me do it. Some of them are thick as bricks. Some aren't even about African-American themes.

It gets worse. I have no natural rhythm, no criminal record and can correctly pronounce the word "ask." I don't curse nearly as much as I ought to. Oh, and I went and married my baby mama. Obviously, my blackness is on life support.

Many of us have been taught that it is demeaning and delimiting when someone presumes to say who you are, how you will behave, what you think, what you like, and how intelligent you are, from the color of your skin. We have been taught that such behavior abridges the other person's individuality. But apparently, that's only when white people do it to black people. When black people do it to black people, it's called assessing your blackness, making sure you aren't some "cornball brother."

How enlightening to learn that. It is even more enlightening to discover that we have such easy-peasy rubrics to go by. You can't be black if you are a Republican? That means Colin Powell isn't black. Neither, if published reports are to be believed, are rappers LL Cool J and 50 Cent. Who'd have thought?

Poor Frederick Douglass has a double whammy. He was a Republican and had a white wife. Who'd have thought this former slave, one of the towering heroes of African-American history, wasn't black enough?

It is this kind of bold insight and trenchant analysis ESPN loses in sacking Rob Parker. What is the network thinking? Parker, who also contributes commentary to WDIV television in Detroit, defended himself in an interview with the station that aired just before ESPN dropped the ax. He pronounced himself shocked by the fallout and suggested his comments were taken out of context.

"You can't be afraid to talk about race," he said. He's exactly right. In discussing race, we must be fearless. We must also be thoughtful. And informed. And exact. And alive to the ramifications of what we say. Surely, Parker knows this. Or if he didn't before, he does now.

As for being black enough, he is probably a greater expert than he was before. He is, after all, a man out of work. It doesn't get much blacker than that.

Questions for Discussion

1. How does Pitts attack Parker's contention that you aren't *really* black unless you fit a particular criteria? Do you find his response effective? Why?

2. Pitts enlists his own black stereotypes to show he doesn't fit the mold: blacks don't read, swear too much, have wedlock children, and don't have jobs. Is such stereotyping of blacks by a black man defensible in any way?

3. Discuss racial stereotypes of blacks, whites, Asians, and Latinos. What are such stereotypes based on and how are they harmful?

Unit Five
Problems and Solutions

One of the greatest contributions that writers make is addressing the myriad of problems that confront us and providing solutions to help solve those problems. On any day in the newspaper you might find an article on the dangers of global warming and how it can be combated, on the recent local drought and how residents can help by reducing water usage, on a solution to a marital problem posed by a reader to "Dear Abby," and on how local school districts facing a decline in student enrollment can survive the unexpected shortfall.

Since problems confront us all of the time - the loss of a job, not getting the classes we need, the unhealthy effects of increasing pollution, the rising cost of tuition, textbooks, gasoline, and housing - there is always something to write about. In addition, writing about problems helps to develop our problem-solving abilities, which we can apply at school, in the workplace, and in our personal relationships.

Writing about problems and solutions is a complex task which may involve determining exactly what the problem is, what caused the problem, what its effects are, who or what is affected, and what possible solution or solutions could eliminate or reduce the problem. Since most problems worth writing about don't have any simple, obvious solution, one of the greatest challenges is coming up with solutions that can work and that people are willing to try.

In this unit, you write about a particular problem and how it might be solved. You can write about any problem you want, from the personal to the universal. The purpose of this assignment is to engage you in a complex writing task which draws upon your evaluative, analytical, and creative thinking skills. In addition, writing about problems and solutions can often help the writer, who may find a new solution to a nagging problem, and the readers, who may have similar problems and benefit from the writer's ideas.

Prewriting

Since a problem/solution paper contains a number of different elements, each element requires some attention during the prewriting process. A prewriting activity introduced in this section helps writers analyze those elements: asking questions. The traditional journalistic questions of who, what, where, when, and why help writers probe a subject and generate material for a paper.

Selecting a Topic

Writers can usually find problems to write about since they are seldom in short supply. The decision to be made is which problem stands out as the best topic for your upcoming paper. To help you decide on a problem to write about, consider the following criteria.

1. Choose a problem that is affecting you in some way and that may affect others as well.

2. Choose a problem that is serious enough to engage readers' interest. For example, if the problem is that you can't find a dry cat food that your finicky cat will eat, readers may find the problem more amusing than engaging.

3. Choose a problem that doesn't have an obvious solution that you have discovered. One purpose of this paper is to try and find solutions to a problem where no simple solution is apparent. For example, if the problem is that your car has a flat tire, the solution - to get it fixed - is a bit too obvious.

4. Choose a problem that is nagging and persistent rather than passing. For example, if you are short on cash this month because your financial aid check is late, you have a temporary problem that will soon take care of itself.

5. You may choose any kind of problem: personal, family-related, school-related, work-related, or a particular local, state, national, or universal problem.

6. Since this is not a "research" paper, choose a topic that you are knowledgeable about.

Prewriting Activity 5.1

To generate possible topics for your paper, brainstorm some ideas, writing down any problems that come to mind without evaluating them. From this list, you may find your writing topic.

Sample Brainstorming Session

loneliness at new school	lack of school activities	lack of jobs for students
making budget work	managing time better	required health fee
probation for grades	violence where I live	lack of computer labs
living with roommate	cliques of local students	city pollution
torn up city streets	not having a car	sharing a computer

Prewriting Activity 5.2

Choose a topic for your upcoming problem/solution paper keeping in mind the criteria presented and your brainstormed list of problems.

Sample topic selection: working and going to school

Tentative topic:

Analyzing the Problem

Now that you have selected a problem to write on, you can begin analyzing the problem with the goal of finding a workable solution. To help you analyze the problem, you answer questions that will help you probe its various elements.

Asking Questions

Asking and answering questions helps writers think more deeply about a topic and analyze its different parts. The following questions will help you dissect the problem you are writing about.

1. What exactly is the problem? How would you describe it in one sentence?

2. When did the problem begin, and how did it get started?

3. What are the causes of the problem?

4. Who or what is affected by the problem?

5. What are the effects of the problem?

Prewriting Activity 5.3

To help you analyze the problem and generate some material for your upcoming paper, answer the five questions just presented. Take some time to consider each question since your answers may help lead you to a solution.

Sample Answers

Topic: working and going to school

1. What exactly is the problem?

   The difficulty of working and going to college at the same time.

2. When did the problem begin, and how did it get started?

The problem began when I started college and had to work to pay for everything. I got a job at a supermarket in town to make some money.

3. What are the causes of the problem?

    I have to pay for tuition and books and other fees, which add up to quite a bit of money. In addition, I have car payments and insurance and gas and food to buy. To make enough money to pay for everything, I work thirty to forty hours a week along with taking a full load at the college.

4. Who or what is affected by the problem?

    I'm obviously affected by the problem but so are a lot of other students who are doing the same thing: working and going to college at the same time. I've met a lot of students whose schedules are pretty similar to mine.

5. What are the effects of the problem?

    It seems that I don't have enough time to do everything: go to classes, work, study, get enough sleep. I'm tired most of the time and I have to stay up late studying. I'm not as sharp and focused at work or at school as I'd like to be. I also don't have much social life since I'm always busy and don't have extra money. I think I could be doing much better in school if it weren't for work.

Answers to questions:

1.

2.

3.

4.

5.

_____

Finding Solutions

Solving difficult problems isn't easy. Sometimes unresolved problems between a brother and sister, a parent and child, an employee and supervisor, or even neighboring countries can go on for years, poisoning relationships and damaging lives. While some problems eventually work themselves out with time, others stubbornly persist despite the best efforts to solve them.

In seeking solutions to a problem, the following suggestions will help you consider different possibilities and evaluate their chances for success.

Solution Guidelines

1. Exactly what does solving the problem mean? What do you hope to accomplish? For example, if there is a parking problem for students on campus, does solving the problem mean that every student would be able to find a parking place or that the problem would be alleviated enough to satisfy most students?

2. How can the solution get to the roots of the problem, its underlying causes? If a solution doesn't address the causes of a problem, it seldom succeeds. For example, solutions to the Israeli-Palestinian conflict may have failed over the years because they haven't adequately addressed the underlying cause: both groups believing that they have the historical right to the same land.

3. What are possible alternative solutions to the problem? Often with difficult problems, different solutions have to be tried before something works, or different combinations of solutions. For example, with the parking problem, a possible solution might include car pooling incentives for students, tram rides for students parking farthest from classes, and the creation of a new parking lot.

4. Is compromise an important part of the solution? With problems involving individuals, groups, or even nations, there often has to be some give on both sides for a solution to work. If the solution is good for one party and not the other, it probably won't work. For example, any solution to the Israeli-Palestinian conflict will probably involve Israel giving up more land than they want and Palestinians getting less land than they would like.

5. What is a realistic solution to the problem? Can the right solution completely eliminate the problem, or can it make a bad situation better? For example, with college enrollments increasing and parking areas being limited by space, parking problems may remain with a particular college for a long time, but that doesn't mean that solutions that reduce the problem and make the situation tolerable shouldn't be tried. On the other hand, it appears that there is no half-way solution to a problem like the Israeli-Palestinian conflict. Either Palestine will become a sovereign nation alongside Israel or the conflict will continue.

6. What do other people think? Often there are people to turn to when seeking solutions to thorny problems. That person may be an interior designer if your problem is too little living space and too much furniture, a college advisor if you can't seem to work your class schedule around your work schedule, a marriage counselor if your marriage is in trouble, or a time management expert if you never have enough time to do what you need. Sometimes part of the solution is seeking out someone who may help you find it.

Prewriting Activity 5.4

Based on the six suggestions presented, consider some possible solutions to your problem. Generate a number of solutions without evaluating their relative worth. At this point, you don't need to decide on a particular solution or solutions for your first draft. Get some ideas on paper to think about, and be open to discovering different solutions as you give the problem more thought.

Sample Alternative Solutions

Topic: working and going to school

Solutions: Cut back on work hours
             Look into night and weekend classes
             Find someone to study with
             Cut back on number of units
             Eliminate the split schedule of going from work to class and back again
             Take some pills to help keep me awake to study
             Sell my car and get a bike

Possible solution(s):

First Drafts

Now that you have selected a problem to write about, analyzed the problem in some depth, and considered possible solutions to the problem, you are ready to write your first draft. Before you begin, consider the people you want to read this paper -your reading audience -and your reason for writing to them -your purpose.

Audience and Purpose

Since most writing is a form of communication, the people that will read your writing and your reasons for writing to them help shape the content of your paper. Your audience and purpose influence what you include in your paper, what you emphasize, the tone of your writing, the types of examples you provide, and how you open and conclude the paper. Writing for a reading audience with a purpose in mind brings meaning to your writing that writing as an exercise can never provide.

In deciding on your audience and purpose for your paper, consider these suggestions.

1. Whom would I like to read this paper?

2. Who might benefit from reading the paper?

3. By reading this paper, who might help in some way to solve the problem?

4. What is my purpose in writing to this audience? What do I hope to accomplish?

5. What is the best tone for this paper to help accomplish my purpose?

Drafting Activity 5.5

Decide on a reading audience and purpose for your paper, and a writing tone that will help you accomplish your purpose.

Sample audience/purpose/tone

Topic: Working and going to college

Audience: college students

Purpose: to share my work/school experience with others in the same situation and perhaps provide some solutions they might consider

Tone: serious, understanding (of readers' problem)

Audience:

Purpose:

Tone:

Drafting Guidelines

As you write your first draft, keep the follow considerations in mind.

1. Introduce the problem in your opening paragraph, its significance, and why readers should be aware of it.

2. In the middle paragraphs, incorporate material from your question-and-answer activity to help readers understand when and how the problem started, its causes, who is affected, and what the effects are.

3. Conclude the draft by suggesting a solution or combination of solutions to the problem which may eliminate it or reduce its impact.

4. Change paragraphs as you move to different aspects of the problem: its beginnings, its causes, its effects, possible solutions.

5. As you write, keep your reading audience in mind and your purpose: what you want to accomplish.

6. Give your draft a simple title that tells what it is about.

Drafting Activity 5.6

Write the first draft of the problem/solution paper following the guidelines presented.

Sample First Draft

Working and Going to College

Working and going to school at the same time is challenging to say the least. I work thirty-to-forty hours a week and take a full load of classes at the college. Talking with other students, their schedules are frequently similar to mine, and they have the same complaints. It's a problem that's not going away for me, and one that I'm going to have to try and deal with better than I am.

The reason for working and going to school at the same time is the same for everyone: the need for money. We need money to pay for tuition and books, to make car and insurance payments, to buy food, and so on. Some students also need money for apartment rental and to help take care of a family. I can't imagine how difficult it would be to have family responsibilities on top of work and school, but a lot of students are in that situation.

The effects of working and going to school are somewhat obvious. First, time is the biggest factor. I'm rushing from job to classes or from classes to work every week day, trying to squeeze in time for lunch or dinner during my break times. If there were more hours in the day, that would be a big help. Since there aren't, I have to get along with the time I have and try to do a better job of managing it.

Second, working fairly long hours leaves you significantly less time to study, which makes it harder to do well in classes. My study time is basically restricted to evenings, and I often end up studying until 1:00 or 2:00 a.m. and then getting up by 6:00. Sometimes I'm too tired for long study sessions and I just blow off studying for the night or end up falling asleep while I'm studying and not waking up until morning. I usually end up paying for it when I do poorly on a test or don't get a paper turned in on time.

Third, students who work and go to school are tired much of the time. The lack of sleep affects you at work and at school. It is harder to have the energy to do your best and much easier to lose focus while at work or trying to take notes in class. It's no fun to always wish that you could get in a few more hours of sleep or a much needed nap, but it's just something you try to get used to.

Finally, if you have to work and go to school at the same time, you can pretty well forget a social life. First, you don't have the time. Second, you seldom have the energy. By the time a Friday or Saturday night comes around, I look forward to nothing more than getting some much needed sleep, not going to a concert or movie. In addition, when all of your money is going towards school, your car, insurance, gas, and food, who has the extra money that a social life requires?

Since I'm not going to be able to quit working while going to school any time soon, I'm going to have to live with it. However, I definitely want to think of ways to handle the situation better than currently. First, I've never really kept a budget or kept track of how I spend my money. I'm going to keep track of my expenditures for a month and see where I might be able to cut back. The only way that I can reduce my work hours would be to spend less each month. If I can figure a way to cut back on my spending, I'd love to cut back on my hours, which my boss would allow, and which would give me more time for school and sleep.

Second, I'm starting to study with a partner who is in a similar situation as myself. Instead of studying at home where the nice, soft sofa is always calling me to fall asleep, we meet in the library three evenings a week, get a study room, and study until the library closes. Not only does this keep us from the temptations at home, we push each other to keep going and stay with it. My study partner has more energy than I do, and she'll say, "Come on, suck it up!" when I slack off or come up with excuses to go home.

Third, I'm going to stop doing any type of split schedules, where I have to go back and forth from school to work or vice-versa. For some time, I've been going to early morning classes, then to work, then back to school for classes later in the day. It seemed like a good idea to break up the work and school, and I've been able to get the classes I needed, but it's just too much time wasted. Therefore, I'm going to set up a schedule which doesn't require the split scheduling.

To that end, I'm going to try taking some night and weekend classes, which I have avoided in the past. Here's the big advantage to night and weekend (Saturday) classes: evening and weekend classes meet just once a week, or at least the classes I'm going to take. Rather than spend an hour in class on three different days, I can spend three hours in one evening or on a Saturday. Going to classes with larger blocks of time and fewer meetings leaves me with larger blocks of non-class time to do other things. Granted, I'd have less time to study in the evenings, but more time to study during the day when I'm more awake and have more energy.

Three things I'm not going to do which are tempting but can lead to trouble are taking out loans, popping pills, or lengthening my stay in college. I could probably get a student loan, but I don't want to get caught in that trap, where at the end of my schooling, I owe thousands of dollars in loans and don't have the means to pay them off. I know of students who have gone that route and later regretted it. I've also heard stories of students whose loan payments have followed them for many years after college, a burden that they can't get out from under. I'm not going to let that happen.

A lot of students pop pills like no-doze or pro-plus or other caffeine-laced pills to keep them awake for the long study sessions. Two things can happen: you can get physically addicted to them or you can get psychologically addicted, meaning you feel you need them to keep awake even if you don't. Either way, no matter what kind of stay-awake pill you take, you're putting drugs into your system and trying to artificially make up for what you really need: some sleep. I'm not going to risk my health by getting wired on drugs, even the seemingly harmless types.

The stretching-out-my-college-stay option is sometimes tempting. If I just took six or nine units a semester rather than fifteen or more, my life would be more manageable. However, I would be in school two or three years longer, prolonging the time before getting my degree or getting a job. I see students who take fewer units, perhaps because they have no choice, and they are resigned to being in school for a number of years, chipping away at the required courses a few at a time. To me, that is not a good option. I want to get out of school as soon as I can with my degree, not hang around for a few additional years.

In the end, there are two things that will not solve my problem but make it at least tolerable. First I know that there is a light at the end of the tunnel, that I'm not going to be on this crazy schedule forever. And every semester that I complete means I'm that much closer to the light. That helps me keep going.

Second, I'm intent on keeping my eye on the prize: a college degree which will lead to a good job and a good future. Any time I get really down, I look at the alternative: not making it. That provides me with the strongest motivation to keep going no matter how difficult life gets. Quitting is not an option

Revisions

Now that you have written the first draft of your problem/solution paper, you are ready to revise it and make any changes you feel would improve its content, organization, or wording. As you reread your draft, you may find a better way to organize your middle paragraphs, better wording options for some of your sentences, and perhaps a new solution that you hadn't previously considered. As you revise, be open to new ideas that may come to you, and feel free to incorporate new material as you improve what you have already written.

Varying Sentence Structures

Writers sometimes get into ruts, relying too much on the same sentence structures and connecting words. In the following example, the writer has a tendency to overuse compound sentences joined by and or but.

> We flew into Los Angeles at night from New Orleans, and we noticed flames on the ground. The flames were on the far western side of the LA basin, and they appeared to cover a large stretch of area. I thought it might be a controlled weed burn in the foothills, but the flames appeared to stretch lower than that. I tried to determine the exact city where the fire might be burning, but we were too high to tell. I read the paper the next morning, and the fire was in the Malibu area. It covered over 10,000 acres, and hundreds of residents had to evacuate their homes. A number of people were treated in hospitals, but there were no fatalities. The fire was caused by an arsonist, and it spread due to powerful Santa Ana winds and extremely hot Southern California weather.

As you can see, the writer relies solely on one sentence structure, the compound sentence, and on two joining words: *and* and *but*. The following revised version of the paragraph provides some structural variety.

> Flying into Los Angeles at night from New Orleans, we noticed flames on the ground. The flames, which were on the far western side of the L.A. basin, appeared to cover a large stretch of area. I thought it might be a controlled weed burn in the foothills, but the flames appeared to stretch lower than that. Although I tried to determine the exact city where the fire might be burning, we were too high to tell. I read in the paper the next morning that the fire was in the Malibu area. It covered over 10,000 acres, and hundreds of residents had to evacuate their homes. A number of people were treated in hospitals; however, there were no fatalities. The fire was caused by an arsonist and spread by powerful Santa Ana winds and extremely hot Southern California weather.

As you can see, the revised paragraph contains a variety of sentence structures and is more interesting to read. When a writer relies too heavily on one or two structures and a limited number of joining words, the writing can become monotonous to read and detract from the writer's ideas.

Commonly Used Sentence Structures

Writers have a variety of sentence structures at their disposal, including the following.

1. Simple sentence - a sentence with one subject and one verb:

   <u>Joaquin</u> *hates* working out at a gym. (Subject underlined, verb italicized)

   Variations:

   Simple sentence with an introductory phrase:

   During the hot summer months, <u>Joaquin</u> *hates* working out at a gym.

   Simple sentence with a *compound subject* or *compound verb*:

   <u>Joaquin</u> *hates* working out at a gym but *enjoys* running on the campus track.

   <u>Joaquin</u> and <u>Angie</u> both *hate* working out at a gym.

2. Compound sentence - two complete sentences joined by *and, but, or, so, for, or yet*:

   <u>Alchemists</u> *believed* they could turn base metals into gold, but <u>they</u> never *succeeded.*

   <u>Isaac Newton</u> *was* a seventeenth century scientist, and <u>he</u> *was* also an alchemist.

3. Complex sentence - two sentences joined by subordinate conjunctions like *although, if, when, because, since, unless while, as, before, after, until,* or *whenever.* The conjunction may begin the first half or the second half of the sentence:

   Examples (subordinate conjunction in italics):

   While you were waiting at the E line subway, I was upstairs at the F line. I enjoy going boating on the ocean *although* I get seasick rather easily. *Unless* the weather clears up soon, we should scrap our plans to study outside.

4. Sentence with a *relative clause* - a sentence containing a group of words beginning with a *relative pronoun - who, which, whom, that,* or *whose* - that modifies the word or group of words it follows.

   Examples (*relative pronoun* in italics):

   The Brooklyn Bridge, *which* connects Manhattan with Brooklyn, is a walking and a driving bridge.

Last semester my grade point average was above 3.0, *which* shocked my parents.

The students *who* organized the canned food drive on campus did a great job.

5. Sentence containing a compound and complex sentence structure, two complex sentence structures, or two compound sentence structures.

Examples:

Although the weather report calls for rain, the sky has been clear all morning, and there are no clouds on the horizon. (Complex/compound combination)

Lobotomies were an accepted operational procedure on mentally ill patients in the 1950's, and the barbaric practice continued into the '60's although the outcomes were often disastrous. (Compound/complex sentence)

The recent fires in Southern California forced over 500,000 people to evacuate their homes, and they raged over 50,000 acres from San Diego to Santa Barbara, but fortunately, no one was killed as a direct result of the fires. (compound/compound sentence)

If you are driving to the football game on Saturday, plan on coming at least an hour before game time because the parking lots will fill quickly. (complex/complex sentence)

6. Sentence beginning or ending with a *participial phrase* beginning with a *participle*: *walking* to the park, *waiting* beside the library, *sleeping* in the bough of the tree, *troubled* by her son's behavior, *thwarted* by the opponent's defense.

Examples (*Participles* in italics):

Walking to the park, Gretchen was drenched by a sudden downpour.

Sleeping in the bough of the tree, the baby monkey was barely visible.

Troubled by her son's behavior, Gladys met with his 5th grade teacher.

Thwarted by the opponent's defense, the football team resorted to trick plays.

Revision Activity 5.7

Combine the following sentences to create the different sentence structures provided.

Example: complex sentence

I don't think I would like eating sushi. I might give it a try.

Although I don't think I would like eating sushi, I might give it a try.
(complex sentence beginning with subordinate conjunction *although*)

Compound sentences (joining words: *and, but, so, for, yet, or*)

1. A lot of alternative rock music today sounds the same. That could be said of rock music from any time period.

     _____

     _____

2. The new river walk on the east bank of the Thames is easily accessible. Tourists and locals take the walk from the London Eye ferris wheel to the new restaurants farther down river.

     _____

     _____

3. Disneyland in Los Angeles still attracts more visitors than Disney World Orlando. It is located in a more heavily populated area.

     _____

     _____

Complex sentences (joining words: *although, if, when, because, since, unless, of, while, before, until, whenever, as*)

4. You may want to get a 4.0 GPA this semester. It will be difficult carrying twenty units.

     _____

     _____

5. For a few hours, the river actually reverses directions at its mouth. The ocean tide rises higher than the river that feeds it.

192

6. I have been traipsing all over the library looking for books on the Druids. You have been wisely researching the ancient religious sect on the Internet.

_____

_____

7. You want to get the best seats possible for the concert. Go on-line to Ticketron a month in advance.

_____

Sentences with a relative clause (relative pronouns: *who, whose, whom, which, or that*)
Delete or replace unnecessary words, and move words or phrases around if necessary.

8. The Brooklyn Bridge connects Brooklyn with Manhattan. It is a walking bridge and a driving bridge.

_____

_____

9. St. Johns, New Brunswick was settled in 1781 by British loyalists. They had been living in the New England colonies before the Revolutionary War.

_____

_____

10. I'd suggest taking the Washington D.C. subway to Georgetown. That is the fastest way to get there.

_____

_____

11. The Dalai Lama has been hired as a professor at Emory University in Atlanta. He is an internationally famous former Tibetan monk.

_____

_____

Simple sentences with compound subjects and/or verbs

12. Freda is doing well in Dr. Taylor's calculus class. Matthew is also doing well. Their friend Felix is also doing well.

   _____

   _____

13. Samantha enjoys visiting her grandma on holidays. She also likes browsing yard sales on weekends. Finally, she relishes taking long walks with her dog in Central Park.

   _____

   _____

Compound/complex, complex/compound, compound/compound, or complex/complex sentences

14. Freeman likes doing experiments in his chemistry class. He gets bored sitting through lectures on chemistry. He prefers the active, hands-on learning which the experiments provide.

   _____

   _____

15. The razing of the World Bank complex occurred over four years ago. Workers are still clearing the site. Construction on a replacement building won't begin for many months.

   _____

   _____

16. I'm going to register on-line for classes for the fall semester. It will be easier than going through on campus registration. I will also have the best chance of getting the classes and times that I need.

   _____

   _____

17. I've been studying for tests earlier in the morning. I've gotten better grades. The material is fresh in my head.

   _____

   _____

18. The Chicago Cubs haven't won a World Series in over fifty years. Their record is improving almost every year. They may have a good chance in the next five years.

_____

_____

Sentences with a beginning or ending *participial phrase* (You may delete words or move them around.)

19. Joanna returned to work after a two-week vacation. She had over two-hundred e-mails awaiting her.

_____

_____

20. Malcolm didn't get to the subway station until after midnight. He hoped to catch the last train to the airport.

_____

_____

_____

Revision Activity 5.8

The following paragraph contains a number of similarly structured sentences that could bother readers. Combine groups of related sentences into single sentences using a variety of sentence structures and joining words. Add, delete, and replace words and move them around to combine sentences most effectively.

Example:

My roommate and I set the thermostat in our apartment at eighty-two degrees in the summer. We set it there so that the air conditioner won't run all the time. In the winter we set the thermostat at sixty-eight degrees. We set it there to save on our heating bill. I go around the apartment in shorts and a t-shirt in the summer. It is always a little warm. I go around the apartment in sweats in the winter. It is always a little cool. It is difficult to adjust to a fourteen-degree change in temperature. That change occurs between summer and winter. It is necessary. We save a lot of money on utilities.

Revised:

My roommate and I set the thermostat in our apartment at eighty-two degrees in the summer so the air conditioner won't run all the time. In the winter, we set the thermostat at sixty-eight degrees to save on our heating bill. Since it is always a little warm, I go around the apartment in shorts and a t-shirt in the summer while in the winter, I wear sweats since it is always a little cool. It is difficult to adjust to the fourteen-degree change in temperature that occurs between summer and winter, but it is necessary because we save a lot of money on utilities.

Example:

My five year old nephew is in kindergarten, but he is already reading at 4th grade level. He also has a great memory. He has memorized all of the planets. He also knows all of the states and their capitals. He also knows the order in which they were admitted into the Union. He can also add and subtract two-column figures in his head. He can do basic multiplication and division. He won't have that in school for two years. Kindergarten is extremely easy for him. He already knows everything that they are doing, and that makes school boring at times. Kindergarten is where he belongs socially. He is an average five year old. He likes to play and have fun. He would be out of place in a higher grade. He could certainly do the work. There are no gifted programs for kindergarten students, so his teacher gives him extra work for home. That includes more challenging reading. It also includes more advanced math. His mother serves as his tutor at home. She is a high school teacher. Home is where he does most of his learning.

Revised:

Revision Activity 5.9

Revise the first draft of your problem/solution paper by applying the following guidelines.

Revision Guidelines

1. From your opening, do readers clearly understand the problem you are writing about and its significance? Is there anything that you can add or change in your opening to engage the readers' interest further?

2. From your middle paragraphs, can readers clearly understand the causes of the problem? Do they see its effects and understand who is affected and how? What might you add or change to strengthen the paragraphs that deal with the problem's causes and its effects?

3. Read your draft to see whether your ideas are organized in the most effective way. Does one paragraph follow logically from the preceding one? Is there any paragraph or sentence that seems out of place and could be moved to a more effective location?

4. Read your conclusion to see whether you have presented your solution(s) clearly and effectively. Evaluate your solution one last time, making sure that it is the most sensible, workable solution to the problem, one that addresses its causes.

5. Read your sentences to see whether you have used a variety of structures to present your ideas most effectively. Revise sentences as you have done in the sentence variety activities to improve sentence variety and eliminate repetitive structures and joining words.

6. Read your sentences and eliminate unnecessary words or phrases, reword vague sentences, smooth out any awkward sentences, and replace questionable word choices.

7. Check your paragraphing to make sure that you have changed paragraphs as you move

to new ideas in your paper. Divide overly long paragraphs and combine strings of short paragraphs that have related content.

8. Read your paper with your audience and purpose in mind. Make any changes that would make the draft more interesting, meaningful, or informative for readers, or that would help you accomplish your purpose.

Revision excerpts from "Working and Going to College" draft *(last 3 paragraphs)*

~~The~~ Stretching out my college stay ~~option~~ is sometimes tempting. If I just took six or nine units a semester rather than fifteen or more, my life would be ~~more manageable~~ **much easier**. However, I would be in school **at least** two or three years longer, prolonging the time before getting my degree or getting a job. I see students who take fewer units, perhaps because they have no choice, and they are resigned to being in school for a number of years, chipping away **slowly** at the required courses ~~a few at a time~~. ~~To~~ **For** me, that is not a good option. I want to ~~get out of school as soon as I can with~~ **complete** my degree **as soon as possible**, not hang around for a few additional years. **I want to get on with my life.**

In the end, there are two things that ~~will not~~ **don't** solve my problem but make it ~~at least~~ **more** tolerable. First, I know that there is a light at the end of the tunnel, that I'm not going to be on this crazy schedule forever. ~~And~~ **E**very semester that I complete means I'm that much closer to the light. That helps me keep going.

Second, I'm ~~intent on~~ **going to** keep~~ing~~ my eye on the prize: a college degree which will lead to a good job and, **hopefully,** a ~~good~~ **bright** future. Any time I get really down, I look at the alternative: not making it **through college**. That **gives** ~~provides~~ me ~~with~~ the strongest motivation to keep going no matter how difficult **my daily** life gets. Quitting is **simply** not an option.

(Revisions made to improve wording, to delete unnecessary words and phrases, to add detail, and to provide new thoughts.)

198

Editing

The final phase of the writing process is to correct any errors in punctuation, spelling, or grammar usage in your paper before passing it on to readers. With all of the work you have put into writing and revising your paper, you owe it to yourself and your readers to produce an error-free final draft.

In this section you review the elements of punctuation and grammar usage covered in previous units. You are also introduced to new punctuation marks - colons, semicolons, and dashes - and to a new grammar consideration - comparative and superlative adjectives. The use of colons, semi-colons, and dashes gives you more options for expressing yourself most effectively, and using the correct comparative and superlative adjectives forms will help you make comparisons in your writing and avoid common usage errors.

Colons, Semi-Colons, and Dashes

While colons, semi-colons, and dashes are used somewhat sparingly by most writers, they nonetheless serve useful functions. Once you clearly understand how to use them, you will find ways to insert them into your writing naturally and effectively. The following guidelines will help you use colons, semi-colons, and dashes effectively in your writing.

1.   A colon (:) is used to set off a word or group of words that follows it and relates to the complete statement preceding the colon.

    Examples:

    There is one thing that most students look forward to: Christmas break. We will need several items for the camping trip: tents, sleeping bags, food, and flash lights.

    I usually get my best grades on one type of test: multiple choice.

    One misnomer leads to disappointment among many first-time stock market investors: unrealistic expectations about making fast money.

    One trait stands out among people who are successful in the sales business: perseverance.

    There are several things that trouble us about Theodore: his slovenly appearance, his poor hygiene, his sarcastic manner, and his habit of borrowing books and not returning them.

2.   A semi-colon (;) joins two sentences that are closely related in meaning. A transitional word such as *however* or *therefore* often follows the semi-colon.

    Examples:

    I'm going to pull weeds in the front yard for a while; you can continue planting bulbs if you want.

The morning has been warm and mild; however, a powerful storm is coming in later this afternoon.

There is no way to study for Dr. Garcia's philosophy tests; therefore, you just have to relax and do the best that you can.

I don't really want to go to a movie this evening; I'd much rather stay and home and watch TV.

Sam got a speeding ticket in a 35 mile an hour zone; consequently, he has to go to traffic school.

(Note: For clarity, semi-colons can also be used in place of commas to separate series of long phrases or clauses. Example: The feeding frenzy created by the huge school of grunion included thousands of small seafaring birds that blackened the water; hundreds of pelicans dive bombing the surfing area; waves of seagulls launching their attacks from the beach; and numerous dolphins encircling their prey like sharks.)

3. A dash (-) is used similarly to a colon, setting off information referred to in the statement preceding it, and can be used in place of a colon in more informal writing. More frequently, however, dashes are used in pairs, before and after the information referred to, and the sentence continues after the second dash.

    Examples:

    Most of the migratory birds on the lake -mallards, coots, geese, and mergansers -feed off of the thousands of minnows that populate the waters.

    Three are many ways to cook chicken -bake, fry, boil, grill, or roast -but my favorite is to barbecue.

    Everyone who attends plays on campus -students, townspeople, parents, and school officials -raves about the quality of the performances.

    The most frequent errors that writers make -running sentences together, misspelling words, omitting commas -are usually caught and corrected during the proofreading phase of the writing process.

    One thing that my history professor harped on -never waiting until the night before a test to study -finally sunk in before I took my mid-term exams.

The following paragraph provides example of how colons, semi-colons, and dashes can be incorporated into your writing.

Working full-time and going to college is really hard. I attend school in the morning and work from 1:00 p.m. until 8:00 p.m. at a fast-food restaurant. Most evenings follow the same routine: eat, study, and go to bed late. I'm always tired. I also work the same shift on Saturdays, so I have little time to spend with my friends. After I spend the money I make on necessities -college expenses, car payments, and insurance -I have little left for other things. However, without the job, I wouldn't be in college or have a car; that is the reason I work. While some students may look forward to going out partying, I look forward to something a little different: sleep.

Editing Activity 5.10
Punctuate the following sentences correctly using colons, semi-colons, or dashes.

Example: You will need the following ingredients to make tacos hamburger meat, taco flavoring mix, tomatoes, onions, cheese, lettuce, avocados, corn tortillas, and salsa.

Corrected: You will need the following ingredients to make tacos: hamburger meat, taco flavoring mix, tomatoes, onions, cheese, lettuce, avocados, corn tortillas, and salsa.

1. To make tacos, put a pound of hamburger meat in a skillet then break up the meat with a fork.

2. When the meat is browned, add one ingredient taco mix to flavor the hamburger meat.

3. Next, cut up your vegetables tomatoes, onions, lettuce, and avocados and grate your cheese.

4. Then put a thin layer of cooking oil in a second skillet cook your tortillas in the skillet one at a time.

5. Next, take a tortilla and fill it with all of your ingredients hamburger meat, cheese, and vegetables and then add salsa on top.

6. Make sure not to fill the tortilla too full of meat the bottom could fall out while you are eating it.

7. You have now learned to make the best kind of meal delicious, easy to make, and inexpensive.

8. If you get tired of hamburger meat, replace it with something else chicken, fish, or even shrimp to add variety to your tacos.

Editing Activity 5.11

Write six original sentences, two of which include colons, two with semi-colons, and two with dashes.

Examples:

With my schedule, there's one thing I often neglect: sleep.

I'm not thrilled at waking up at 5:00 every morning; I also don't love getting home from work at 10:00 p.m.

Balancing three responsibilities – school, work, and family – is more than a full-time job.

Editing Activity 5.12
Read the following paragraph and insert colons, semi-colons, or dashes where they are needed.

Example:
At the natural art museum, the side-by-side skeletons of a young gorilla and an eight-year old boy who lived 20,000 years ago are eerily similar the same skeletal frames with the exception of the gorilla's longer arms and bigger feet. The other difference is the size of the skull the boy's skull is larger and rounder, housing a larger, more advanced brain.

Corrected:
At the natural art museum, the side-by-side skeletons of a young gorilla and an eight-year old boy who lived 20,000 years ago are eerily similar: the same skeletal frames with the exception of the gorilla's longer arms and bigger feet. The other difference is the size of the skull; the boy's skull is larger and rounder, housing a larger, more advanced brain.

We have a large family living in a three-bedroom rental four kids and two parents. A few months ago, my aunt and uncle immigrated to the U.S. with their kids. They moved in with us until they could find a place to stay, and they are still here. Now there are ten people living the house. The obvious problems three kids to a bedroom, no privacy, constant noise will only be solved when they move out. They are nice people and we get along well, but with that many people in one small house, things are going to come up. My uncle is a smoker he keeps it out of the house, but he brings the smell in on his clothes. My aunt does a lot of the cooking, and she's not a very good cook. It's hard having my boyfriend over because wherever we go, my little nieces have to be there, giggling all the time. It's crazy around the house, and studying is impossible. There's one thing that I'd pay to have peace and quiet.

Comparative and Superlative Adjectives

Writers frequently use adjectives to describe things in their papers: hungry children, ominous clouds, a talented pianist, a difficult test. They also use adjectives to compare things: the higher humidity in Atlanta than in Chicago, the more difficult problem of global warming compared to pollution, the lower price of gas in the U.S. compared to Europe, or the tallest mountain peak in the world compared to all others. Adjectives that compare have a number of different forms, depending on how many things are being compared and how many syllables the adjective has. Some basic grammatical rules govern the forms these adjectives take, and once you learn them, you will have little problem using the correct forms in your writing.

Comparative Adjectives

Comparative adjectives compare one thing to another. The following rules apply to comparative adjectives.

1. Add *er* to one-syllable adjectives.

   I am *shorter* than you are.
   Sam is *thinner* than Phil.
   Mercury lights are *brighter* than florescent lights.

2. Add *more* in front of adjectives with two or more syllables.

   I am *more* introverted than you are.
   Samantha is *more* graceful than Phyllis.
   Mercury lights are *more* effective than florescent lights.

   Exception: Add *er* to two-syllable words ending in *y* or *ow*.

   I am *lonelier* than you are.
   Margo is *sillier* than her brother.
   Mercury lights are *prettier* than fluorescent lights.
   The river is *shallower* along the banks than in the middle.

Superlative Adjectives

Superlative adjectives compare three or more things. The following rules apply to superlative adjectives.

1. Add *est* to one-syllable adjectives.

   I am the *tallest* person in my family.
   Sam is the *smartest* gorilla in the zoo.
   Mercury lights are the *brightest* lights for football fields.

2. 2. Add *most* in front of adjectives with two or more syllables.

   Felipe is the *most* dependable person in the family.
   Sam is the *most* curious gorilla in the zoo.
   Mercury lights are the *most* expensive lights for outdoor home lighting.

   Exception: Add *est* to two-syllable words ending in y or ow.

   I am the *rowdiest* person in my family.
   Sam is the *heaviest* gorilla in the zoo.
   Mercury lights give off the *loveliest* glow on dark nights.
   The Dead Sea is the *shallowest* ocean in the world.

Editing Activity 5.13

Each of the following sentences compares two things. Fill in the correct comparative form of each adjective in parentheses. Determine the number of syllables the adjective has, and add *er* to one-syllable adjectives and two-syllable adjectives ending in *y* or *ow*, and add *more* in front of adjectives of two syllables or more.

Examples: (quick)   You are a <u>quicker</u> thinker than I am.

      (beautiful) The elm trees on campus are <u>more beautiful</u> in the spring than in the summer.

1. (interesting)   The first week of school was _____ than I thought it would be.

2. (friendly)   The students were _____ than I imagined.

3. (fascinating)   The classes were _____ than my high school classes.

4. (short)   The classes were also _____ than usual, since it was the first week.

5. (fast)   The whole day went by _____ than I expected.

6. (tedious)   I thought the school work would be _____ than it was.

7. (enthusiastic)   Now I am _____ than ever about school.

8. (long)   However, next week's classes will be _____ than this week's.

9. (difficult)   The homework will get _____ as the semester progresses.

10. (typical)   The next weeks will be _____ of the rest of the semester.

Editing Activity 5.14

Each of the following sentences compares three or more things. Fill in the correct superlative form of each adjective in parentheses. Determine the number of syllables the adjective has; add *est* to one-syllable adjectives and two-syllable adjectives ending in *y* or *ow*, and add *most* in front of adjectives with two syllables or more.

Examples: (quick)   That was the <u>quickest</u> that Ricardo has ever completed a biology experiment.

      (unusual) The modern art display in the library is the <u>most unusual</u> display of the year.

206

1. (interesting)   The first week of school was one of the _____ weeks I've spent.

2. (unusual)   I met some of the _____ teachers I've had.

3. (fascinating)   The class subjects were the _____ I've been exposed to.

4. (long)   The classes were also the _____ I have ever attended.

5. (fast)   It was the _____ week of school I've been through.

6. (tedious)   I thought biology would be the _____ class of the semester.

7. (enthusiastic)   Now I am the _____ I've ever been about taking biology.

8. (hard)   Although the classes are the _____ I've had, I enjoy them.

9. (difficult)   Although the homework is the _____ I've done, I don't mind it.

10. (typical)   Students say that the fourth and fifth weeks of school are the _____ weeks to judge school by.

Editing Activity 5.15

Fill in each of the following blanks with an appropriate comparative or superlative adjective by following the rules presented. Include both one-syllable and two-or-more syllable adjectives.

Examples: In winter the evenings grow *shorter* while in summer they grow *longer*.
That is the *most expensive* textbook I've ever bought.

1. The oboe is _____ to play than the clarinet.
2. The saxophone is the _____ woodwind instrument to play.
3. The alto saxophone has the _____ sound of any woodwind.
4. The French horn is _____ than the trumpet.
5. The tuba is the _____ brass instrument.
6. The band director appeared the _____ every time the woodwind section took over the melody.
7. When a woodwind squeaks, it is one of the _____ sounds there is.
8. A French horn can produce the _____ sound of any brass instrument.
9. Percussion instruments are often the _____ to play.
10. The snare drum is _____ to play than the timpani.

Editing Review

Throughout the text, you review elements of punctuation, spelling, and grammar that give writers problems. The purpose of these review activities is to give you more proofreading and editing practice and ultimately to eliminate such problems in your writing. Even writers who make few mistakes find an occasional error to correct during the editing process, and all writers can profit from editing practice.

Editing Activity 5.16

Proofread the following draft for errors involving run-on sentences or comma splices, sentence fragments, irregular verbs, comma usage, subject-verb agreement, subject pronouns, or pronoun-antecedent agreement, and make the necessary corrections. Read the draft several times, looking for different types of errors each time.

Example:

The stucco on the outside of my aunt's house is cracking, there is several long cracks running across the walls. The house is relatively new and the cracks occurred when the stucco on the walls were drying. The cracks on the front of the house is particularly noticeable, it runs long and deep from the sides to the front door. One of the cracks are jagged instead of straight and they are very noticeable. My aunt and me plastered over the biggest cracks and once the plaster on the walls are dry we will paint over them. We smoothed out the plaster so that it blends in smoothly with the stucco, once we paint over them the walls should look as good as new if you don't stand too close.

Corrected:

The stucco on the outside of my aunt's house is cracking. There are several long cracks running across the walls. The house is relatively new, and the cracks occurred when the stucco on the walls was drying. The cracks on the front of the house are particularly noticeable. They run long and deep from the sides to the front door. One of the cracks is jagged instead of straight, and it is very noticeable. My aunt and I plastered over the biggest cracks, and once the plaster on the walls is dry, we will paint over it. We smoothed out the plaster so that it blends in smoothly with the stucco, so once we paint over it, the walls should look as good as new if you don't stand too close.

Unique Campus

Our school campus is built on a hill. At the top of the hill is two small ponds which provides water for the water features on campus. Some of the water from the ponds run down several copper troughs which are located on each side of several stairways that runs from the top of the hill to the bottom across the campus. Water from the ponds also create several small waterfalls throughout the campus which feeds into small water basins. Water is pumped back up the hill from the basins and they are recycled into the ponds on top of the hill.

With all the water features you can hear water running everywhere on campus, they create a relaxing sound. In addition the beauty of the waterfalls and the water running down the copper troughs makes the campus very special. Unlike any campus I've ever seen. With the ponds above the campus the water features throughout the campus the hilly environment and the pine and eucalyptus trees growing between the buildings our campus almost feel like a resort area, students enjoy just hanging out here after his or her classes.

Editing Activity 5.17

Proofread your paper for errors by applying the following guidelines, and make any necessary corrections. Read the draft several times, looking for different types of errors each time.

Editing Guidelines

1. Check your sentences to make sure you haven't run any sentences together or put a comma between sentences instead of a period. Correct run-on sentences or comma splices by separating longer sentence with periods and combining shorter, related sentences with a joining word.

2. Check your draft for any sentence fragments: incomplete sentences with a period after them. To correct fragments, attach them to the sentence they belong with, or add words to make them complete.

3. Check your use of irregular verbs, making sure you have used the correct irregular forms and spelled them correctly.

4. Check your comma usage, making sure you have inserted commas into your sentences correctly and not in places they aren't required.

5. Check the spelling of any word you are uncertain of, or run the spell check on your word processing program, to eliminate any spelling errors.

6. Check your verbs in each sentence to make sure that they agree with their subjects.

7. Check your pronouns in each sentence to make sure they agree with their antecedents, and make sure you are using the correct subject pronoun forms.

8. Check your use of colons, semi-colons, and dashes to see whether you are using them correctly and effectively. If you have used none, see whether there may be an occasional sentence that you might improve by revising it to require a colon, semi-colon, or dashes.

9. Check your use of comparative and superlative adjectives, and make sure that you have used the correct forms following the usage rules in this section.

Applying the Writing Process

At the end of each unit, you write a second paper applying what you have learned without interruptions for instruction or activities. The purpose of this assignment is for you to work independently on your writing, to gain more experience writing problem/solution papers, and to continue improving your writing skills.

Writing Assignment

Select another problem to write about, something very different from the topic of your first essay. Working independently, follow a similar writing process that you used to develop your first paper. (Refer back to the drafting, revision, or editing guidelines in the unit as needed.)

- Select a problem to write about.
- Consider how the problem got started, what caused it, who is affected, what the effects are, and some possible solutions.
- Write a first draft.
- Revise by making sure all aspects of the problem are covered thoroughly (causes, effects, people affected, solutions), by focusing on clear sentence wording and effective paragraphing, and by adding whatever will improve the draft.
- Edit the draft by correcting any errors that you find.
- Write the final paper.

Before revising, share first drafts with a classmate or two, and ask each other questions about anything that seems unclear in the draft or that you'd like to know more about. Consider your classmates' input as you revise your paper.

Readings

Are You A Procrastinator?
By Julianne Kuroda

Are you a procrastinator? Sure you are, just like every other human being. We all put off doing something at one time or another, whether it be making the bed, studying for a test, or paying the bills. What varies from one person to another is the frequency with which we procrastinate, the kind of tasks we put off until tomorrow, and the extent that it affects our lives. Among individuals, procrastination ranges from an occasional random act to a habitual, chronic pattern. For people who fall towards the latter end of the spectrum, procrastination can be a serious problem.

Procrastination is familiar to us all. We know the car needs washing badly. We'll do it this morning but after we read the morning paper. Then there's something on TV to watch, so the car can wait a little longer. It's starting to get hot outside, and the car could spot badly if it isn't dried off quickly after rinsing. Tomorrow morning will be cooler, so it would be smarter to wash it tomorrow. Besides, there's a 10% chance of rain tonight, which could ruin the wash job. So tomorrow morning it is.

It is not difficult to understand why people procrastinate. We prefer avoiding things we don't particularly enjoy doing. For most of us, it is not great fun washing dishes, cleaning out the garage, beginning a research paper, or confronting someone we have a problem with. Instead of tackling the task, we put it off by substituting a more pleasurable activity: watching TV, taking a nap, or playing a video game.

Laziness is certainly a culprit in much of our procrastination. Lying around and relaxing sounds a lot better than beginning the thirty-page reading assignment for biology class. Fear of failure or rejection is another, like putting off a job interview or failing to call someone you're attracted to. Indecisiveness can also lead to procrastination, like letting a deadline pass for a college application. Anxiety is also responsible for our putting off certain tasks, so we reschedule the dentist appointment or feign illness on the night we are to have dinner with our boyfriend's parents. As you can see, a range of negative emotions often lie behind our procrastination, and to change the situation, we must at some point overcome them.

Is procrastination really a problem that we need to address? After all, if everyone procrastinates at one time or another, what's the big deal? For some people, procrastination isn't a problem. If you occasionally put off some everyday task but still get it done, your life probably isn't the worse for it. However, if you put tasks off until the kitchen sink is stacked high with dishes or loads of dirty clothes lie around for days or you have to cram two weeks of assigned reading into one night, procrastination is controlling your life in negative ways. And like most procrastinators, you probably carry around your share of guilt.

Procrastination can also have more devastating effects. For people who put off the more important things in life, the consequences can be severe: loss of a job, flunking out of school, divorce, lost job opportunities, a negative credit rating, a knock on the door by the IRS, a court date for outstanding parking tickets. For chronic procrastinators, life can be one long series of mishaps and failures resulting from their chronic pattern of putting things off. And all too often procrastinators don't think of the negative impact that their actions, or inactions, can have on those around them: husbands, wives, friends, roommates, or co-workers. Frequently other people end up doing for the procrastinators what they should have done themselves.

There are some people for whom procrastination is but a symptom of some deeper psychological or emotional problem, and such people need professional help. However, for most of us, procrastination is simply a bad habit that we've allowed ourselves to fall into and done little to escape. The fact is that procrastination is a choice we make, and we always have an option. As we choose to procrastinate, we can also choose not to.

To stop procrastinating, as the Nike commercial says, Just Do It! We all know when we procrastinate, so there is seldom a problem identifying the situation. We look out the window and see weeds growing taller than the shrubs in the flower bed. We walk across the bedroom and step over clothes and shoes that we stepped out of the night before. We see the pile of bills sitting on the kitchen table. We see the gas gauge needle on the car sitting near the big E. We know the mid-term geography test is scheduled for this Friday. We notice our computer printer is printing out faint gray letters and pinkish-purple pictures. We smell an odor of urine from our toddler's diapers. We know Mother's Day is tomorrow and we don't have a card or flowers.

When you see something that needs to be done and you are the person responsible to do it, jump right in. Getting started is the hardest part; if it wasn't, we wouldn't procrastinate. Frequently the task doesn't take long -loading the dishwasher, taking the garbage bins to the street for pick-up, doing the bills, filling the car with gas -so getting started is more than half the battle. If it's a bigger task, like filling out a lengthy job application, studying for a final exam, or cleaning the apartment, start with the idea of putting in at least twenty minutes before taking a break. More often than not, you will keep working longer than you planned, sometimes to the point of completing the task.

Of course, "just doing it" is easier said than done, particularly against a lifetime of "just doing it later." There are always those more pleasurable instant-gratification options that frequently win out, and they aren't going to go away. So try reversing the order of action. If there is something you really want to do -see a particular movie, go out with the guys or girls, watch a particular TV program, play some basketball, continue reading your romantic page-turner, play Wii Fitness -reward yourself by doing it after you complete what needs to be done. Give yourself some positive reward for doing the task, something to look forward to on its completion.

There is one way almost certainly to fail in your attempt to stop procrastinating, and that is to go to extremes. When you think about it, there is almost always something that could be classified as "needs to be done." You could go from room to room of your house or apartment and find things to do all the time. You could do the same with your studies, your job, your relationships. If you try to do too much at once, you will wear out quickly and fail utterly, lapsing in relief to your previous pattern of procrastination. Start by taking one thing that you previously would have put off and get it done. You will feel good about it and get a little more done the next day.

While it's probably impossible to end all procrastination, it is something that we can certainly bring under control so that it doesn't hurt our lives or those around us. We can replace our habit of procrastination with new habits: paying the bills within the first week of the month, keeping the bedroom picked up, getting a start on a school or work assignment the day it is assigned. People actually do these things, and so can we. The good news is we don't have to do away with any of the pleasurable things in our lives. We just have to put them off for an hour or two occasionally.

If you are a hardcore procrastinator with an absolute anathema about starting something you don't want to do, try this: give the task an immediate five minutes of your time. Five minutes is nothing out of a 1440-minute day. Stop after five minutes if you want to, and try it again the next day on a different task. Your greatest problem is not doing the work but getting started on it, and the five-minute approach is a start.

The upside of taking control of our procrastinating ways is significant: greater feelings of self-worth, greater chances of success, more things accomplished, improved work habits, decreased feelings of guilt, greater feeling of accomplishment, better relationships, more enjoyment of pleasurable activities. In short, less procrastination can change our lives for the better, sometimes dramatically, so isn't it worth a try? If you're thinking, "Well, maybe I'll think about changing and decide tomorrow," you know what's in control. Try deciding today.

Questions for Discussion

1. When, according to the author, is procrastination a problem? Do you agree?

2. What are the causes of procrastination? Which causes do you identify with?

3. What are the effects of procrastination? Which affects do you identify with?

4. What solutions does the author present? Does the essay compel you to try them?

A Positive Solution for Plagiarism
by Jeff Karon

We know that students plagiarize. We suppose that plagiarism, as well as academic dishonesty in general, has increased over the past few years, decades, or century—depending on which academic ax we choose to grind.

The caveats are familiar: Perhaps cheating just is easier than it used to be (most honors students who are caught plagiarizing say they did so because it was "easy"). Perhaps we are better at detecting plagiarism because of software such as Google and Turnitin. Or perhaps we forget that every generation, at least since the ancient Romans and Greeks, complains that the next one is composed of lazy, possibly illiterate, youngsters willing to cut ethical corners.

But a good dose of skepticism toward the doomsayers doesn't make the worry go away. For example, a July 21 article in *The Chronicle* on a New York University professor who vowed to stop pursuing plagiarists has drawn 249 comments, several of which were impassioned denunciations of institutional responses to the problem. Dealing with student plagiarism is a nagging, seemingly endless problem for academics, judging from the number of articles, blog posts, and forum discussions on the topic. Indeed, I've contributed to some of those discussions but have yet to find any consensus emerge.

I've organized and participated in conference panels on plagiarism, held workshops for college instructors and schoolteachers on the subject, and for several years have used the methods I'm about to describe. I also began my teaching career with a zero-tolerance policy, which meant that I have been involved in campus judicial proceedings, a step that drains just about everyone touched by the accusation.

But as the Internet has matured, I decided that I did not want to spend time as a cyber-cop. More important, my goal should be to help inculcate honor and integrity rather than build a culture of fear and accusation.

It's easy to find excellent articles and Web sites on dealing with plagiarism. From those sources, we can develop four general guidelines for an effective response:

- The solution should be positive; that is, show students how to act as responsible scholars and writers. The same tone should be reflected in the syllabus. I have seen many syllabi in which the penalties for plagiarism are laid out in excruciating detail, with no positive models or behavior mentioned. Surely by now we know that positive motivation trumps the negative variety.

- It should help students avoid plagiarism rather than focus on our catching it.

- The solution should objectively strengthen both students and teachers.

- It should also make students and teachers feel as though they are stronger.

Those seem to me to be minimal requirements, yet they often are not met in practice. Before laying out a workable solution, let's review some approaches whose weaknesses contribute to the seemingly endless discussions of plagiarism:

Draconian consequences. The instructor who threatens maximum damage if plagiarism is detected usually stakes out the moral high ground. Syllabi and accompanying class discussions list everything that will befall the student, including possible expulsion.

Strength: If applied consistently, without regard for extenuating circumstances, this approach seems to work particularly well for teachers who are both imperious and admired by their students. I knew one colleague, a tenured professor of literature and writing, who threatened to ruin, as nearly as possible, the reputations of offending students. Somehow he still inspired them.

Weakness: Instructors who use this tactic set an adversarial tone at the beginning of a course. Although some can inhabit the Professor Kingsfield character from The Paper Chase, many simply come off as nasty or suspicious. And approaching plagiarism this way is dispiriting—it never energizes students or teachers. In the end, it often doesn't prevent enough plagiarism to counter its weaknesses.

Preventive construction. A teacher who is concerned about plagiarism and has read about strategies may attempt to construct every assignment in a way that precludes plagiarism.

Strength: Rethinking assignments—freshening them up—often produces new energy in a course. Those who reflect often on pedagogy will be attracted to this approach.

Weakness: The approach often means devising assignments with a narrow scope. But it's important to train students to explore widely. They need to be able to sift through all sorts of sources, and closely tailored assignments may be too restrictive. Such assignments certainly don't simulate the strengths needed in graduate or professional school. And sooner or later, we either will run out of ideas for assignments or will be lulled into a false sense of security.

Dedicated discussion. Some teachers discuss extensively in class the nature and consequences of plagiarism, believing that such time is well spent.

Strength: Some students may not understand what constitutes plagiarism or its consequences. By discussing it carefully in class, instructors demonstrate an awareness of that problem.

Weakness: Merely talking with students, especially about a critical topic, is a poor way to ensure that they will act correctly. Giving quizzes on the topic is a move in the right direction. But a quiz still encourages passivity. Plagiarism and academic dishonesty are actions taken by people; powerful lessons about it require actions as well.

A workable solution. The first writing assignment I give students in my writing courses involves plagiarism as a topic. I ask them to investigate and read resources on the Web assembled by experts on the subject such as Nick Carbone, a new-media consultant for Bedford/ St. Martin's, and Bruce Leland, a professor emeritus at Western Illinois University. I ask students to take notes on the readings, especially on how both authors are unhappy with standard approaches to preventing plagiarism and academic dishonesty. I tell them to pay special attention to Carbone's discussion of Dos and don'ts, a list he developed after deciding that his previous approaches to fighting plagiarism adopted an inappropriate tone, and to Leland's extensive list of resources that instructors can use to deal with plagiarism.

Then I ask students to find a Web site that offers free essays for download. I provide a central source, such as "Cheating 101: Internet Papers" though there are many others. Each student has to download one paper (or as much of one as is permitted by the site) and analyze its strengths and weaknesses. They must bring to class a copy of the paper as well as their notes on their reading, and deliver oral reports.

The idea is for students to read materials written by teachers for teachers, rather than something written just for students. The explicit lesson is for them to learn about plagiarism and academic dishonesty. An implicit lesson is that instructors already are aware of free papers and other Internet dodges. Even if a faculty member is not particularly computer-savvy, students will assume from this assignment that he or she understands how to track down plagiarism.

By analyzing these "free essays" before the class, students learn firsthand that the papers available over the Internet often are far inferior to what they could produce on their own. When they occasionally happen on a strong paper, they will remark that it is too good: No professor would believe that such a professionally written piece had come from a student for a course assignment.

You need not guide the students' choices of papers: Their own interests and majors will do that. Through this assignment, they are engaging in research from the first day of the course, and are practicing critical reading. They understand that you will treat them like adults, since you have assigned them to read authoritative, friendly articles from Web sites that speak to adult professionals. And other than require that they concentrate on a paper's strengths and weaknesses, you need not guide the analyses: Students of all writing levels will demonstrate that they can pick apart someone else's work.

Faculty can substitute other Web sites or articles, of course. But they should give students separate credit for their Web-site notes and for their critique of the downloaded paper—both of which should be physical copies. Students who took notes can be distinguished easily from those who did not, which allows instructors to teach the lesson that strong scholars or professionals take notes. The physical copies also allow instructors to collect the assignments if they run short on time for the oral reports, though I encourage faculty to allow everyone to present.

This assignment builds: (1) a direct awareness of plagiarism and its responses; (2) research skills, since students immediately follow and analyze reliable Web sources; and (3) presentation skills, all without creating a hostile or adversarial atmosphere. The assignment can be adapted for large (or online) courses by creating a blog or online discussion area, although nothing beats the in-person connection. (I also ask students to introduce themselves by name every time they present. My philosophy is to maximize what any assignment can achieve.)

I have employed this approach with undergraduate and graduate, traditional and nontraditional students. During the past two semesters, I used it in online classes to great effect. Any method that makes both students and professors feel strong is worth trying.

Questions for Discussion

1. Discuss the various approaches to plagiarism Karon presents that instructors tend to use. What is your opinion on each approach and how effective it would be?

2. Evaluate Karon's approach to plagiarism: the assignment he gives to counter plagiarism and the positive approach he uses. Do you feel that his approach is better than the other ones presented in combating plagiarism? Why?

3. What is your opinion on academic cheating (plagiarism and cheating on tests)? Is such cheating commonplace at your school? Why do many students cheat, and how do they justify it?

Getting Guys to the Altar
by Lionel Collins

"All the good men are taken." "Men just want to be players today." "Men are afraid to commit." "Men don't want to grow up and take responsibility." "Why don't they make more men like my dad anymore?"

Ah, the lament of unwed women. And it is, after all, a woman's lament. How often do we hear men saying, "Where are all the good women hiding?" They don't, because they see good women all over the place. They just don't want to marry them, well at least for now.

What's the matter with today's men? Since society doesn't frown on them living with women, having children with them, or even leaving them to raise the children on their own, why should they go to the trouble of getting married? Where's is the incentive? What's the reward?

Assuming that marriage is a still a good thing, let's figure out some creative ways to get guys to the altar and to commit to their marriages. Social scientists have come up with some potential solutions based on attacking the root causes, but they haven't gone nearly far enough in their thinking. Here are some ideas that could produce the desired results faster.

Marriage or Prison
Not married by your thirtieth birthday? Off to prison 'til you change your mind. Let's put those laggards in jail where they belong. Let's put them in solitary confinement where they don't hear the sound of a human voice for days. Then on intervals, let's pipe in the sweet sound of a lady's voice cooing, "Marriage is wonderful. Some woman out there loves you and can't wait for you to get out of prison."

If men think that marriage is a prison, wait 'til they spend a few months in the real thing. The message: shape up and ship out. Once a man commits, the prison chaplain will perform the marriage ceremony and the jailors will double as best men. The women can wear orange wedding gowns to complement their men's attire. The prison will pay for the ceremony and a weekend vacation at Alcatraz. The recidivism rate should be quite low.

Aversion Therapy
Let's shock men into marriage, literally. In the privacy of an asylum with a nicely manicured lawn, an avuncular psychiatrist will ask the man, "How do you feel about getting married?" If he responds, "It's not for me," or "I'm not keen on it," he gets a jolt of electricity to the head. If asked, "Are you planning on getting married by the time you are thirty?" and he says "Probably not," he gets a stronger jolt. Over a period of days, the man will not only respond with answers like, "I like the idea of getting married" and "I want to get married this year," he will respond before he is even asked the questions, salivating like Pavlov's dog.

Once released from therapy, he will be required to wear the metal shock helmet until he is married, a constant reminder of those mind-jarring jolts, but he may remove the helmet for the marriage ceremony. His wife will then keep the helmet in a safe place and only bring it out when her husband needs a gentle reminder.

The Carrot
Men love beer. Beer can work as the positive reinforcement for men that candy does for children.

Offer a man a free beer and he's your friend for the afternoon. Offer him a case and, well, you see where this is heading.

The Federal government, or each state with a Federal subsidy, will guarantee a man one case of beer of his choice upon marriage and a subsequent case each month that he remains married. He will receive twelve beer stamps a year that will be honored at any Safeway, Albertson's, Winn-Dixie, or Piggly Wiggly. He will also receive a list of Alcoholics Anonymous chapters in his area. Men who abuse their privilege by driving drunk, losing their job, or streaking their neighborhood will receive twelves cases of O'Douls for the next year.

The Bill of Rights

A Married Man's Bill of Rights will be passed by Congress and signed into law by the President, probably a woman. This Bill of Rights will spell out the rights that every man who marries is entitled to. Chief among these rights will be the following:

- The right to snore without getting kicked in the ribs.

- The right to at least one home-cooked meal a week (working moms, you know).

- The right to watch Monday night, Thursday night, and Sunday NFL football games provided there are at least two television sets in the house.

- The right to attend no more than one dinner with the in-laws every two months and to call the in-laws Sam and Alice rather than Dad and Mom.

- The right to leave the house for two hours any time one of the following TV programs are being watched: The View, Oprah, Real Housewives of Anywhere, any award's show (other than on ESPN), any show with a Kardashian, Project Runway, or Dancing with the Stars.

- The right to attend any really cool, violent adventure movie starring Stallone, Denzel, Arnold, Jackie, Samuel Jackson, or Danny Trejo in exchange for attending a rom-com with the wife, provided the rom-com receives at least a 51% positive rating on Rotten Tomatoes.

As stated at the end of the bill, "All other rights not expressly enumerated herein or otherwise guaranteed by the Constitution are arbitrable, and if disputed by husband and wife, shall be subject to decision by binding arbitration, which both parties shall abide by." Husbands anticipating such disputes will be wise to move to Utah.

Harassment

Harassment teams will be formed to badger men into marriage. The teams will be comprised of men and women known to the man, including friends, ministers, IRS workers, and drug addicts, all paid for their services by the League of Women Voters. The harassment will be constant through face-to-face confrontations, e-mails, late-night phone calls, and Skype. The harassment will include the following such comments, repeated many times a day.

Guy friend: I'm so much happier being married. Not being married sucks, doesn't it? Man, you really look bad. Is that your normal skin color?

Gal friend: I'm so much more sexually liberated since I got married. My husband is the luckiest guy around. Are you getting it 3-4 times a day? Oh. That's too bad.

Minister: Our couple's retreat to Tahiti is going to be awesome. Get that romantic spark back! Oops, I forgot. You're not married. Well, we've got Solitary Singles Day Saturday in the church basement. We'll read from the book of Job and enjoy Mrs. Krudlove's egg salad sandwiches and chamomile tea. And our conjoined twins are going to perform! Come early, stay late.

IRS guy: The married couple deduction is $9,738 a year. The child deduction, per child, for married filers is $3,252. With joint filing, you receive yet another tax break when your combined income equals that of two single filers. If you are single, of course, the IRS screws you royally. You're still single? Hahahahahahahahahahahahahahahahahah!

Drug addict: Hey dude, got any Quaaludes? A little pot? Come on, dude. You're a single guy. Hook me up, man. You don't have an old lady to rat you out. I'll be back tomorrow with my buddy Slash. Have a little taste ready for us. Us single guys stick together, right?

When All Else Fails

While the solutions provided have not been legally sanctioned in the U.S., they have reportedly achieved considerable success in the Barbituros Islands and Berzerkistan. Such favorable precedents bode well for their employment in the U.S.

However, if worse comes to worse, and these measures, once sanctioned, don't drive men to the altar in frothing droves, we might consider the legal right of fathers in Elbonia to club a reluctant suitor to death. ("Marry my daughter or I club your brains out!") Of course, several legal hurdles would need to be cleared in the U.S. before suitoracide were legalized, but no stone should be left unturned, if not thrown. In addition, there is the problem of importing clubs from Elbonia, given the tight airport security these days. Perhaps they could be airdropped in baseball bags from unmanned drones. Getting the military involved could be the answer. Which brings to mind the uncharted uses of waterboarding.

All that said, is any Neanderthal guy who has to be dragged or enticed to the altar really worth the effort? Don't wonderful, attractive, smart women deserve much better? Well of course they do! But let's keep that shock helmet available just in case.

Questions for Discussion

1. The essay, of course, is satirical, not to be taken seriously. Who or what is being satirized (poked fun at), and what examples in the essay support your viewpoint?

2. What material do you find humorous in the essay? Why do satire and humor often go together?

3. Do you agree with the essay that men today are reluctant to marry and that women are concerned about the situation? What is your own attitude towards marriage and family?

Cyber Bullying
by Anton Hout

Home sweet home is no longer a sanctuary into which victims of bullying can escape their tormentors. Bullies can now stalk their prey after school hours long after their targets have gone home.

Social isolation, public humiliation and malicious gossip have long been the stock in trade of bullies. With the advent of modern communications such as email, chat, text messaging and cell phones as well as the ability to publish online on websites, blogs and social networking sites such as Facebook and MySpace making their message instantly available to millions, the bully's reach and powers of social manipulation have been increased exponentially.

Parents are well advised to pay close attention to how this new threat can impact their children. We have already seen too many cases of children subjected to a cyber bullying attack who have been so traumatized that they have committed suicide as a direct result. "Bullycide" is the term that has been used to describe suicides caused by relentless bullying. "Cyberbullycide", to coin a phrase, would describe someone driven to suicide following a cyberbullying attack.

In the book *Bullycide In America: Moms Speak Out about the Bullying/Suicide Connection*, compiled by Brenda High, the story of Jeffery Johnston serves as a warning about cyber bullying. Jeffrey's mother Debbie Johnston writes,

> "A bully doesn't have to be eye to eye to bully someone. Sometimes he or she gets into cyberspace, and then there's no place to hide from their torment. With the keyboard as his weapon, the bully violated the sanctity of my home and murdered my child just as surely as if he had crawled through a broken window and choked the life from Jeff with his bare hands. It was not a death that was quick and merciful. It was carried out with lies, rumors and calculated cruelty portioned out day by day."

Cyber bullies, like any bully, want to feel power and control over their victim. They want to get under their victim's skin. Many kids live and breathe the internet. It is essential to how they see themselves and how they socialize with their peers. The computer is as essential a social tool today as the telephone was decades ago.

This is part of why a cyberbullying attack can be so devastating. Cyber bullies cut to the core of their victim's social life and self-image. Targets are faced with threats and intimidation in emails and instant messages, but it is not only fear that the cyber bully can instill over the web. It is not good enough anymore for bullies to simply beat up their victims. With digital video becoming ubiquitous, beatings are now digitally recorded and uploaded so everyone can have a front row seat and the bloodlust can be enjoyed again and again.

How can cyber bullies be so heartless? Perhaps the internet lends itself to this indifference. Bullies don't have to see their victims or answer for their actions. Like the cowards they are, they hide behind their computers - behind a veil of anonymity.

Even though the effects of cyberbullying can be every bit as dangerous as offline bullying, if not more so, parents are even less likely to hear about it happening to their child.

To understand why, you have to understand how important access to the Internet is for many kids. They will remain silent about cyberbullying because they are afraid if their parents find out they will go off the deep end and cut off access to their computer, Internet and/or mobile phone. Years ago this would be the equivalent of a child who complained of bullying being grounded and losing their telephone privileges. Loss of Internet access would be deemed by many kids now to be the cruelest of punishments.

The first step in combatting cyber bullying is to stop responding to the cyber bully. Do not reply to emails, posts, IM's or text messages. This is what the bully wants. They want you to engage with them. They want to manipulate you into responding.

If you respond in any way that is emotional or lets them know that they are getting to you and are able to make you upset, it only encourages the cyber bully.

Remember, bullies often suffer from low self-esteem and they want to feel better about themselves. Instead of doing something positive or succeeding at something or making a new friend, a bully has learned to make themselves feel better by controlling, abusing and tearing down others. This gives them a sense of control and power they don't have in their lives. Most bullies are actually quite weak and the same is true of cyber bullies. If you respond in a way that lets the bully know that you are angry, upset or afraid, they will only be happy because they have managed to control your emotional state. Even if you do feel like that, don't give the cyber bully the satisfaction and encouragement by letting them know.

It is especially important not to respond emotionally because this could make you send a reply that you might regret later. Messages sent on the Internet are almost impossible to take back. If you lash back in anger you could find yourself the one who is being accused of being a cyber bully and the tables could be turned against you.

Bullies are hoping to get you upset so you slip up and make a mistake. Don't send flames and don't get into flame wars.

While you should not respond to the cyber bully online (or offline), you should also not delete their messages. That's right, do NOT delete their messages. Cyber bullies are especially cowardly and like to hide behind the anonymity that the Internet gives them. Or does it? Messages sent on the Internet are traceable. Make sure to keep all messages as the police will be able to use this information to track down the culprit. Do not delete any messages and save as much information you can about chats, IM's, text messages, blog posts, websites, etc.

This will also help show just how often the cyber bullying takes place, at what times and even from which location. Every computer, server and device connected over the (TCP/IP) network has a unique IP (Internet Protocol) address. Police along with the cyber bully's ISP (Internet Service Provider) can use this information to trace the bully right to his or her house.

You need to let appropriate authorities know about the cyber bullying or they cannot take corrective action. Cyberbullying is not something you want to ignore. It is your responsibility to report this behavior so the perpetrators can be dealt with. This helps not only to protect you (or your child, if you are a parent) but to intervene before the cyber bully harms even more kids. Bullies often behave in a serial fashion attacking multiple victims either at the same time or one after another. Once the high of abusing one victim is over they move to their next prey.

While bullies may have had a free ride up until now, they are more and more running into the long arm of the law. Cyber bullying needs to be brought to the attention of the police. Be sure to provide them with as much information as you can. They can then contact the cyber bully's ISP and track them down.

If you are a parent, inform your child's school if the cyber bully is a student. While the school administration may say they have no legal obligation as the bullying is taking place outside of school hours and off school property, many schools are adopting code of conduct-type contracts with their students and parents. This allows for schools to take action in such cases where the bullying still impacts on another student while he or she is at school. Targets of cyberbullying are traumatized and often lose focus on their schoolwork as a direct result of the harassment. Even if your child's school does not have such a policy, they still need to be made aware of the abuse so they can be alerted to potential further bullying that may be taking place while your child is at school.

If you are a parent or older sibling, pay close attention to your kids or younger siblings. Are they acting strangely? Are there unexplained pictures or odd messages on their computers or cell phones? Are they having trouble sleeping or falling behind at school? Do they seem depressed or more aggressive? Are they being evasive and don't want you to know who they are talking to, or do they close windows on their computer screen whenever you come near? Don't ignore what your instincts are telling you. If you think something is wrong, don't wait until it is too late.

Cyber bullying can be every bit as dangerous as face-to-face bullying, more so in some cases. Awareness is the key. And children need to know that cyber bullying is not their fault. It is not because of something wrong with them. The fault and the problem both lie with the cyber bully.

Discussion Starters

1. What is Hout's depiction of a cyber bully's make-up? Does it fit the make-up of bullies as you perceive or have encountered them?

2. What are Hout's recommendations for dealing with cyber bullying? Are there any that you question or any that you would add?

3. Have you had any personal experience with cyber bullying (as victim or assailant)? How did the experience affect you? How did you deal with it? How would you suggest that other victims deal with it?

Unit Six

Making Decisions

Every day we make decisions based on the choices available. Sometimes the decisions are relatively simple and inconsequential: where to eat lunch, what to watch on T.V., what to do on a Friday night. Other times the decisions are more important: where to attend college, what classes to take for the semester, what car to lease, or where to work part time. In either case, such decisions usually involve considering the different options available and making the best choice.

For example, a student may be interested in the medical profession, due in part to her interest and in part to the job opportunities available. Within the medical profession, of course, there are a number of different jobs: physician, registered nurse, nurse practitioner, medical transcriber, radiology technician, phlebotomist, and so on. In evaluating the different options, the student may take into account the years of schooling required, the average salary for the job, the type of work entailed, the job opportunities in the area, and which job would best suit her interests. Based on that evaluation, she would no doubt choose a job track that seems the best fit for her.

Comparing and evaluating similar subjects and making decisions based on your evaluation provides the writing emphasis for this unit. You will select a subject of interest, evaluate different options within that subject, and make a decision as to which option is the most desirable. Making informed decisions based on comparing and evaluating options provides another challenge in your continued writing development and a process to apply to any decision-making you may do.

Prewriting

In preparing to write your comparative essay, you will decide on a topic for comparison and on the subjects to compare within that topic. Then you will select a *criteria* by which to compare them, evaluate the subjects based on that criteria, and draw conclusions that will help you make a decision.

Comparing Subjects

Writers compare similar subjects for a variety of purposes: to present their similarities and differences, to evaluate their relative quality, to suggest to readers the best decision to make, or to make a decision for themselves: which car to buy, mayoral candidate to support, or college to attend. The most effective comparative essays usually cover critical points of comparison, provide details that reveal the differences between subjects, present accurate, objective information, and draw insightful conclusions for readers based on the comparative information presented.

An important aspect of comparative writing is deciding on the *criteria* on which to base the comparison: the set of standards, rules, qualities, or features used to compare and evaluate your subjects.

For example, if you were comparing presidential candidates, your comparative criteria might include the candidates' political experience, positions on key issues, integrity, and leadership qualities. If you were comparing singers, your criteria might include their quality of sound, strength of voice, performance ability, and song choice. Deciding on a criteria for your comparison is an important step in writing a comparative essay.

Comparative Criteria

When a friend recommends a particular restaurant, encourages you to see a particular physician, or says that a particular quarterback is the "best" in college football, you would probably want to know *why* he believes as he does. His response would indicate his *criteria* for making each judgment: the things that he feels are most important in a restaurant, physician, or quarterback. For example, his "restaurant" criteria might include the quality of food, the range of choices, the atmosphere, and the quality of service. His "physician" criteria might include the doctor's friendly manner, her expertise, and the quality of treatment she provides. His "quarterback" criteria might include percentage of passes completed, touchdown-to-interception ratio, and the success of his team. How closely your friend's criteria corresponds to your own could influence whether you agree with him.

To write the most convincing comparative essay, the criteria you decide on should include those elements that are most important in evaluating your subjects. To that end, consider the following suggestions:

1. **In deciding on a criteria to evaluate your subjects, ask yourself, "What are the most important considerations for comparing these subjects?** For example, if you are comparing two different driving routes to get to a particular destination, the most important considerations may be the length of time each takes, the quality of the roads, the relative amount of traffic, and the easiest route to navigate.

2. **More comparative points are better than fewer.** You never know what comparative point may interest some readers, so it is better to be more inclusive rather than leave out a point or two that some readers may be looking for. For example, in the "driving routes" criteria, some readers may only care about how long each route takes, others may prefer the easiest route, and still others may prefer the nicest freeway route even if it takes longer. You never know what consideration may be most important to readers.

3. **When deciding on your criteria, look at your subjects from different perspectives.** For example, for some readers, the cost of a product may be most important. For others, the quality may be most important. For others, the durability may be most important: how long will it last? Depending on your subjects, there may be a "fairness" component (Should cheaper non-union carpenters be hired over more expensive union carpenters?), or a "right-and-wrong" component (Should foreign students pay the same college tuition as American students?).

4. **Keep your readers in mind when considering your criteria.** In making the comparison, ask yourself, "What can I include to help readers, as well as myself, make a decision on what to buy, whom to vote for, or what to believe?" Regarding your subjects, consider what you think your particular readers would think most important, which could vary among different reading audiences: high school students, young working adults, senior citizens, or people just scraping by financially.

Prewriting Activity 6.1

For any three of the following comparative topics and reading audiences, decide on a criteria by which to evaluate the subjects. Include what you feel are the most important points of comparison, keeping in mind the four suggestions presented. Then share your criteria with a classmate or two, and explain why you chose each criteria. Note how your criteria are similar to or different from your classmates', and decide whether you might change (add to or delete) any criteria.

Example:

Topic: Comparing apartment and dormitory living

Audience: College students

Criteria: Cost (rent, food, transportation)
            Convenience
            Freedom
            Space
            Choice of roommates
            Privacy

Topic: Comparing local community colleges

Audience: High school seniors

Criteria: Size of college
            Programs offered
            Quality of instructors
            Social life
            Facilities
            On-campus resources (library, computers, Internet access, tutors, etc.)

1. Topic: Comparing two teams (any sport, any level)

   Audience: College students

   Criteria:

228

2. Topic: Comparing two similar stores (e.g. Target and Kmart)

          Audience: College students

          Criteria:

3. Topic: Comparing two similar cars (e.g. Toyota Camry and Honda Civic)

          Audience: Young adults shopping for cars

          Criteria:

4. Topic: Comparing two fast-food restaurants

          Audience: Junior high students

          Criteria:

5. Topic: Comparing two gaming stations (e.g. Wii, X Box, Play Station)

          Audience: College students

          Criteria:

Writing Assignment

In your upcoming essay, you will compare two-to-four similar subjects and evaluate them based on your criteria. To help you decide on what to compare, consider these suggestions:

1. **Compare subjects that your reading audience wouldn't already be knowledgeable about.** For example, comparing fast-food restaurants like McDonald's, Burger King, and Wendy's would be of little value since most people are familiar with fast-food restaurants. Compare subjects that would provide your readers with some new and useful information.

2. **Compare subjects that interest you and that you are knowledgeable about or want to learn more about.** Think of subjects that you are familiar with and have perhaps compared for yourself. If you are interested in knowing more about some subjects - e.g. different LED television brands, colleges you may transfer to, or similar jobs, such as licensed practical nurse, registered nurse, and nurse practitioner – you might learn more and compare those subjects.

3. **Compare subjects that are substantial enough to warrant a comparison.** For example, comparing different brands of bottled water wouldn't produce much of an essay. However, comparing three or four different sport's drinks that have different ingredients, flavors, prices, and results might be of interest to people who work out a lot.

4. **Make sure to compare similar subjects.** For example, you could compare different models of SUV's or different models of mid-sized sedans, but don't compare SUV's to mid-sized sedans, an "apples to oranges" comparison. You could compare different brands of pianos or different brands of keyboards, but don't compare pianos to keyboards, another dissimilar comparison.

5. **Consider a number of different areas where you could find comparative subjects: school, jobs, products, music, politics, sports, technology, etc.** Scan a range of potential subjects before deciding on the best comparison for your essay.

Prewriting Activity 6.2

Take your time deciding on a topic you'd like to write on, and ultimately, choose a comparison that both you and your readers could learn something from. Then decide on your criteria for comparing subjects: the most important considerations in comparing subjects.

Example:

Topic: Comparing electric cars (the Chevy Volt and Nissan Leaf)

Criteria: Cost and savings
            How they work
            Range (driving distance between recharges)
            Size

Looks
Performance
Relative "greenness" (how environmentally friendly)

Topic:

Criteria:

Researching Subjects

Do you need to find out more about your subjects to write a well-informed essay? If you are writing about subjects that you need to learn more about, decide the best way to get information and proceed from there. To find out more about your subjects, if necessary, consider these suggestions.

1. **Find *objective* information on your subjects.** For example, if you are comparing Sony, Toshiba, and Mitsubishi camcorders, pamphlets put out by Sony and Toshiba would probably provide the most favorable, least objective information. Look for sources that would provide the most objective information, like in-store experts on camcorders.

2. **Use your criteria to find relevant information.** Look specifically for information that compares your subjects in the areas you have decided on. You might also find some new criteria based on what you learn about your subjects.

3. **Find local "experts" that may be able to provide good information.** They may be college instructors, fellow students with experience with your topic, local car dealers, or store employees at a Best Buy, Home Depot, or bookstore.

Prewriting Activity 6.3

If necessary, find out more on your topic before proceeding, taking notes on any information that you may use in your essay to help compare subjects.

Audience and Purpose

By now, you may have a good idea on the best reading audience for your essay: readers who would have the most interest in it. It may be people who are looking for a good used car, deciding on what college to transfer to, deciding which adventure reality show to watch on television, or wondering which mayoral candidate to vote for in the upcoming election. Choose a reading audience that you feel would be interested in your topic, that would learn something from it, and that might benefit from reading about it.

Your writing purpose for this essay depends on your subject. If you are comparing two musical groups, your purpose may be to recommend to readers which group's concert to attend in your city. If you are comparing three candidates for mayor, your purpose may be to encourage readers to vote for none of them and instead support a "write-in" candidate of your choice. If you are comparing different brands of HD 35-inch televisions, your purpose may be to help readers decide which brand to buy if they are shopping for a TV.

Prewriting Activity 6.4

Decide on a tentative audience for your comparative essay and your purpose in writing to them.

Example:

Topic: Comparing the Chevy Volt and Nissan Leaf

Audience: Anyone who is interested in electric cars and may consider buying one now or in the future.

Purpose: To help readers decide which electric car would be the best choice for them.

Audience:

Purpose:

First Drafts

As you progress through the lessons, each drafting experience presents some new and some familiar considerations. For your current comparative essay, the new considerations include doing a point-by-point comparison of similar subjects and drawing conclusions for readers based on your comparison. The familiar considerations include providing an interesting topic introduction, developing your main points in the middle paragraphs, providing a strong conclusion, and keeping your reading audience and purpose in mind.

Organizing a Comparative Essay

There are two basic ways that writers organize most comparative essays. The organizational method that you decide on depends on how you believe you can present your comparisons most effectively to readers.

One way to organize your essay is to compare the subjects point-by-point throughout the essay. For example, let's say that you are comparing organically and non-organically grown fruit, and your criteria include looks, size, taste, cost, and environmental impact. After your opening, your essay organization may look like this:

Paragraph one: Compare the looks of your two subjects.
Paragraph two: Compare their size.
Paragraph three: Compare their taste.
Paragraph four: Compare their cost.
Paragraph five: Compare their environmental impact.

Look at the first draft of "Comparing Electric Cars" in Drafting Activity 6.7 for a point-by-point comparison.

A second way to organize your essay is to take one subject at a time, cover all of the criteria for that subject, and then do the same for the next subject. For example, with the same fruit comparison, your organization may look like this:

Paragraph one: Present the looks and size of organically grown fruit.
Paragraph two: Present the taste and cost of organically grown fruit.
Paragraph three: Present the environmental impact of organically grown fruit.
Paragraph four: Present the looks and size of non-organically grown fruit.
Paragraph five: Present the taste and cost of non-organically grown fruit.
Paragraph six: Present the environmental impact of non-organically grown fruit.

An advantage of this organizational method is that you get all of the information on a subject at one time. A disadvantage is that you don't get a "side-by-side" comparison of the two subjects and may have to read back and forth to see how they compare.

Most comparative essays lend themselves best to a "side-by-side" comparison of subjects on each point. However, there can be exceptions, such as comparing the health care systems in two countries or comparing two famous singing groups, which may be more effectively presented one subject at a time.

Drafting Activity 6.5
Decide on the best organization for your comparative essay based on your topic, purpose, and reading audience.

Sample organization:
Topic: Comparing Electric Cars

Organization: Comparing subjects together point by point

Reason: Readers can get the best sense of the differences and similarities between the two cars if I compare them together on each point.

Organization:

Drawing Conclusions

In the opening of your draft, you introduce your subjects for comparison. In the middle paragraphs, you compare them in a number of different areas. What remains in the ending is to draw conclusions for readers that may help them, and you, make a decision. Based on your subjects and how they compare, you might draw any of the following conclusions:

1. **Clear-cut conclusion.** With a "clear-cut" conclusion, you have one recommendation to make for all readers: vote for Dominguez, lease an apartment rather than rent it monthly, take Dr. Cheney for Biology II. If one subject stands out over the other(s), you may single it out for readers.

2. **Qualified conclusion.** With a "qualified" conclusion, rather than make a single recommendation, you may make recommendations based on a reader's circumstances or preferences. For example, with the organic/non-organic fruit comparison, a writer might conclude, "If price or looks of the fruit are your most important considerations, buy non-organic fruit. If you are concerned about the environment and the effects of chemical fertilizers and pesticides used in non-organic farming, you should buy organic fruit. For another example of a "qualified" conclusion, read the ending of the upcoming "Comparing Electric Cars" draft.

3. **Flip a coin.** If after evaluating the subjects you don't see a great difference between or among them, your conclusion should reflect that opinion. For example, if you find that the top three brands of 52" HD televisions are comparable in price, picture clarity, looks, and warranty length, you might conclude that readers can't go wrong with any brand. On the other hand, if neither gubernatorial candidate in your state measures up in your evaluation, you might conclude that readers could send a message by sitting out this election or supporting a write-in candidate.

Drafting Activity 6.6
Considering your subjects and reading audience, what type of conclusion are you most likely to draw? If you might write a qualified conclusion, think of the readers' circumstances and preferences that could influence your recommendations.

Sample Conclusion:

Topic: Comparing electric cars

Conclusion: Qualified

Reason: Which electric car a reader might buy depends on different factors: what they can afford, how far they drive every day, how much seating room they need, how important looks are, and how "green" they want their car to be. I'll make different recommendations based on people's circumstances.

Conclusion:

Drafting Guidelines

As you write the first draft of your essay, consider the following suggestions:

1. **In your opening, introduce your subjects and give readers an idea of why you are comparing them and why they may be interested in the comparison.** How might readers benefit from reading this essay?

2. **If you need to provide some background or explanatory information about your subjects, include it after the opening.** For example, the writer of the "Comparing Electric Cars" draft explained to readers the kind of electric cars she was comparing in her second paragraph.

3. **In the middle paragraphs, present your points of comparison in the most effective order, and make sure to compare both (or three or four) subjects on each point.** In general, develop each comparative point in a separate paragraph, with its first sentence indicating the point of comparison. (See the middle paragraphs of the "Comparing Electric Cars" draft.)

4. **End your draft by drawing a conclusion for readers based on your evaluation, which may help them make a decision.** Your conclusion should take in mind your reading audience and your purpose in writing to them, and should follow logically from the comparative information you have provided on the subjects.

> 5. **As you write, be open to including new ideas that may come to you: a new point of comparison, the explanation of a particular term, a different conclusion than you had planned on.** The drafting process is a thinking process, which can lead to new, sometimes critical discoveries. No matter how much preparation you do for a draft, new connections and insights may come to you as you write.

Drafting Activity 6.7

Read the following first draft "Comparing Electric Cars," noting its introduction of subjects, explanation of what electric cars are in the second paragraph, points of comparison in the middle paragraph, including details provided to make the comparisons, and the "qualified" conclusion that takes into account the reader's circumstances and preferences. Then write the first draft of your essay, keeping the five drafting considerations in mind.

Sample First Draft

Comparing Electric Cars

Reading audience: Anyone who is interested in electric cars and may consider purchasing one at some time.

With the price of gasoline constantly rising and auto emissions contributing significantly to global warming, more Americans are seriously looking into buying electric cars. Many companies are beginning to come out with electric car models, but two models stand out at this time: the Chevy Volt and the Nissan Leaf. The Tesla Roadster is a third electric vehicle that is getting a lot of attention, but with a price tag of $110,000, it is not in a price range that most people can afford.

Unlike hybrid vehicles such as the Prius and Ford Focus, which use electric and gasoline power in combination to improve gasoline mileage, the Volt and Leaf are electricity-first cars. The Leaf is a pure electric car with no gasoline engine and has a 100 mile driving range. The Volt is an electricity-first, gasoline-second vehicle which has a 40 mile electric driving range, after which its gasoline engine kicks in and can extend the range to 400 miles. However, each time the electric engine is recharged, it powers the car for 40 miles. In other words, the gas engine is a "safety valve" for longer drives between recharges. Both the Leaf and Volt can be recharged in a few hours by simply plugging into a 120 volt wall plug in a garage.

Both the Leaf and Volt are 5-door hatchbacks, but the Leaf holds five passengers while the Volt holds four. The interior and seating space in both is similar to most compact cars, with comfortable front-seat space and a little tight sitting in the back. Both cars also have the same technological dash features of most autos today, including GPS navigation and blue tooth phone systems.

As far as performance, the Volt is smooth and quiet, it rides well, and it has good acceleration. There is little difference between the Volt's performance and that of gas-powered compacts. The Leaf, which is not as quick as the Volt, also has a quiet, smooth, pleasant drive. As far as performance, there is little to choose between the two. Both cars handle well and possess similar safety features to gas-powered compacts.

If you are into looks, you'll probably find the Volt more pleasing to the eye. It has a sleek, sedan-like look despite being a hatchback while the Leaf definitely looks like a hatchback with its boxy rear end. The Leaf also has a higher top, accentuating its boxiness and giving it a mini-SUV look.

When it comes to price, the Leaf definitely has the Volt beat, which may explain why it has outsold the Volt two-to-one in the last year. The Leaf's base price is $33,000 while the Volt's is $41,000. It's duel-engine set-up may contribute to the higher price than the Leaf's single electric engine. As sales and production go up in the future for both cars, their prices will undoubtedly fall nearer the price of comparable gas-powered compacts.

There is no question that both the Volt and Leaf outperform all hybrids when it comes to gas consumption and emissions. The Leaf uses no gasoline and the Volt only uses gas when it's 40-mile electric range is exceeded, which may seldom occur during daily around-town driving. While the price of the Volt and Leaf exceeds that of comparable gas-powered compacts, the savings in annual gas cost can be in the $2000-$4000 range. Since the cost of running a car on electricity is a small fraction of the cost of gasoline, the savings is significant when factoring in the cost of electricity.

Whether the Volt or the Leaf is the best choice depends on your situation. For a family of five, the five-seated Leaf obviously seems the best choice. For someone whose commute exceeds 100 miles, the Volt with its gas-powered engine that kicks in after 40 electrical miles makes the most sense. For looks-conscious drivers, the Volt is also the sleeker-looking car. For someone wanting the "greenest" car, the Leaf is a clear choice since it burns no gasoline and emits no carbon dioxide into the atmosphere. If cost is a big consideration, the Leaf is also about $8,000 less expensive.

Whichever car you may consider buying, the prices could come down appreciably in the future, putting them on the radar for more prospective buyers. There may also be more electric car models in production, but for now, the Volt and Leaf are the best choices on the market.

Revision

Each draft that you write has some revision considerations specific to that essay and some broader considerations that apply to most essays you write. For example, with your current comparative essay, the specific considerations include evaluating the criteria that you used for your comparison, the effectiveness of each point of comparison, and the appropriateness of your conclusion based on your comparison.

The broader revision considerations include improving your sentence wording, evaluating your paragraphing and organization, considering what you might add to strengthen the essay, checking your use of transitional wording, and determining how you might improve your opening or ending. By this time, most of these considerations are probably built into to your revision process as you become increasingly adept at revising your drafts.

Revision Guidelines

To revise your current draft, consider the following suggestions:

1. **Read your entire draft once to get an overall sense of its strengths and possible weaknesses.** You may notice that you have spent too much time on some areas of comparison and too little on others, buried one comparison in an overly long paragraph, or left readers unclear as to which subject was superior or the better option. Keep such concerns in mind as you begin revising your draft.

2. **Check your opening to see how effectively you introduced your topic and created interest for readers.** Make any changes that will pique readers' interest in the topic.

3. **Check to see whether you have provided explanations for anything your readers might not understand.** For example, the writer of the "Comparing Electric Cars" draft explained what an electric car and a hybrid car were so readers would understand the difference. Check for any terms or concepts in your draft that may require some explanation for your readers' understanding.

4. **Check your criteria - the points of comparison you presented - to see whether you have covered the most important comparisons and ordered them effectively.** If a new point of comparison comes to mind, you may want to include it. If a point in your draft seems rather minor, you may want to delete it. In addition, evaluate the order in which you presented your criteria, and determine whether a different order may be more effective.

5. **Check your use of details and examples to develop each comparison between subjects.** What might you add to make a particular comparison clearer or show a sharper distinction between subjects?

6. **Check the wording of each sentence.** Delete unnecessary words or phrases, reword awkward or vague sentences, and replace questionable word choices.

7. **Check your use of transitional wording to tie thoughts together and help readers navigate your paper.** Since you are presenting a number of different comparative points,

you might find use for transitions such as "first," "next," "another," or "lastly," as well as transitions that show different relationships such as "however," "nevertheless," "therefore," or "consequently."

8. **Check your conclusion to see whether it follows logically from the comparisons you made and takes into account your reading audience.** Does your conclusion make the most sense based on your evaluation of subjects? Does it take into account the different circumstances or preferences that your readers may have? Your comparative points lead to what may interest readers the most: the recommendations that you make in the conclusion.

9. **Evaluate how well you achieved your writing purpose.** Viewing your draft from a reader's perspective, what changes might you make to ensure that your purpose is clear and that you have accomplished it successfully?

Revision Activity 6.8

Look at the revisions below for the "Comparing Electric Cars" draft, noting how the changes improve each paragraph. Then revise your own draft, keeping the previous revision suggestions in mind. For the best results, you may want to read your draft several times, covering one or two revision areas at a time.

Revision excerpts from "Comparing Electric Cars" *(First two paragraphs)*

With the price of gasoline constantly rising and auto emissions contributing significantly to global warming, **many** Americans are ~~seriously looking into~~ **considering for the first time** buying **an** electric ~~cars~~. Many companies are beginning to ~~come out with~~ **introduce** electric car models, but two models stand out at this time: the Chevy Volt and the Nissan Leaf. The Tesla Roadster, ~~is~~ a third electric vehicle ~~that is~~ getting a lot of attention, **is out of most people's price range at $110,000.** ~~but with a price tag of $110,000, it is not in a price range that most people can afford.~~ **However, the Volt and Leaf give drivers two reasonable electric car options to consider.**

Unlike hybrid vehicles such as the Prius and Ford Focus, which use **a combination of** electric and gasoline power ~~in combination to improve gasoline mileage~~, the Volt and Leaf are electricity-first cars. The Leaf is a pure electric car with no gasoline engine and has a 100 mile driving range ~~between charges~~. The Volt is an electricity-first **car** ~~gasoline-second vehicle~~ which has a 40 mile ~~electric~~ driving range **between charges**, after which its gasoline engine kicks in and ~~can~~ extends the range to 400 miles. ~~However, each time~~ **Once** the electric engine is recharged, it **again** powers the car, ~~for 40 miles. In other words~~ the gas engine ~~is~~ **being** a "safety valve" for longer drives between recharges. Both the Leaf and Volt can be recharged in a few hours by ~~simply~~ plugging **them** into a 120 volt wall plug ~~in the garage~~.
(Revisions made to improve wording, add information, eliminate unnecessary words or phrases, and provide detail.)

(Final two paragraphs)

Whether the Volt or the Leaf is the best choice depends on your situation. ~~For a family of five, the five-seated Leaf obviously seems the best choice.~~ For someone whose commute or regular travel exceeds 100 miles **daily**, the Volt with its **"safety valve"** gas-powered engine ~~that kicks in after 40 electrical miles~~ makes the most sense. For looks-conscious drivers, the Volt is also the sleeker-looking car. For someone ~~wanting the "greenest" car, and~~ whose daily driving remains under 100 miles, the Leaf is a clear choice since it burns no gasoline. **It is the "greenest," most environmentally friendly car, emitting no carbon dioxide into the atmosphere.** ~~and emits no carbon dioxide into the atmosphere.~~ **For a family of five, the five-seated Leaf also seems the best choice.** If cost is a big consideration, the Leaf is about $8,000 less expensive.

Whichever car you may consider buying, the prices could come down appreciably in the next couple years, ~~putting them on the radar for a lot more prospective buyers,~~ **making them more affordable**. There may also be more electric car models in production by then, but for now, the Volt and Leaf are the best choices on the market **and the first viable electric car options that Americans have had**.

(Revisions made to reorganize information, presenting Volt information first and Leaf information second, to add detail, to improve wording, and to provide new information.)

Revision Activity 6.9

Exchange drafts with a classmate or two to get some reader feedback. Ask questions about anything that you don't understand or would like more information on, including additional areas of comparison. Make any revision suggestions that you feel would improve the draft for readers. Then based on your classmate's feedback, make any revisions that you feel would further improve your essay.

Editing

Now that you have revised your draft, you are ready to correct any errors to produce a final error-free essay for your readers. While error correction is your top priority, to some degree, writers are always in the "revision mode," and if you notice a way to improve your paper while you are proofreading for errors, make the revision.

In this lesson, you are first introduced to apostrophe usage in possessive words and contractions. Then you do a review activity covering the grammatical and punctuation areas from previous lessons. Finally, you proofread your draft for errors to complete the writing process.

Apostrophe Usage

Apostrophes are used in possessive words to indicate "ownership" (Maria's dress) and in contractions to replace the letters that are omitted when the two words forming the contraction are combined (you + are = you're).

Omitting an apostrophe in a possessive word is a fairly common error, usually caused by the writer not noticing the possessive form of a word. For example, in writing the sentence, "Todays weather is supposed to be much milder than yesterdays," a writer may pay little attention to the possessive words "todays" and "yesterdays" and omit the required apostrophes: *Today's* weather is supposed to be much milder than *yesterday's*.

Using apostrophes correctly in contractions is less of a problem for most writers since most contractions don't "look right" without their apostrophe. For example, a contraction such as "haven't" or "I'm" doesn't look right to most writers without its apostrophe: "havent" or "Im." You may have little problem with contractions and if so, needn't spend much time on them.

To use apostrophes correctly in possessive words and contractions, follow these basic rules and suggestions:

Possessive Words

1. **A possessive word shows** *ownership* - **something** *belongs* **to a person or thing: cat's instinct, rainbow's colors, Bernadette's wig, freedom's power.**

2. **If a** *singular* **word is possessive, it ends in** *apostrophe* + **"s" ('s): car's windshield, Malcolm's toothbrush, tomorrow's headline.**

   If a *plural* **word is possessive, it ends in "s" +** *apostrophe* **(s'): several cities' budget deficits, thirty students' math scores, boxes' lids.**

   (Exception: If a word forms its plural without adding "s" (children, geese, men, women), its possessive form ends in apostrophe + "s:" children's books, geese's pond, men's clothing, women's prerogative.)

3. **Apostrophes are not used in possessive pronouns such as** *his, hers, theirs, yours, ours.* However, apostrophes are used in *indefinite* possessive pronouns: someone's umbrella, everybody's business, no one's fault; somebody's coat.

4. **A possessive word may** *follow* **the word it possesses:** That credit card is Fran's. That newspaper is yesterday's. The coat I borrowed is my mother's.

Contractions

1. **A *contraction* is a word formed by combining two words:**

    I + am = I'm   you + are = you're

    has + not = hasn't   they + are = they're

    will + not = won't   we + are = we're

    you + have = you've   he + will = he'll

2. **An apostrophe replaces the letters that are omitted when the words are combined:**

    you're (apostrophe replaces "a" in "are")

    they'll (apostrophe replaces "wi" in "will")

    she's (apostrophe replaces "i" in "is")

3. **Contraction problems occur most frequently with the following word mix-ups:**

    Its time to change the calendar in the kitchen. (*Its* is a possessive pronoun.)

    Correct:

    It's time to change the calendar in the kitchen.

    I don't think *were* going to the concert. (*Were* is a past tense verb.)

    Correct:

    I don't think *we're* going to the concert.

    Amal hopes that *your* not angry with him. (*Your* is a possessive pronoun.)

    Correct:

    Amal hopes that *you're* not angry with him.

    Theirs no better debater than Therese. (*Theirs* is a possessive pronoun.)

    Correct:

    There's no better debater than Therese.

Editing Activity 6.10
The following paragraph contains some possessive words and contractions in need of apostrophes and some incorrect words that need to be replaced with contractions. Insert apostrophes where they are needed and replace the incorrect words with contractions.

Example:
The Italian cruise ship rammed into a reef and turned onto its side. Theres reason to suspect that the captain steered too close to the port islands reef before turning into its harbor. Many of the ships lifeboats were incapacitated, so hundreds of island residents boats anchored in the harbor sailed to the sinking ship to rescue the 4,000 passengers and ships crew. Its the first major cruise ship disaster in over fifty years.

Corrected:
The Italian cruise ship rammed into a reef and turned onto its side. *There's* reason to suspect that the captain steered too close to the port *island's* reef before turning into its harbor. Many of the *ship's* lifeboats were incapacitated, so hundreds of island *residents'* boats anchored in the harbor sailed to the sinking ship to rescue the 4,000 passengers and *ship's* crew. *It's* the first major cruise ship disaster in over fifty years.

Science Experiment

Amalias science project didnt turn out the way she had hoped. She and a friend collaborated on

an experiment to try and prove that greenhouse gases, most notably CO2, were responsible for

climate change. They built a large, rectangular plastic box with a hole in its side for inserting

a rubber hose into the box. The boxs dimensions were three-feet long, two-feet wide, and two-

feet high. The rubber hoses outside end was attached to a pump that theyd borrowed from the

chemistry lab. The pumps chamber was filled with CO2 gas, and when they turned on the pump,

the boxs interior filled with the gas. As the CO2 gas trapped heat inside the box, they theorized

that the temperature inside the box should increase, as a thermostat placed inside the box would

indicate. They awaited anxiously for the thermostats red bubble to begin to rise.

Its clear that their experiment had a significant flaw, however. CO2 traps heat in the earths

atmosphere which would otherwise escape into space. The gas acts like a giant lid that retains

244

more heat in the atmosphere and consequently warms the air. And theres the problem with the experiment. The "atmosphere" inside Amalia and her friends plastic box already had a lid on it, allowing no heat to escape. Therefore, whatever heat was inside the box was already trapped, so adding CO2 to the box had no effect.

Rather than abandoning the experiment, their looking into ways to allow heat to escape from the box, such as drilling some holes in its lid, to try and duplicate the heat loss in the earths atmosphere. Theyve put a lot of time and effort into the experiment, and theyd love to be able to provide a working model of mankinds contribution to global warming.

———————————————————————————————————

Editing Activity 6.11
Proofread your paper focusing specifically on possessive words and contractions, and insert any apostrophes you may have omitted.

Editing Activity 6.12
This review activity provides some proofreading practice involving run-on and comma-splice sentences, sentence fragments, subject-verb agreement, subject pronouns, pronoun-antecedent agreement, and comma usage. Proofread the follow paragraphs for errors and make the necessary corrections.

Example:
The parking pass validation rules at the shopping mall is tricky. Which means that you need to read the fine print. First a shopper can only get their parking pass validated if they spend at least $20 in a store. Second only certain stores on the mall accepts parking validations, you need to check the list of participating stores. Finally, if you leave your parking pass in the car which is very easy to do you are out of luck.

Corrected:
The parking pass validation rules at the shopping mall is *are* tricky, *which* means that you need to read the fine print. First, a shopper *shoppers* can only get their parking pass validated if they spend at least $20 in a store. Second, only certain stores on the mall accepts *accept* parking validations. *You* need to check the list of participating stores. Finally, if you leave your parking pass in the car, which is very easy to do, you are out of luck.

Campus Maze

Not one of the internal campus roads get you from one side of the campus to the other. Each road in the structural maze dead-end at some point, you are forced to turn around and try a different route. Which is a waste of precious time when you're trying to get to class. In addition, most of the roads are one-way. It is sometimes difficult to find a road going the direction you want, a student can literally get stuck mid-campus trying to navigate their way across the college. Me and my friends have given up on using the campus roads to get to class and that is the intent of the college's crazy road maze. If college officials wanted students on the roads they would have devised a more workable system. In my opinion the college trustees and president wants to

246

maintain the roads primarily for faculty, campus security staff, and administrative use. It prefers that students walk or ride bikes around campus instead of driving. Making it difficult to get to class on time if your next class is across the campus.

Editing Guidelines

1. Check your sentences to make sure you haven't run any sentences together or put a comma between sentences instead of a period, and make any necessary corrections.

2. Check your draft for any sentence fragments: incomplete sentences with a period after them. To correct fragments, attach them to the sentence they belong with, or add words to make them complete.

3. Check your comma usage, making sure you have inserted commas correctly into your sentences.

4. Check the spelling of any word you are uncertain of, and run the spell check on your word processing program, to eliminate any spelling errors.

5. Check your verbs in each sentence to make sure that they agree with their subjects.

6. Check your pronouns in each sentence to make sure they agree with their antecedents, and make sure you are using the correct subject pronoun forms.

7. Check your use of colons, semi-colons, and dashes to see whether you are using them correctly and effectively.

8. Check your use of comparative and superlative adjectives, and make sure that you have used the correct forms.

9. Check your possessive words to make sure you have inserted apostrophes correctly.

Editing Activity 6.13

Following the "Editing Guidelines," proofread your draft for errors, focusing on the types of errors you most frequently make. Make sure to run the spell-check on your word processing program, and also check for spelling errors involving similar-sounding words the spell-check may not catch: their/they're/there, know/no, to/too/two, affect/effect, then/than, your/you're, its/it's.

Applying the Writing Process

Working independently, follow a similar writing process that you used to develop your first comparative paper. (Refer back to the drafting, revision, or editing guidelines in the unit as needed.)

- Select a topic for comparison and the subjects to compare. Select a very different topic from the one that you wrote your first essay on.
- Decide on your criteria for comparing subjects.
- If necessary, do some research to learn more about your subjects.
- Decide on the best organization for your comparative essay.
- Write your first draft.
- Revise by focusing on the thoroughness of your comparison (whether you covered each subject in detail for each criterion), the appropriateness of your conclusion based on your comparison, your organizational structure, your paragraphing, and the quality of your sentences.
- Edit your draft by correcting any errors that you find.

Before revising, share first drafts with a classmate or two, and ask each other questions about anything that seems unclear in the draft or that you'd like to know more about. Consider your classmates' input as you revise your paper.

Readings

Why Chinese Mothers Are Superior
by Amy Chua

A lot of people wonder how Chinese parents raise such stereotypically successful kids. They wonder what these parents do to produce so many math whizzes and music prodigies, what it's like inside the family, and whether they could do it too. Well, I can tell them, because I've done it. Here are some things my daughters, Sophia and Louisa, were never allowed to do:

- attend a sleepover

- have a playdate

- be in a school play

- complain about not being in a school play

- watch TV or play computer games

- choose their own extracurricular activities

- get any grade less than an A

- not be the No. 1 student in every subject except gym and drama

- play any instrument other than the piano or violin

- not play the piano or violin.

I'm using the term "Chinese mother" loosely. I know some Korean, Indian, Jamaican, Irish and Ghanaian parents who qualify too. Conversely, I know some mothers of Chinese heritage, almost always born in the West, who are not Chinese mothers, by choice or otherwise. I'm also using the term "Western parents" loosely. Western parents come in all varieties.

All the same, even when Western parents think they're being strict, they usually don't come close to being Chinese mothers. For example, my Western friends who consider themselves strict make their children practice their instruments 30 minutes every day. An hour at most. For a Chinese mother, the first hour is the easy part. It's hours two and three that get tough.

When it comes to parenting, the Chinese seem to produce children who display academic excellence, musical mastery and professional success - or so the stereotype goes. Despite our squeamishness about cultural stereotypes, there are tons of studies out there showing marked and quantifiable differences between Chinese and Westerners when it comes to parenting. In one study of 50 Western American mothers and 48 Chinese immigrant mothers, almost 70% of the Western mothers said either that "stressing academic success is not good for children" or that "parents need to foster the idea that learning is fun." By contrast, roughly 0% of the Chinese mothers felt the same way. Instead, the vast majority of the Chinese mothers said that they believe their children can be "the best" students, that "academic achievement reflects successful parenting," and that if children did not excel at school then there was "a problem" and parents "were not doing their job." Other studies indicate that compared to Western parents, Chinese parents spend approximately 10 times as long every day drilling academic activities with their children. By contrast, Western kids are more likely to participate in sports teams.

What Chinese parents understand is that nothing is fun until you're good at it. To get good at anything you have to work, and children on their own never want to work, which is why it is crucial to override their preferences. This often requires fortitude on the part of the parents because the child will resist; things are always hardest at the beginning, which is where Western parents tend to give up. But if done properly, the Chinese strategy produces a virtuous circle. Tenacious practice, practice, practice is crucial for excellence; rote repetition is underrated in America. Once a child starts to excel at something—whether it's math, piano, pitching or ballet—he or she gets praise, admiration and satisfaction. This builds confidence and makes the once not-fun activity fun. This in turn makes it easier for the parent to get the child to work even more.

Chinese parents can get away with things that Western parents can't. Once when I was young—maybe more than once—when I was extremely disrespectful to my mother, my father angrily called me "garbage" in our native Hokkien dialect. It worked really well. I felt terrible and deeply ashamed of what I had done. But it didn't damage my self-esteem or anything like that. I knew exactly how highly he thought of me. I didn't actually think I was worthless or feel like a piece of garbage.

As an adult, I once did the same thing to Sophia, calling her garbage in English when she acted extremely disrespectfully toward me. When I mentioned that I had done this at a dinner party, I was immediately ostracized. One guest named Marcy got so upset she broke down in tears and had to leave early. My friend Susan, the host, tried to rehabilitate me with the remaining guests.

The fact is that Chinese parents can do things that would seem unimaginable—even legally actionable—to Westerners. Chinese mothers can say to their daughters, "Hey fatty—lose some weight." By contrast, Western parents have to tiptoe around the issue, talking in terms of "health" and never ever mentioning the f-word, and their kids still end up in therapy for eating disorders and negative self-image. (I also once heard a Western father toast his adult daughter by calling her "beautiful and incredibly competent." She later told me that made her feel like garbage.)

Chinese parents can order their kids to get straight As. Western parents can only ask their kids to try their best. Chinese parents can say, "You're lazy. All your classmates are getting ahead of you." By contrast, Western parents have to struggle with their own conflicted feelings about achievement, and try to persuade themselves that they're not disappointed about how their kids turned out.

I've thought long and hard about how Chinese parents can get away with what they do. I think there are three big differences between the Chinese and Western parental mind-sets.

First, I've noticed that Western parents are extremely anxious about their children's self-esteem. They worry about how their children will feel if they fail at something, and they constantly try to reassure their children about how good they are notwithstanding a mediocre performance on a test or at a recital. In other words, Western parents are concerned about their children's psyches. Chinese parents aren't. They assume strength, not fragility, and as a result they behave very differently.

For example, if a child comes home with an A-minus on a test, a Western parent will most likely praise the child. The Chinese mother will gasp in horror and ask what went wrong. If the child comes home with a B on the test, some Western parents will still praise the child.

Other Western parents will sit their child down and express disapproval, but they will be careful not to make their child feel inadequate or insecure, and they will not call their child "stupid," "worthless" or "a disgrace." Privately, the Western parents may worry that their child does not test well or have aptitude in the subject or that there is something wrong with the curriculum and possibly the whole school. If the child's grades do not improve, they may eventually schedule a meeting with the school principal to challenge the way the subject is being taught or to call into question the teacher's credentials.

If a Chinese child gets a B—which would never happen—there would first be a screaming, hair-tearing explosion. The devastated Chinese mother would then get dozens, maybe hundreds of practice tests and work through them with her child for as long as it takes to get the grade up to an A.

Chinese parents demand perfect grades because they believe that their child can get them. If their child doesn't get them, the Chinese parent assumes it's because the child didn't work hard enough. That's why the solution to substandard performance is always to excoriate, punish and shame the child. The Chinese parent believes that their child will be strong enough to take the shaming and to improve from it. (And when Chinese kids do excel, there is plenty of ego-inflating parental praise lavished in the privacy of the home.)

Second, Chinese parents believe that their kids owe them everything. The reason for this is a little unclear, but it's probably a combination of Confucian filial piety and the fact that the parents have sacrificed and done so much for their children. (And it's true that Chinese mothers get in the trenches, putting in long grueling hours personally tutoring, training, interrogating and spying on their kids.) Anyway, the understanding is that Chinese children must spend their lives repaying their parents by obeying them and making them proud.

By contrast, I don't think most Westerners have the same view of children being permanently indebted to their parents. My husband, Jed, actually has the opposite view. "Children don't choose their parents," he once said to me. "They don't even choose to be born. It's parents who foist life on their kids, so it's the parents' responsibility to provide for them. Kids don't owe their parents anything. Their duty will be to their own kids." This strikes me as a terrible deal for the Western parent.

Third, Chinese parents believe that they know what is best for their children and therefore override all of their children's own desires and preferences. That's why Chinese daughters can't have boyfriends in high school and why Chinese kids can't go to sleepaway camp. It's also why no Chinese kid would ever dare say to their mother, "I got a part in the school play! I'm Villager Number Six. I'll have to stay after school for rehearsal every day from 3:00 to 7:00, and I'll also need a ride on weekends." God help any Chinese kid who tried that one.

Don't get me wrong: It's not that Chinese parents don't care about their children. Just the opposite. They would give up anything for their children. It's just an entirely different parenting model.

Here's a story in favor of coercion, Chinese-style. Lulu was about 7, still playing two instruments, and working on a piano piece called "The Little White Donkey" by the French composer Jacques Ibert. The piece is really cute—you can just imagine a little donkey ambling along a country road with its master—but it's also incredibly difficult for young players because the two hands have to keep schizophrenically different rhythms.

Lulu couldn't do it. We worked on it nonstop for a week, drilling each of her hands separately, over and over. But whenever we tried putting the hands together, one always morphed into the other, and everything fell apart. Finally, the day before her lesson, Lulu announced in exasperation that she was giving up and stomped off.

"Get back to the piano now," I ordered.

"You can't make me."

"Oh yes, I can."

Back at the piano, Lulu made me pay. She punched, thrashed and kicked. She grabbed the music score and tore it to shreds. I taped the score back together and encased it in a plastic shield so that it could never be destroyed again. Then I hauled Lulu's dollhouse to the car and told her I'd donate it to the Salvation Army piece by piece if she didn't have "The Little White Donkey" perfect by the next day. When Lulu said, "I thought you were going to the Salvation Army, why are you still here?" I threatened her with no lunch, no dinner, no Christmas or Hanukkah presents, no birthday parties for two, three, four years. When she still kept playing it wrong, I told her she was purposely working herself into a frenzy because she was secretly afraid she couldn't do it. I told her to stop being lazy, cowardly, self-indulgent and pathetic.

Jed took me aside. He told me to stop insulting Lulu—which I wasn't even doing, I was just motivating her—and that he didn't think threatening Lulu was helpful. Also, he said, maybe Lulu really just couldn't do the technique—perhaps she didn't have the coordination yet—had I considered that possibility?

"You just don't believe in her," I accused.

"That's ridiculous," Jed said scornfully. "Of course I do."

"Sophia could play the piece when she was this age."

"But Lulu and Sophia are different people," Jed pointed out.

"Oh no, not this," I said, rolling my eyes. "Everyone is special in their special own way," I mimicked sarcastically. "Even losers are special in their own special way. Well don't worry, you don't have to lift a finger. I'm willing to put in as long as it takes, and I'm happy to be the one hated. And you can be the one they adore because you make them pancakes and take them to Yankees games."

I rolled up my sleeves and went back to Lulu. I used every weapon and tactic I could think of. We worked right through dinner into the night, and I wouldn't let Lulu get up, not for water, not even to go to the bathroom. The house became a war zone, and I lost my voice yelling, but still there seemed to be only negative progress, and even I began to have doubts.

Then, out of the blue, Lulu did it. Her hands suddenly came together—her right and left hands each doing their own imperturbable thing—just like that. Lulu realized it the same time I did. I held my breath. She tried it tentatively again. Then she played it more confidently and faster, and still the rhythm held. A moment later, she was beaming.

"Mommy, look—it's easy!" After that, she wanted to play the piece over and over and wouldn't leave the piano. That night, she came to sleep in my bed, and we snuggled and hugged, cracking each other up. When she performed "The Little White Donkey" at a recital a few weeks later, parents came up to me and said, "What a perfect piece for Lulu—it's so spunky and so her."

Even Jed gave me credit for that one. Western parents worry a lot about their children's self-esteem. But as a parent, one of the worst things you can do for your child's self-esteem is to let them give up. On the flip side, there's nothing better for building confidence than learning you can do something you thought you couldn't.

There are all these new books out there portraying Asian mothers as scheming, callous, overdriven people indifferent to their kids' true interests. For their part, many Chinese secretly believe that they care more about their children and are willing to sacrifice much more for them than Westerners, who seem perfectly content to let their children turn out badly. I think it's a misunderstanding on both sides. All decent parents want to do what's best for their children. The Chinese just have a totally different idea of how to do that.

Western parents try to respect their children's individuality, encouraging them to pursue their true passions, supporting their choices, and providing positive reinforcement and a nurturing environment. By contrast, the Chinese believe that the best way to protect their children is by preparing them for the future, letting them see what they're capable of, and arming them with skills, work habits and inner confidence that no one can ever take away.

Questions for Discussion

1. Discuss the differences between the Chinese and Western "mothering" in the essay. Do you find one method superior to the other? Why? What kind of a balance between the two methods might be best?

2. Chua has said that the essay is intended to be satirical. Reading the essay as satire, what is being satirized and what is being praised?

3. Discuss your own parental upbringing regarding school and achievement. How do you feel it affected (affects) your life? How would you raise (or do you raise) your own children?

Wedding Bliss

By Ramon Sandoval

What woman doesn't love attending a wedding? And what man doesn't have to be dragged by the collar, hoping the ceremony is a couple short, sweet "I do's" followed immediately by an open bar? Women and men attend weddings with polar opposite attitudes, offering a glimpse into some basic differences between the genders.

First, women look forward to being married from childhood on, role-playing the prince and princess wedding ceremony with a female friend since no self-respecting 8-year old boy will play the groom. Growing up, boys seldom if ever think about getting married, with more pressing concerns like running, jumping, and smashing into things. Wedding dress magazines take on greater interest as girls grow older. Ever see a tuxedo magazine on a coffee table? For women, attending a wedding is just part of a lifetime interest that men have never shared.

Next, women love to dress, and what better place than for a wedding? Getting a new dress for the wedding is a must. That requires days, perhaps months, of shopping and trying on dresses. But this is not an arduous process for most women; it's fun. After all, if the bride is going to look like a million dollars, no woman wants to look like a buck ninety-nine. And notice whose heads are turning around as soon as the wedding music begins: the women's, craning to see what everyone in the wedding party has on, especially the bride!

Men, on the other hand, couldn't care less about getting "dressed up." They don't shop for a new suit for the wedding. They go into the closet, find the suit they wore to the last wedding two years ago, and hope that the pants still fit. At the end of the night, they couldn't tell you what one man was wearing or what color the maid of honor's dress was. Women love dress up. Men can't wait to unbutton their collars and get those coats off.

Then there are all of those wonderful wedding speeches. The personal vows that brides and grooms often recite, gazing lovingly into each other's eyes, are heartfelt and emotional. The more emotional and romantic the vows, the better that women like them. Men are squirming in their seats and wondering first, why any guy would want to write his own vows and second, whether he's faking the tears. Women are wiping their eyes; men are more than slightly embarrassed.

Of course, later come the maid-of-honor and best-man speeches and often speeches by the fathers of the bride and groom. These tend to go on for some time, particularly if the best man has had a few, and their essential content can be found in every wedding speech ever given. Women hang onto every word like hearing them for the first time. By now, men are bored out of their gourds and ravenously hungry: "Are we ever going to eat dinner?"

Who drinks more at a wedding? That, of course, is easy to answer. Just look at the line at the bar as soon as the wedding ceremony is over. See many women? Men feel that they have earned a few drinks for sitting through yet another grueling wedding. They fortify themselves to get through the next two or three hours. Women have been thoroughly enjoying themselves and have no interest in dulling their senses – "just a glass of white wine please" - as there is still much to look forward to: the mother-son dance, the father-daughter dance, the bride-groom dance, the cake cutting, the garter toss! In anticipation of all of those awkward events, men don't stray too far from the bar or from a buddy to commiserate with.

There is one thing that men and women have in common at weddings: they are both looking at the women. Women don't look at men at weddings; they are barely aware of their existence.

They want to see what all the women are wearing - their dresses, their shoes, their accessories, how they are coiffed. And they want to talk to each other about all of that stuff. Men, in various stages of inebriation, are looking at the women too but not to admire the color or style of their shoes. Guys will be guys.

Unquestionably, women are more romantically wired than men, and the wedding is the romantic zenith of their lives, as close to the prince-and-princess fairytale romances of childhood as they will come. Men have no such romantic grounding, favoring those funny little dwarfs over Snow White and the prince kissing. Yuck! Whether through evolution or upbringing, women are programmed to love weddings and men are programmed to give them a big yawn.

Nothing reveals the differences between women's and men's attitudes towards weddings more than listening to them talk at a wedding – any wedding. Women say stuff to each other like, "The bride looked absolutely radiant." The flowers were gorgeous." "Everything was just perfect." "The wedding cake looked amazing." "How cute was that flower girl!" Men say stuff to each other like, "Can we get a second piece of cake?" "Man, it's hot in here." "Are we still playing golf tomorrow?" "They're watering down the drinks!" Women love to talk about the wedding – every detail - in glowing terms. Men talk about anything but the wedding, other than trying, albeit unsuccessfully, to plot an early escape.

Why then, wedding after wedding, do women drag their men along, and why are men, after some griping, always willing to go? For the same reasons, perhaps, that women go to football games and tractor pulls. In most relationships, the art of compromise means that if you'll let me drag you along to this, then you can drag me along to that. That's the deal: the misery quid pro quo. It's what makes relationships work. An afternoon at the stock car races, an evening at the wedding. Enough romance for everyone.

Questions for Discussion

1. According to the essay, what differences between men and women are revealed through their attitudes towards going to weddings? Do you agree?

2. The essay contends that women's and men's attitudes towards weddings begin in childhood experiences. Do you agree based on your own experience?

3. Do you agree with the essay's assessment about how women and men view weddings? Do you think it applies to the majority of women and men? How do you personally feel about attending weddings?

Colleges Confront a Gender Gap in Student Engagement
by Libby Sander

For decades, women have enrolled in college in greater numbers than men, and, by many measures, have outperformed them in the classroom. But in recent years, as social scientists and student-affairs offices have focused on other differences between the genders, they have documented patterns that could explain how engagement influences student development.

Women tend to study abroad, volunteer in the community, and spend longer hours preparing for class, some experts have noted. Men spend more time playing video games, relaxing, and watching television. But men have more substantive engagements with their professors, are more likely to do undergraduate research, and tend to major in fields that steer them into better-paying jobs. And although women do many of the things that researchers have identified as positive influences on a college experience, they also report higher levels of stress and lower levels of confidence than men.

"It's not necessarily that men are not engaged and that's bad, and women are very engaged and that's good. The real story is much more nuanced than that," says MaryAnn Baenninger, a scholar of gender and cognition and president of the College of Saint Benedict. Girls and boys are treated differently from the day they're born, Ms. Baenninger says, and the disparities playing out on college campuses say as much about how men and women are socialized before they get to campus as they do about what happens once they're there. "They're different," she says. "But there is probably something to be learned from both the women and the men in terms of how they navigate in college."

Looking at student-engagement trends in the aggregate—men and women together—can mask some important differences between the genders, researchers say. Men and women, it turns out, tend to view college differently—and those differences often shape their willingness to get invested in academic pursuits and other activities.

"When left to their own devices in an academic environment, women are excelling," Ms. Baenninger says. But she's noticed that that doesn't always translate into professionally oriented tasks like career fairs, where men often schmooze more readily with prospective employers. The disconnect makes her wonder if the ideal lies somewhere between the women's academic gusto and the men's more laid-back approach. "What good is Phi Beta Kappa if you don't know how to go through that job interview?" she asks. "And suppose you know how to go through that job interview—wouldn't it be great if you had Phi Beta Kappa on your résumé?"

When Demetri Morgan was a student at the University of Florida, he observed that his female friends were active on the campus and excelled academically as a way to assert themselves and find their footing at the large institution. Not so for the guys. "That wasn't how they were defining themselves," he says. "Their social capital came from how many women they were sleeping with or how good they were at sports or what job they were aspiring to."

Today, Mr. Morgan, who graduated in 2011 and is now pursuing a master's degree in higher education and student affairs at Indiana University at Bloomington, sees a conflict between what he has learned from research on student engagement and what he has seen in his own life. "I know plenty of guys who were only involved in the fraternity—and they weren't even really involved in that—and they're doing fine," he says. On many occasions, he'd get deep into discussions with other men about why it was important to get involved. They'd often meet his pleas with a pragmatic comeback: "If I'm here to get a degree, why are you talking to me about involvement?" he recalls them saying. "Sometimes I try to argue back about all the positive outcomes about engagement," he says. Other times, he felt they had a point: "I'm like, 'Yeah, you are here to get a degree.'"

The gender differences tend to become evident early on, usually during students' first year of college, says Jillian Kinzie, associate director at the National Survey of Student Engagement, based at Indiana. At that time, survey results have shown, female students are participating at very different levels than male students are. The women are volunteering in the community, spending more time each week preparing for class, and caring for dependents; male students, meanwhile, spend more time relaxing and playing intramural sports.

Many of those trends equalize over time, Ms. Kinzie says. But she is troubled by other contrasts. Women work harder to meet expectations, spending more time on drafts of papers, say, before turning them in. But men spend more time interacting with faculty on research projects and other serious academic endeavors.

"Women are doing more of the things that are beneficial for them in college," says Linda J. Sax, a professor of higher education at the University of California at Los Angeles and one of the authors of The Gender Gap in College. But the fact that men spend more time on leisure is "not necessarily a bad thing."

The diligence and motivation that many female students display, though, often belies a complicated vision of their own skills and abilities. Women appear to be harsher—or perhaps just more realistic—critics of themselves than men are.

In the 2011 freshman survey, administered each year by UCLA's Higher Education Research Institute, men claimed to be above average at certain skills at rates higher than women—in some cases, much higher. They saw themselves as above average in academic ability, popularity, mathematical ability, physical and emotional health, and in negotiating controversial issues, to name a few. In some cases, the gender disparities were more than 15 percentage points. (Women viewed themselves as "above average" more than men did in only a handful of categories, including artistic ability and "drive to achieve.")

Men and women also respond differently in academic settings. Women may spend more time revising papers and hitting the books, but the impact of academic engagement on students' overall success tends to be stronger for men, Ms. Sax says. "We know that men spend less time studying. But we know that if we can increase their homework time, they're going to reap greater benefits," she says. "There's something about the academic engagement that's a bit more eye-opening for men than for women when it comes to their thinking about their place in the larger world."

Ms. Sax has found that interacting with professors is a powerful influence on how women view themselves. It can cut both ways, though. If women feel that faculty are taking them seriously, they tend to feel better about themselves. But if they think they're not being taken seriously, that impression can undermine their confidence.

Although women outwork and outperform men in college, the gender gap still appears to favor men. They still earn more than women, and they tend to dominate positions of power and prestige in government and the private sector. But Frank Harris III, an associate professor of postsecondary education at San Diego State University who has studied engagement among male college students for a decade, says that such eventual success doesn't let colleges off the hook now. "Men are absolutely still more advantaged in society than are women," Mr. Harris says. "But I don't think that should be a reason for us not to do the work necessary to help men become better people."

The work that colleges do with men in their college years, he believes, could help them make better decisions later in life. But first, colleges need more men to show up.

Questions for Discussion

1. What are some of the major differences cited in the essay for how "engaged" men and women are in college? What do you think the main reasons are for this "gender gap?"

2. How do you reconcile the contradictory contention that women work harder and are more successful in college but that men get the better jobs upon graduation?

3. The essay suggests that women and men approach college differently because they are raised differently. What differences in upbringing would lead to the educational disparities that reveal themselves in college (and before)?

Baseball and Football

by George Carlin

Baseball is different from any other sport, very different. For instance, in most sports you score points or goals; in baseball you score runs. In most sports the ball, or object, is put in play by the offensive team; in baseball the defensive team puts the ball in play, and only the defense is allowed to touch the ball. In fact, in baseball if an offensive player touches the ball intentionally, he's out; sometimes unintentionally, he's out.

Also, in football, basketball, soccer, volleyball, and all sports played with a ball, you score with the ball and in baseball the ball prevents you from scoring.

In most sports the team is run by a coach; in baseball the team is run by a manager. And only in baseball does the manager or coach wear the same clothing the players do. If you'd ever seen Coach John Madden in his Oakland Raiders uniform, you'd know the reason for this custom.

Now, I've mentioned football. Baseball and football are the two most popular spectator sports in this country. And as such, it seems they ought to be able to tell us something about ourselves and our values. For that reason, I enjoy comparing the two:

Baseball is a nineteenth-century pastoral game.
Football is a twentieth-century technological struggle.

Baseball is played on a diamond, in a park. The baseball park!
Football is played on a gridiron, in a stadium, sometimes called Soldier Field or War Memorial Stadium.

Baseball begins in the spring, the season of new life.
Football begins in the fall, when everything is dying.

In football you wear a helmet.
In baseball you wear a cap.

Football is concerned with downs - what down is it?
Baseball is concerned with ups - who's up?

In football you receive a penalty.
In baseball you make an error.

In football the specialist comes in to kick.
In baseball the specialist comes in to relieve somebody.

Football has hitting, clipping, spearing, piling on, personal fouls, late hitting and unnecessary roughness.
Baseball has the sacrifice.

Football is played in any kind of weather: rain, snow, sleet, hail, fog...
In baseball, if it rains, we don't go out to play.

Baseball has the seventh inning stretch.
Football has the two minute warning.

Baseball has no time limit: we don't know when it's going to end - might have extra innings.
Football is rigidly timed, and it will end even if we've got to go to sudden death.

In baseball, during the game, in the stands, there's kind of a picnic feeling; emotions may run high or low, but there's not too much unpleasantness.
In football, during the game in the stands, you can be sure that at least twenty-seven times you're capable of taking the life of a fellow human being.

And finally, the objectives of the two games are completely different:

In football the object is for the quarterback, also known as the field general, to be on target with his aerial assault, riddling the defense by hitting his receivers with deadly accuracy in spite of the blitz, even if he has to use the shotgun. With short bullet passes and long bombs, he marches his troops into enemy territory, balancing this aerial assault with a sustained ground attack that punches holes in the forward wall of the enemy's defensive line.

In baseball the object is to go home! And to be safe! - I hope I'll be safe at home!

Questions for Discussion

1. Baseball and Football" is a classic comic routine by comedian George Carlin. Based on his comparison, which sport do you think he favors and why?

2. Look at the individual comparisons that Carlin makes. Which do you find most amusing and why?

3. Carlin compares football to war by using a number of military terms to describe the game. Do you agree that football has a war-like quality? Which sport do you favor?

Unit Seven
Discoveries

Before writing a particular essay or article, writers often need to learn more about their subject. Most of us, for example, would need to do some research on a subject such as global warming before we could write about it knowledgeably.

Many of the subjects that interest us as writers go beyond our personal experience and knowledge, so the first step in preparing to write on a particular subject may be to find out more about it. We may have read, for example, that the fighting in Iraq involves Sunni and Shiite Muslims, members of Al Quaida, foreign insurgents, Iraqi soldiers, and American soldiers. However, exactly who is fighting whom and for what reasons is a complex subject that would require considerable research.

As writers, we research a particular topic to learn more about it, to evaluate different viewpoints on the subject, to help formulate our own viewpoint, and to expand our knowledge of the world around us. A wide range of topics may require some research: comparing models of hybrid cars, evaluating the effects of sex education on students' behavior, or analyzing the impact of a political candidate's race on voters.

In this final unit, you write on a topic that will require you to do some research. The purpose of the assignment is for you to learn to research a topic effectively, to write a research-oriented paper, to express and support your viewpoint based on your research, and to apply everything you have learned to writing an effective paper. In addition, this assignment will help prepare you for future research writing.

In this unit, you are introduced to the basic elements of research writing: investigating several sources, incorporating research material into your paper, acknowledging the sources as you use them, quoting some sources and paraphrasing others, formulating a thesis statement that expresses your viewpoint and is supported by your research, and maintaining your writer's voice throughout the paper.

All of this may sound more daunting than it actually is. As you research your topic, you compile the information that forms the core of your paper. Once your research is completed, the remaining task is to incorporate the material into your paper in a way that distinguishes the research material from your own ideas and that supports your thesis. At this point in the course, you are up to the task.

Prewriting

The prewriting emphasis for a research-oriented paper is on the research: finding sources for your topic, reading the material, and taking notes on anything you may include in your paper. Once you have completed the research, you are ready to evaluate the information and formulate a viewpoint on the topic. Your first task, of course, is to select a topic to research.

Selecting A Topic

To select a topic for your research-oriented paper, follow these guidelines.

1. Select a topic that you are interested in and would like to know more about.

2. Select a topic that you can research in the library and on the Internet.

3. Select a topic that you believe some reading audience would like to know more about. Steer away from traditional topics -abortion, child abuse, legalization of marijuana -that students frequently write about.

4. Select a topic that is limited enough to cover in a three-five page paper. For example, while the general topic of "steroid use among athletes" could fill a book, the more limited topic of "steroid use among high school football players" could be a manageable subject for a paper.

5. Select a topic that other classmates aren't writing about.

The following sample topics show the range of writing possibilities.

Should there be college football playoffs?	High cost of a college education
Steroids in junior high school	Private vs. public grade schools
Is loud rock music harmful to hearing?	Should minors be tried as adults?
The dangers of global warming	Bullying in the schools
The best hybrid car available	TV's effects on children
Do children grow up too fast?	Pre-school: key to success?
Childhood obesity: a solvable problem	Is there any diet that really works?

Prewriting Activity 7.1

Select a topic for your research paper following the guidelines presented. Consider a couple different topics in case you can't find adequate research sources for one or the other. Make sure that you decide upon a specific enough topic for your research paper. For example, the sample topic "TV's Effect on Children" is overly broad for a limited research paper. However, a more specific topic such as "The Effect of TV violence on aggressive children" may work well. You may want to check with your instructor on the specificity of your proposed topic before moving forward.

Sample Topic:

Gang violence is a big issue in our community. You read about gang-related killings and drive-by shootings in the newspaper frequently. The situation seems to getting worse everywhere, no matter how much police try to crack down. I think it's worth investigating and perhaps writing about.

Tentative topic:

Researching Your Topic

A good research paper is based on reliable information from credible sources. For example, if you wanted to know which car performed better, the Honda Accord or Toyota Camry, you wouldn't get the most objective information from an advertising brochure at a Honda or Toyota dealership. Instead, you would be better off reading consumer magazines that do road testing on comparable vehicles and analyze the results.

Using credible research sources is one of several considerations when researching a topic. The following suggestions will help you find the best sources and harvest the most relevant information.

Finding Sources

1. Your college librarian can be of great help. When in doubt, seek out a librarian, tell him or her the topic you are researching, and ask the best way to proceed.

2. Most colleges index their books by topic on computers. The computers have simple instructions for entering the name of your topic and finding what books are available.

3. Many colleges have computer programs that locate information on topics in periodicals or newspapers, with the articles found on line. Ask your librarians about programs such as Proquest, Lexis Nexus, SIRS, and GALE, and learn how to access them on the library computers to research your topic.

4. You may find information on your topic on the Internet by using a topic search engine such as Google or Yahoo. When you find information on line, print the articles so that you can read them at your leisure, highlight important parts, and take notes.

5. Use credible sources for your research: articles from respected periodicals or newspapers, books from experts, and studies from well-known journals.

Taking Research Notes

1. Make sure to write down the following information for each source that you use to reference in your paper.

Book:	name of author, title of book, publishing company, publishing location, date of publication.
Periodical:	author (if given), title of article, title of periodical, volume number, date of publication, page numbers of article.
Newspaper:	author (if given), title of article, title of newspaper, volume/edition number, date of publication, page number(s) of article.
Interview:	name of interviewee, title of interviewee (medical doctor, marine biologist, county health inspector), date of interview.
Online article:	author (if given), title of article, title of periodical or newspaper, volume/edition number, date of publication, page numbers (if available), address: http://www.Newsweek.com.
From a website:	author (if given), title of article, name of organization providing article (Cancer Foundation, Bureau of Statistics), name of website, date of publication, page numbers, address: http://www.CancerFoundation.com.

2. Take notes from each source that contains relevant information on your topic, including anything that you might use in your paper. Write down the exact words from the article or book so that you can quote from them in your paper. Keep information from different sources separate so that you can identify each source as you use it in your writing. Use lined note cards for your note-taking with the source identified at the top of each card.

3. Note the date of each article or book you find, and use the most recent information you can find. For example, statistics on teenage pregnancy from articles in the early 1990's compared to the 2000's may be quite different, and you want the most updated findings.

4. Since you are writing a limited research paper of three-five pages, you aren't expected to investigate dozens of sources. However, you should use information from at least four or five different sources in your paper. To find that many good sources, you may have to research at least ten since they won't all contain relevant or current information.

5. As you read through various articles or books, consider what you want to include in your paper. For example, if your topic is later-life pregnancies, you may want to know exactly what "later life" means, the risks for the woman and for the baby, how the risks might be minimized, what doctors recommend regarding such pregnancies, and how common they are. You would look for information in those areas as you read through your research materials.

If you are writing on gang violence, you may want to know how pervasive gang activity is, who comprises the gangs and where they live, what kinds of violence are associated with gangs, what the effects are, and how gang violence can be reduced. You would look for sources containing such information.

Prewriting Activity 7.2

Following the research suggestions provided, research your topic using library sources, the Internet, and experts on your subject, if available. Find at least five good sources containing information you can use in your paper. Make copies of articles and check out books.

As you read, take notes on any information that you might use in your paper, keeping material from each source separate, and compile enough information for a three-five page double-spaced paper. Keep in mind what you want to know about your topic, and try to find information on each aspect.

Student sample (notes from one of five sources)

Topic: Gang Violence

Things to find out:

How big of a problem is gang violence in the country?
Who joins gangs and why do they join?
What kind of violent activity are gangs involved in?
What are the effects of the violence, and who is affected?
What can be done to reduce gang violence?

Research source #1:

Grabianowski, Ed. "How Street Gangs Work," HowStuffWorks, p. 1, http://people. howstuffworks.com/street-gang.htm

Research notes from "How Street Gangs Work:"

Gang violence is a problem in every major city in the United States and membership is on the rise. According to the Department of Justice's 2005 National Gang Threat Assessment, there are at least 21,500 gangs and more than 731,000 active gang members. While gangs are less prevalent in rural areas, in major cities, gang violence is responsible for roughly half of all homicides. Gangs are also becoming more savvy, using computers and other technology to commit crimes.

Thesis, Audience, and Purpose

As you read through your research material, you will undoubtedly form opinions about your topic that will help you decide on a thesis for your paper, the best reading audience, and a purpose for writing to them. Depending on your topic, you may form opinions on its seriousness or importance, its positive or negative effects, the people who most need to be aware of it, why they should be aware of it, and the research information that you most want to share with them.

To help you decide on a thesis, an audience, and a purpose for your paper, consider the following suggestions.

Thesis

Your thesis statement expresses the main conclusion that you have reached on your topic. This viewpoint will be supported by your research material as it is presented in your paper. It represents your opinion on the topic that you formed from reading and analyzing the research material, and it unifies your paper by giving you something definite to support throughout the essay.

The follow thesis statements express the conclusions that writers reached on a variety of topics based on their research findings.

1. Breast feeding is the preferred way to nourish your baby, but if you are unable to breast feed, bottle feeding your baby will have no harmful effects.

2. We will continue to lose American's "war on drugs" unless we greatly reduce the demand for drugs through education and drug prevention programs.

3. The positive results of liposuction surgery far outweigh the risks.

4. While most teenagers may be unaffected by violent video games, it takes just one troubled teenager exposed to video game violence to commit a Columbine-like massacre.

5. Based on results from other countries, the legalization of drugs is not the answer to America's drug problem

6. While AIDS in America is no longer a front page story, it is still a danger to anyone who takes sexual risks.

Audience

For your primary reading audience, consider who would benefit most from reading your paper: Teenagers? Parents with children? Older adults? Women? African-Americans or Asians? Educators? College students? The general population? Select a particular audience that would be most interested in your topic and most likely to benefit from reading about it.

The following are examples of primary reading audiences for different research papers.

Topic: Effects of global warming on wildlife
Thesis: Global warming is changing the environment of many animal species and
           endangering their existence.
Audience: general population

Topic: College football playoffs
Thesis: It is time that football follows other collegiate sports and has a national championship
           playoff system.
Audience: NCAA governing body that determines post-season play for football

Topic: Loud rock music
Thesis: Rock music played at high decibels can permanently damage the hearing of teenagers.

Audience: Teenagers who listen to rock music

Topic: Health insurance for children
Thesis: Millions of American children have no health insurance and are dangerously at risk.
Audience: general public

Purpose

Considering your thesis and your audience, what is the purpose of your paper? What do you want people to think or do as a result of reading it? The following purposes are for papers generated from the six thesis statements in the preceding "Thesis" section.

1.   To educate women on the effects of breast feeding and bottle feeding, and to help them make an informed choice when they have a baby.

2.   To get readers to support more legislation and programs that educate people to the dangers of drugs, similar to the education programs that have reduced smoking in America.

3.   To educate people on the benefits and risks of liposuction surgery, and recommend it as a viable alternative for chronically obese people.

4.   To educate everyone on the effects of violent video games on troubled teenagers, and to get the government to regulate their sale and use in some way.

5.   To reach anyone who thinks that drug legalization would be a positive step and convince them that it would do more harm than good.

6.   To educate teens and young adults on the dangers of AIDS, the kinds of sexual activity that lead to infection, and what they can do to eliminate the risk.

Prewriting Activity 7.3
Based on your topic, your research findings, and the suggestions presented in the text, decide on a thesis statement, audience, and purpose for your paper.

Sample topic: Gang Violence
Thesis: Gang violence is a plague upon America that must be eliminated.
Audience: General public, local city council
Purpose: To get the public to understand the serious effects of gang violence and to get the city to do something about it.

Tentative thesis:

Audience:

Purpose:

First Drafts

Now that you have selected a topic, done considerable research, and decided on a thesis, audience, and purpose for your paper, you are ready to learn more about writing a research paper. The following sections on "Source Acknowledgment," "Paraphrasing, Quoting, and Responding," and "Works Cited" will prepare you to write your first draft.

Parenthetical References

Any time that you incorporate research material into a paper, you acknowledge its source. Source references let readers know where the material came from, lending it credibility and distinguishing it from your own ideas and responses. When a writer correctly acknowledges sources, readers always know when the information is "borrowed" from research and when it comes from the writer herself.

Following the MLA format, you will use parenthetical references in your research paper to acknowledge sources. More complete bibliographical information for each source will appear in the "Works Cited" section at the end of the paper. To reference your sources correctly, follow these guidelines:

1. **Include a parenthetical reference at the end of the research material to acknowledge your source.**

   a. Include the author's last name and the page number of the material, if available:

   Hand guns cause over 90% of homicides in the U.S. (Witherow 11).

   b. If the author is anonymous, include the title of the article and page number.

   Animals continue to evolve to survive in changing environments ("How Animals Evolve" 8-9).

   Children raised in threatening environments often become more timid, less trusting adults ("The Psychology of Fear" 131).

   c. If page numbers aren't available, as with some online articles, include the author's name, or if anonymous, the title of the article:

   In some teen sub-cultures, there is no stigma attached to becoming pregnant ("Proud, Pregnant Teens").

   Proponents of universal health care insist that the requirement for all Americans to have health insurance is essential (Vasquez).

   d. If the research material includes several consecutive sentences, put the parenthetical reference at the end of the last sentence:

   The housing bubble that burst in 2008 and led to the nation-wide recession also had an upside. Housing prices had become ridiculously high, and the recession created a "correction" which dropped housing values dramatically. While this didn't please current homeowners, it allowed millions of future home buyers into the market that could have never afforded the higher prices (Corminger 32).

2. While source introductions aren't required along with parenthetical references, they can still be used, particularly if the source lends credibility to the material (e.g. a renown expert, an esteemed periodical, an influential study).

    a. If you include the author in the source introduction, put only the page number of the article or book in parentheses:

        According to Harvard historian Dr. Evan Grayson, accounts of historical events are often colored by the perspective of the writer (32).

    b. If the author is anonymous and you include the title of the article or book in the source introduction, put only the page number in parentheses:

        According to the recent *Times* article "The Fast-Fading Euro," the European monetary system is in free-fall due to the debt crisis in Greece and Portugal (17).

    c. If you introduce the author or title of the article in the source introduction and there is no page number (e.g. online article), do not include a parenthetical reference:

        Children's book author Gwendolyn Mathers believes that young children want to read books that deal with real-life problems.

    d. If you reference a particular study, experiment, or poll found in an article or book, provide a parenthetical reference that includes the author of the article or book, or, if anonymous, the title of the article or book and the page number:

        An experiment conducted by the Mayo Research Clinic revealed that mice who are given chemotherapy for cancer eventually build a resistance to the treatment (Wright 12-13).

    e. Always provide a source introduction as well as a parenthetical reference when you quote from a source:

        According to marine biologist Glenda Wu, "The damage that man has done to the marine ecosystem cannot be undone in a few short years," (3).

        As noted in the Art First 2012 journal, "Art is considered a mainstay in the educational curriculum of many countries and a supplemental diversion in U.S. education," (18).

Drafting Activity 7.4
For practice using parenthetical references, write a sentence that includes a parenthetical reference for each of the following pieces of research material based on the source information provided. *Paraphrase* the material – put it into your own words - unless instructed to use it as a quotation. You will also be asked to include a source introduction for some sentences.

Examples:
Georgia was first settled by former English convicts who worked for years as indentured servants to gain their freedom.
By George Strait, "Our Earliest Settlers," page 3

(Do not include source introduction)

English prisoners were the first settlers of Georgia, working for years as indentured servants before gaining their freedom (Strait 3)

Urban renewal projects have resulted in remarkable turnarounds for blighted urban areas long resistant to improvement.
Mercy Montanez, *Solutions to Urban Decay*, page 36

(Include source introduction)

In her recent book *Solutions to Urban Decay*, Mary Montanez says that long-time areas of urban blight have benefitted greatly from urban renewal projects (36).

1. U.S. dependence on foreign oil has contributed to our government coddling Middle Eastern dictators intolerant of democratic principles.
    Molly Kinkcaid, *U.S. Middle Eastern Policy*, page 112

    (Do not include source introduction)

2. While the majority of college football, basketball, and baseball players aspire to a career in the professional ranks, only a small minority ever make it.
    "Making the Grade: Educating Our College Athletes" (online article, no page numbers, anonymous author)

    (Do not include source introduction)

3. Refined white sugar is a major culprit in the problem of childhood obesity.
    Rachel Marquez, nutritionist, "Obesity in Children," *Today* magazine, page 14

    (Include source introduction)

4. America's thirty-year "War on Drugs" has not produced the desired effects. Drug use in the

U.S. is higher today than when the "war" began, and the flow of illicit drugs into the country has not decreased. Clearly a different approach needs to be tried to alter the drug-taking habit of millions of Americans.

Clarence Collins, "End the Drug War," *Time* magazine, page 47

(Do not include source introduction)

5. Pet owners continue to allow their pets to breed while millions of unwanted dogs and cats are euthanized annually in animal shelters.

Mark Kato, "The Silent Epidemic of Unwanted Animals," *The Atlantic*, page 12

(Use as a quotation, which requires a source introduction)

Paraphrasing, Quoting, and Responding

A research paper typically contains three kinds of writing: paraphrased material from the sources, quotations from the sources, and your own ideas and responses, which include most of the opening and concluding thoughts, the thesis statement, and your responses to the research material: opinions formed, conclusions drawn, and observations made. As your audience reads your paper, they should always know when you are paraphrasing, when you are quoting, and when you are commenting or responding.

The following guidelines will help you incorporate paraphrasing, quoting, and your own ideas effectively in your paper.

Paraphrasing

As you write your draft, you *paraphrase* – put into your own words – most of the research information that you use. For example, in a paper on breast implants, you could retain some key words in the original text – e.g. *breast implants, silicone and saline implants, post-surgical scarring* – since you can't use a synonym for every word in an article, but present most of the information in your own words. The purpose of paraphrasing is to include research material in your paper while maintaining your own voice by using your wording. You don't want your paper to sound like a compilation of writing from different authors.

The following paraphrased material shows the difference between the source material and the paraphrased version. Notice that certain key words are maintained and that the meaning of the original material is unchanged although the paraphrased wording is significantly different.

Source Material

Verbal abuse can be as detrimental to a child as physical abuse. When a parent constantly berates a child, criticizes him for the slightest mistake, never compliments or praises him, and tells him that he is worthless or will amount to nothing, that child will not only have a low opinion of himself, he will often grow up sullen and unresponsive, unable to find any good in others or respond normally to positive comments or kind behavior.

Wilson, Loretta. "What We Say to Children," *Psychology Digest*, Spring, 2000, 18.

Paraphrased

According to psychologist Loretta Wilson, verbal abuse can harm a child just as much as physical abuse. When a parent always puts a child down, scolds him for the least error, never compliments him for anything, and says that he is no good and will never accomplish anything, when he grows up, he will often be silent and gloomy, unable to respond to people or see the goodness in others or react to praise or kindness (Wilson 18).

So that readers can always distinguish between paraphrasing and your own comments, make sure that you always provide a source reference for the paraphrased material.

Quotations

When you quote from a source, you use the exact words from the article or book and begin and end the quote with quotation marks (" "). You typically use a quotation instead of paraphrasing when you are capturing a particularly striking or critical piece of information, and the exact source wording would have the greatest impact. Include both a source introduction and a page reference at the end of all quotes.

Examples:

According to Dr. Peg McDermott, "Liposuction surgery is not so much for weight loss as it is for resculpturing your body," (McDermott 23).

"Our ocean waters are slowly rising," bemoans oceanographer Adam Clayton, "and long-term effects could include the flooding of coastal areas such as Manhattan," (Clayton 12).

Quotations from your source material should be used sparingly and effectively to make important points. Most of your source material should be paraphrased in your paper in order to maintain your own voice.

Responding

The majority of the paper should be in your own words by incorporating paraphrased research material and providing your own comments. When you are commenting yourself, of course, there are no source references, so readers will know when they are reading your own thoughts.

Include your own thoughts in the opening and conclusion so that readers will know that you not only have researched your paper but understood the material, analyzed it carefully, and formed your own judgments. In the middle paragraphs, where you introduce most of your research material, provide your own comments and responses to the material so that readers feel your presence throughout the paper and understand that you are using the research material for your own purposes.

Drafting Activity 7.5

For practice paraphrasing research material, paraphrase the following paragraph by putting it into your own words and maintaining the original meaning. Begin the paragraph with a source acknowledgment, and reference the source and page number in parentheses at the end of the paraphrase.

Source Material

Dieting fails most people because they don't actually change their eating habits. They take in less food for a period of weeks or months, so they generally lose some weight. However, typically, they soon revert to their old eating habits, and the weight reappears or sometimes even increases. Losing weight for good means changing your eating lifestyle permanently: what you eat, how much you eat, how you eat, and how often you eat. It requires tremendous will-power, perhaps equal to that of quitting smoking.

Nagata, Emily. *Why Dieting Fails*, Hammond, Massachusetts: Pembroke Publishing, 1999, 132.

Drafting Activity 7.6

Do three things with the following source paragraph: paraphrase the majority of the material, include a quote from the paragraph, and comment on the information. In addition, provide source introductions and ending source and page references in parentheses to indicate when you are paraphrasing, quoting, and commenting.

Example:

Source material

Significantly more deaths in the home are caused by gun-related accidents than by murdering intruders. One month last year in a single rural county, two boys were killed in gun accidents. One boy killed his friend, pointing his father's gun at the boy and pulling the trigger of an "unloaded" gun. Another younger boy killed himself while playing with his father's gun that he found in an open bedroom drawer. In both cases, fathers were ultimately responsible for the deaths of youngsters whom they were trying to "protect" against would-be intruders. Such fatalities are far from unusual, yet handgun proponents sweep them under the carpet like so much dust.

Elmore, Ellen. "Household Deaths," *Children's Journal*, 3 March 2002, 20-21

Source material paraphrased, quoted, and commented on:

Apparently the hand guns in American homes are more cause for a family's concern than the gun of a possible intruder. According to Ellen Elmore in an article in *Children's Journal*, more fatalities are caused by home gun accidents than by intruders who kill (Elmore 20.) Two deadly accidents occurred in the same rural county in one month. In one, a boy killed his friend with his father's gun that he thought was unloaded, and in the other, a younger boy playing with his father's gun he found in a bedroom drawer shot himself to death. In trying to protect their families against violence, the fathers unwittingly were responsible for the deaths of the boys. Although such accidents occur too frequently, says Elmore, "Handgun proponents sweep them under the carpet like so much dust," (Elmore 21). While such accidents are certainly horrible, what goes unsaid are the number of potential violent acts that may never occur because intruders don't risk going into homes where there may be guns. Is removing the guns from homes the answer, or stricter gun safety laws and prosecution for people who leave guns where children may get to them?

Exercise:

Later-life Pregnancies

While many women today are waiting longer to have children, they need to consider the risks associated with later-life pregnancies. One of the greater risks for women waiting until their mid-to-late thirties is possible birth defects in the baby. Females are born with all of the reproductive eggs they will need in their lifetime to conceive children. However, the older a woman gets, the older her eggs become. The older eggs sometimes develop problems solely due to their age, and one of the problems is the possibility of a baby being born with Down's Syndrome, which results in a combination of mental retardation and physical abnormalities. While the risk of a twenty-five year-old woman having a baby with Down's Syndrome is 1 in 1,250, the risk for a thirty-five year old is 1 in 378, and for a forty-five year old, 1 in 30.

"Pregnancy Risks for Older Women," *Women's Health*, February 2000, 6.

Source material paraphrased, quoted, and commented on:

Works Cited

At the end of your paper, you provide a Works Cited section that lists alphabetically all of the sources that you used in the paper: books, magazines, periodicals, journals, newspapers, or interviews. The purpose of the Works Cited section is for readers to see the sources that you used for your paper and the breadth of research that you did, and to be able to find the books, magazines, or newspapers if they want to read further on the topic.

For the Works Cited section, include the following information for each source in the order and form presented. Notice that a second line or third line is indented five spaces.

book: author (last name, first name). *title of book*. publishing location: publisher, date of publication. Medium of publication (print).

Hinds, Clarence. *The Last Hour*. Cambridge: Camden Press, 1999. Print.

article: (periodical or newspaper): author. "title of article." *Name of periodical or newspaper*, date of publication: pages. medium of publication (print).

Fleming, Nancy. "Blue Skies Behind Us." *Harper's*, 4 August 2001: 12-13. Print.

Rodriguez, Steven. "Reef Destruction in Gulf." *Tampa Bay Register*, 6 September 2. Print.

article online: author (if provided). "Title of Article." *name of website* (date of publication): page(s) (if available). medium of publication (Web). date you accessed website article. Note: insert the abbreviations n.d. if no publication date is provided and n.pag. if no page number(s) is provided.

Dobbs, Dr. Stanley. "Treatment for Squamous Cell Cancer." *International Cancer Foundation* (4 June 2009): n. pag. Web. 8 August 2014.

Drafting Activity 7.7

Go to the "Works Cited" section at the end of the draft of "Gang Violence" on page 240 to see the writer's sources and how they are listed.

Drafting Activity 7.8

Write the first draft of your research-oriented paper with the following guidelines in mind. You may want to read the following sample draft before writing your draft.

Drafting Guidelines

1. Introduce your topic in the opening, create interest for readers, and include your thesis statement.

2. Present your research findings in the middle paragraphs in support of your thesis statement. Cover the main aspects of your topic in separate paragraphs, each beginning with a topic sentence expressing the main idea of the paragraph.

3. Conclude your paper in a manner that reinforces your thesis statement and emphasizes the purpose of the paper. Keep your readers in mind and leave them with something to consider.

4. Organize your middle paragraphs to present your research findings in the most effective order.

5. As the writer, respond to the research material as you write. Your comments throughout the paper – opinions, conclusions, thoughts, feelings -put you in control of the paper, and show that you are incorporating the research material for your own writing purposes. Your responses should also reinforce your thesis statement in some manner.

6. Remember to paraphrase most of the research information, use an occasional striking quote, and provide source acknowledgments for all research material.

7. Conclude your paper with a "Works Cited" section listing alphabetically the sources that you used in your paper.

Sample Draft

Gang Violence

Gang violence brought tragedy in May of 2009. Police say that a group of gang members walked up behind unsuspecting 25 year-old C.J. Davis as he was on his way to the market, and opened fire on him with an assault rifle. While speeding away from the scene with police in pursuit, the Cadillac carrying the gang members slammed into another car at an intersection, killing the other driver instantly. The impact sent the vehicles spinning out of control, striking and killing a pedestrian as well. While three of the gang members have since been apprehended, a fourth is still at large ("How Gang Violence Affects Communities").

This senseless tragedy reveals how far-reaching the consequences of gang-related violence can be to a community, in this case leaving three families devastated. Not only are gang members and their families affected by violence, but also innocent bystanders, who are often the victims of drive-by shootings ("Street Gangs: A Dead End for Our Children"). Residents of thousands of neighborhoods across the country live in constant fear because of violent gang activity. Children grow up in territorial battle zones, often suffering from psychological trauma similar to children living in war-torn countries ("The Effects of Community Violence on Children and Adolescents"). Community members want to take their neighborhoods back and rid them of gang violence and their dire effects, but only a long-term, multi-pronged solution involving police, schools, community services, and neighborhood residents will provide a lasting effect.

Gang violence is a problem in every major city in the United States and membership is on the rise. Department of Justice statistics reveal that there are at least 21,500 gangs and 770,000 active gang members. According to gang expert Ed Grabianowski, "In major cities, gang violence is responsible for roughly half of all homicides and the majority of crimes against property," (Grabianowski, "How Street Gangs Work" 1). Gangs also are on the increase in rural and suburban areas of the country as gang members flee increasing law enforcement pressure in urban areas or seek more lucrative drug markets ("Background on Gang Violence").

According to Grabianowski, 47% of gang members are Hispanic and 37% black, almost all living in the lower socio-economic inner cities across the country. Poverty is a driving force behind gang membership, with many gang members viewing drug dealing and theft as the only ways of making money and escaping poverty. Peer pressure also drives youths into gangs, with older gang members recruiting younger teens. Neighborhood gangs also provide an outlet for bored teens who have nothing to do. Finally, gang members often come from troubled homes with parents who may be addicts, gang members themselves, or simply non-responsive. A neighborhood gang gives teens a sense of belonging and the only real "family" they may have (Grabianowski 1).

According to the article "Background on Ground Violence," gang violence stems from a variety of causes. Gangs stake out their territory and shoot members from other gangs who stray onto it, resulting in retaliatory shootings. Large street gangs employ violence to control and expand drug distribution activities, targeting rival gangs and dealers who neglect or refuse to pay extortion fees. Members also use violence to ensure that members adhere to the gang's code of conduct or to prevent a member from leaving. Authorities throughout the country report that gangs are responsible for most of the violent crime in major U.S. cities. Gangs engage in an array of criminal activities including assault, drive-by shooting, extortion, homicide, identification fraud, money laundering, prostitution operations, robbery, and weapons trafficking ("Background on Gang Violence"). The capability for violence is increasing because gangs are able to pay for more expensive weapons, including military-grade automatic weapons such as AK-47 rifles ("Drugs and Latin Gangs").

The effects of gang violence on individuals, neighborhoods, and communities is devastating. In gang-infested neighborhoods, adults and children live in daily fear, never knowing if the next gun shot might smash through their living room window or hit a friend or relative down the street. Families alter normal living patterns by staying off the streets at night and staying in their houses most of the time that they are home. Practically everyone in the neighborhood knows of a friend, acquaintance, or relative who has been killed in a gang-related shooting. Attending tearful funerals of teenage boys and girls is a common occurrence.

Gang membership extracts a terrible toll from the lives of all who come in contact with the members. Parents and relatives of gang members live in double fear, one for their family's safety and that of their gang-related child, who is 60 times more likely to be killed than a non-gang member ("Street Gangs: A Dead End for Our Children"). Tragically, the inevitable way that many gang members eventually leave a gang is in a body bag (Grabionowski 1).

According to Dr. Carole Goguen, Director of the Traumatic Stress Treatment Center, "Many children and adolescents living in violence-riddled neighborhoods suffer from PTSD, Posttraumatic Stress Disorder," (Goguen, "The Effects of Community Violence on Children and Adolescents"). Children with PTSD display disorganized or agitated behavior and have nightmares that may include monsters. They may become withdrawn, fearful, or aggressive, and they may have difficulty paying attention. They may regress to earlier behaviors such as sucking their thumbs and bed-wetting, and they may develop separation anxiety. They may also engage in play that compulsively reenacts the violence (Goguen)

Adolescents with PTSD also experience nightmares and intrusive thoughts about the trauma. They can become depressed, angry, distrustful, fearful, and alienated, and they may feel betrayed. Many do not feel they have a future and believe that they will not reach adulthood. This is especially common among adolescents who are chronically exposed to neighborhood violence. Other trauma-related reactions can include impaired self-esteem, learning difficulties, and acting out or risk taking behaviors such as running away, drug or alcohol use, suicide attempts, and inappropriate sexual activities (Goguen). In short, exposure to a violence-riddled environment can have severe long-term effects on children and adolescents that children in non-violent environments never experience.

Clearly, the disastrous effects of gang violence on millions of America's children and adults cry out for a solution to rid communities of such violence and free people to live normal, healthy lives. Of course, this is much easier said than done as witnessed by the lack of success that cities have had in curbing the problem. Police crackdowns involving sweeps of gang-infested areas to confiscate weapons and arrest wanted gang members results in a short-term reduction in violence. However, such crackdowns don't get at the root problems of gang violence: poverty, lack of positive outlets for youth, the demand for illicit drugs.

While police presence is vital in keeping neighborhoods safer, a more successful long-term approach requires multiple tactics that all boil down to one thing: give people something to live for other than a gang. This can include helping at-risk youth or current gang members find decent jobs or obtain an education. Block clubs and community centers bring the non-gang members, the majority of people, together to clean and maintain their streets, get rid of graffiti and otherwise show pride in where they live. Community events such as dances, football games and game nights give youth something to do other than hang out on porches with gang members. If held outdoors, they make those areas less attractive for gang activity because of all the non-gang members around (Grabianowski 4).

A preferred method of gang suppression today is the Department of Justice's "Weed and Seed" program. This combines police enforcement (**weeding** out the worst gang members) with community activism and economic opportunities (**seeding** the neighborhood with the means to overcome negative conditions). More than 3,000 Weed and Seed programs are active in the United States. Each site can receive up to $1 million to help fund law enforcement, community policing, prevention, intervention, and treatment, and neighborhood restoration (Grabianowski 4).

One of the most influential areas of a child or young adult's life is at schools. According to the article "Gang Violence as a Social Problem," "Providing more funding for schools specifically for anti-gang programs and including anti-gang messages in the curriculum is essential in creating a non-violent atmosphere." Funding for anti-gang violence is not the only way to promote it in schools. Strict rules of on-campus activity and truancy prevention will create an educational culture that will hopefully leak into students' lives outside school. These same messages and programs should also be reinforced in the communities outside of school. Developing after school youth programs gives children alternative options to gang affiliation ("Gang Violence as a Social Problem").

Preventing the recruitment of new gang members is a solution for the future, but other measures must be taken to curb the violence now. Legislation is the voice that is the most used when we talk about attempts to solve gang violence. We look to legislation and to government officials that have the authority to help protect us from gang violence. Establishing new laws that increase the severity of punishments for gang related violence is essential. Any act of criminality related to gangs should automatically have an increased sentence. Additionally, the recruitment of new members to gangs should have a harsh penalty. Recruiting anybody should be punishable by imprisonment, and recruiting a minor should have an increase in the sentencing ("Gang Violence as a Social Problem").

Clearly, any long-term solution to eradicating gang violence includes police enforcement, education, jobs, activity centers, and neighborhood involvement. However, resources must be available to the communities and schools to build programs and create jobs effectively, which takes money. Unfortunately, in cashed-strapped cities, ending gang violence is not the highest priority since the poor minorities most affected by such violence have the weakest voice among constituents.

The impact of gang violence on many of America's poorest citizens should be a priority from the city to the state to the Federal level, with funding support for anti-gang education programs, community activity centers, and jobs creation coming from all levels. Until we recognize and treat gang violence as the most destructive force on the health, welfare, and future success of millions of American children, the problem will continue to destroy lives. The solutions are available. The public resolve must also be.

Works Cited

Broslin, Curt. "Background on Drug Violence." *Do Something.Org* (August 2006). 4-5. Web. 6 February 2011.

"Drugs and Latin Gangs." *Duke University* (9 December 2008): n. pag. Web. 3 February 2011.

"Gang Violence as a Social Problem." *Social Problems, wikispaces* (May 2011): n. pag. Web. 5 February 2011.

Goguen. Carole. "The Effects of Community Violence on Children and Adolescence," *Traumatic Stress Treatment Center* (4 September 2010): 2-4. Web. 6 February 2011.

Grabionowski, Ed. ""How Street Gangs Work." *How Stuff Works* (May 2009): n. pag. Web. 8 February 2011.

"How Gang Violence Can Affect Your Community." *AMW Safety Center* (5 November 2009): n. pag. Web. 9 February 2011.

"Street Gangs: A Dead-end for Our Children." *Lawton Police Department* (May 2011): n. pag. Web. 9 February 2011.

Revision

The revision process for a research-oriented draft is similar to that of other papers with a few added considerations. One of the most important considerations is making sure that readers clearly understand when you are incorporating research material in your paper and when you are providing your own comments. The following drafting guidelines will help you keep that distinction clear.

Revision Guidelines

Consider the following suggestions in evaluating your first draft.

1. Overview. Read the entire draft once to get a general idea of what you have done well and what areas may need some work. As you revise your paper, keep your reading audience in mind and how you would like them to respond.

2. Introduction. Does the opening introduce the topic clearly, create interest for readers, and include the thesis statement for the paper? How might the introduction be revised to make it more interesting or informative, or to highlight the significance of the topic?

3. Middle paragraphs. Is the research material incorporated effectively into the middle paragraphs? Can readers tell from source introductions and page references when you are using resource materials and when you are expressing your own thoughts? Is most of the resource information paraphrased in your own words? Are quotations used sparingly and effectively? Do most paragraphs begin with topic sentences that express the main idea of the paragraph?

4. Thesis support. Read the middle paragraphs to see how well they support your thesis statement. You formulated your thesis statement based on what you learned from the research, so the research material presented in the middle paragraphs should show readers why you reached the conclusion that you did. Revise your middle paragraphs to support your thesis statement most convincingly.

5. Organization. Are the middle paragraphs organized so that the main aspects of the topic are presented in the most effective order? Does the information in one paragraph follow logically and smoothly from the previous paragraph? Are there any sentences or paragraphs that would fit better in a different location? How might the organization of the middle paragraphs be improved?

6. Writer's input. Do you inject your thoughts into the paper – commenting, drawing conclusions, providing opinions, reacting to the research material – so that readers know you are in control of the paper and clearly understand the research material? In addition, do your comments support the thesis statement in some manner?

7. Conclusion. Does the conclusion reinforce the thesis statement? Does it help you accomplish your purpose? How might the conclusion be improved to make a greater impact on readers?

280

8. Wording. Reread each sentence to see if it can be made smoother, clearer, more concise, or better worded. In addition, check to see whether you are using a variety of sentence structures and joining words, and whether there are transitions such as *however, therefore, first, second, for example, on the other hand, as you can see,* and *finally* in key places to tie sentences and paragraphs together.

9. Works Cited. Check the "Works Cited" section at the end of the paper to make sure that you have included all sources, that the information is presented in the correct format, and that the sources are alphabetized.

Excerpts from "Gun Violence" draft *(last 4 paragraphs)*

One of the most influential ~~areas~~ **places in** ~~of~~ a child or young adult's life is ~~in~~ **his or her** school. According to the article, "Gang Violence as a Social Problem," "Providing more funding for schools specifically for anti-gang programs and including anti-gang messages in the curriculum is essential in creating a non-violent atmosphere." ~~Funding for anti-gang violence is not the only way to promote it in schools.~~ **In addition,** strict rules ~~of~~ **for** on-campus **behavior** ~~activity~~ and truancy prevention ~~will~~ **can help** create an educational culture that ~~will hopefully leak into~~ **positively affect** students' lives outside **of** school. These same messages and programs should also be reinforced in the communities outside of school. Developing **after-school** youth programs **in the community** gives children ~~alternative~~ **positive** options to gang affiliation ("Gang Violence as a Social Problem").

Preventing the recruitment of new gang members is a solution for the future, but other measures must be taken to curb the violence now. Legislation is ~~the voice that is the most used when we talk about~~ **a key in any** attempt to ~~solve~~ **reduce** gang violence. ~~We look to Legislation~~ **Legislators** and ~~to~~ government officials ~~that~~ have the authority to help protect us from gang violence. ~~Establishing~~ New laws ~~that~~ **must** increase the severity of punishment for gang related violence. ~~is essential.~~ Any ~~act of~~ **gang-related** criminal~~ity~~ **act** ~~related to gangs~~ should ~~automatically have an increased~~ **draw a longer** sentence. Additionally, ~~the recruitment of~~ **recruiting** new members to gangs should be a crime ~~have a harsh penalty~~. Recruiting anybody should be punishable by imprisonment, and recruiting a minor should ~~have~~ **draw** an increase~~d in the sentencing~~ **sentence** ("Gang Violence as a Social Problem").

~~Clearly~~ **Obviously**, any long-term solution to eradicating gang violence includes police enforcement, education, jobs, activity centers, and neighborhood involvement. However, resources must be **made** available to ~~the communities and schools~~ schools and communities to build programs and **help** create jobs~~effectively~~, which **means** ~~take~~ money. Unfortunately, in cashed-strapped cities, ending gang violence is ~~not~~ **seldom** the highest priority since the poor**er inner-city** minorities most affected by such violence ~~have the weakest voice~~ **don't have a strong voice** among **voting** constituents.

~~The impact of~~ **Eradicating** gang violence ~~on~~ **that affects** ~~many~~ **millions** of America's poorest citizens, **many of them children,** should be a priority ~~from the city to the state to the Federal government level,~~ at all levels of government, with funding ~~support~~ for anti-gang education programs, community activity centers, and jobs creation coming from ~~all~~ city, county, state, and Federal levels. Until we recognize and treat gang violence as the most destructive force on the health, welfare, and future~~success~~ of millions of American children, the problem will continue to destroy lives. The solutions are available, **but where is** the public resolve? ~~must also be.~~ **While all of us may not be affected by gang violence in our neighborhoods today, the time will come when there will be no "safe havens" from such violence unless we aggressively address the problem now.**

(Revisions were made to improve word choice, to smooth out awkward phrasing, to eliminate unnecessary words, and to make the sentences smoother and more readable.)

Revision Activity 7.9

Revise the first draft of your paper following the revision guidelines presented. Then exchange drafts with a classmate. Indicate any place in the draft where it is unclear whether the information is from a research source or the writer, or where the paper doesn't appear to support its thesis statement. Make any necessary changes, and write the second draft of your paper.

Editing

This final editing section reviews what you have learned in previous units about avoiding errors and introduces some new punctuation marks and spelling concerns.

Punctuating Quotations

Since you may have used quotations from different sources in your research paper, it is important to punctuate them correctly so that readers know exactly what is being quoted. The following rules will help you punctuate quotations correctly.

1. Put quotation marks (" ") around the exact words from the source that you incorporate into your paper, placing the ending quotation mark outside the period:

   According to climate expert Max Shurer, "The warmer air temperatures of the last twenty years do not follow any natural cyclical pattern that we have seen in the past."

2. Always acknowledge the source of the quote along with the quotation, and separate the two with a comma.

   "Standing water of any kind provides a breeding ground for mosquitoes in warm weather," warned public health official Nancy McGowen.

   According to recent Gallop Poll results, "Women are more likely to vote for a woman candidate for President than men are."

3. Punctuate the following quotation situations in the manner shown.

   a. Quoted sentence divided by the source acknowledgment:

      "The best time to catch large-mouth bass on Hawthorne Lake," according to professional bass fisherman Brock Adams, "is at dawn or at sunset." (commas before and after source introduction, quotations marks before and after both halves of the quoted sentence)

   b. Two quoted sentences with source acknowledgment between sentences:

      "You can catch the most fish by fishing four-to-six feet deep," said Adams. "The bigger fish, however, are in the deeper waters." (period after source introduction, quotation marks before and after each quoted sentence)

   c. Source acknowledgment followed by two-sentence quote:

      According to Adams, "Fishing successfully at Hawthorne Lake requires a lot of experience and skill. It is such a big lake that you have to know where to fish at different times of the year."
      (no quotation mark before second sentence of the quote)

d.   Rather than quoting an entire sentence, the quote begins at mid-sentence:

Dr. Abrams believes that most alleged cures for arthritis are "worthless shams that cost desperate people millions of dollars a year."
(small letter begins mid-sentence quote, no comma after source introduction)

4.   Do not put quotation marks around an indirect quotation, which states what someone said rather than quoting his or her exact words:

Indirect quotation: Dr. Hall said that he did not believe in prescribing horse liniments for arthritis sufferers.

Direct quotation: Dr. Hall said, "I don't believe in prescribing horse liniments for arthritis sufferers."

Editing Activity 7.10
Punctuate the following quotations according to the rules presented by inserting quotation marks, commas, and capital letters where they are needed. Do not put quotation marks around indirect quotations.

Example:
Stock market expert Ivan Crookside said there is not enough good news related to the economy to sustain any kind of upward momentum in stocks over the short haul.

Punctuated:
Stock market expert Ivan Crookside said, "There is not enough good news related to the economy to sustain any kind of upward momentum in stocks over the short haul."

1. Anti-war demonstrations have been planned in major US cities for October 28, according to demonstration organizer Lucy Planter.

2. The demonstrations according to Planter will show the government that US citizens don't support the continuing war in Iraq.

3. In particular, the demonstrations will protest against any renewed funding for the war efforts said Planter we are wasting billions of dollars that could be going to education and health care.

4. Planter said she believes that upwards of a million people will protest in ten cities.

5. She said if the government doesn't get the message sent by a million Americans, it is no longer representing the people who elected it.

6. Planter said that she felt Americans were more than frustrated by a war that was unnecessary and harmful. We should have never gone into Iraq in the first place said Planter Every day that we stay just amplifies the problem.

7. News coverage of the upcoming demonstrations has been spotty at best said Planter and there appears to be a pro-war bias among conservative newspaper chains. They are reluctant to publicize the demonstrations at all.

8. The people will be heard said Planter in summation. We are not going away.

Editing Review Activity 7.11

To review what you learned in previous units, proofread the following paragraphs and eliminate errors in the following areas: run-on sentences or comma splices, sentence fragments, comma usage, subject-verb agreement, pronoun-antecedent agreement, subject pronouns, irregular verb forms, colons, semi-colons, and dashes.

Example

The school orchestras concert schedule is the more ambitious ever. They are playing four concerts this school year which is two more than usual. The reason for the increase according to the orchestra instructor are the crowds at last year's concerts which was sold out. The school believes that there is enough interest to attract good crowds to four concerts this year and they will use the added revenue to fund the orchestras summer concert performances in Europe.

Corrected

The school orchestra's concert schedule is the ~~more~~ most ambitious ever. They are playing four concerts this school year, which is two more than usual. The reason for the increase, according to the orchestra instructor, ~~are~~ is the crowds at last year's concerts, which ~~was~~ were sold out. The school believes that there is enough interest to attract good crowds to four concerts this year, and they it will use the added revenue to fund the orchestra's summer concert performances in Europe.

Exercise Paragraph:

One of the amber trees alongside the apartments are shorter than the others. It also loses its leaves more early in the fall. And start to blossom more late in the spring. The tree is definitely the runt of the ambers, it isn't sickly but it's small. The apartment manager has tried giving it extra water and fertilizer but nothing seem to help. The soil is no different where the smaller amber is planted than for the rest of the trees so it is getting the same amount of nutrients from the ground. Apparently some trees are just inherently more small than others it doesn't mean it is less healthy or won't live as long. Some animals of course falls into the same category the runt of the litter. Nature has their runts among all species of plants and animals.

288

Editing Activity 7.12

Proofread your draft for errors by applying the following guidelines and make the necessary corrections. Then type the final draft of your paper.

Editing Guidelines

1. Check your sentences to make sure you haven't run any sentences together or put a comma between sentences instead of a period, and make any necessary corrections.

2. Check your draft for any sentence fragments: incomplete sentences with a period after them. To correct fragments, attach them to the sentence they belong with, or add words to make them complete.

3. Check your use of irregular verbs, making sure you have used the correct irregular forms and spelled them correctly.

4. Check your comma usage, making sure you have inserted commas correctly into your sentences.

5. Check the spelling of any word you are uncertain of, or run the spell check on your word processing program, to eliminate any spelling errors.

6. Check your verbs in each sentence to make sure that they agree with their subjects.

7. Check your pronouns in each sentence to make sure they agree with their antecedents, and make sure you are using the correct subject pronoun forms.

8. Check your use of colons, semi-colons, and dashes to see whether you are using them correctly and effectively.

9. Check your use of comparative and superlative adjectives, and make sure that you have used the correct forms.

10. Check your quotations in the paper, making sure that you have inserted quotation marks around direct quotations, separated quotations and source introductions with commas, and capitalized the first word of any quoted sentence.

11. Check your possessive words to make sure you have inserted apostrophes in the correct places.

Readings

Teen Smoking
by William Chang

A 2008 study by the Center for Disease Control and Prevention (CDC), a Federal agency under the Department of Health and Human Services, found that nearly one in four high school students reported smoking in the last month. The study found an increase in teen smoking compared to a 2003 study when one in five students reported smoking ("Teen Smoking: Statistics and Prevention"). More recent studies show no decline in the number of teens who smoke despite everything that is known about the long-term health effects of smoking. Teenage smoking continues to be a serious problem throughout the country, one which has disastrous effects on the long-term health of millions of American teens.

Teens smoke for a number of reasons. Some feel insecure in social situations, and puffing on a cigarette seems to help them cope. Teens smoke because of peer pressure, wanting to fit in with their smoking friends. Teens are also more apt to smoke if their parents smoke or other older people that they admire ("Why Teens Smoke"). According to Denise Witmar in the article "Why Do Teens Start to Smoke," "They are drawn to the 'forbidden' lure of smoking that also attracts teens to drinking and marijuana use," (Witmar 1). Some teens also smoke because they think they look "cool" with a cigarette dangling from their mouth, a defiant gesture against adult authority.

Smoking can also produce pleasurable feelings and reduce stress. Nicotine in cigarettes activates the brain circuitry that enhances feelings of pleasure in cigarette smokers, and since the pleasurable feelings wear off within seconds of the last drag on a cigarette, smokers are quick to light up the next cigarette ("Nicotine"). Nicotine in cigarettes is also a strongly addictive drug which can hook cigarette smokers early in their usage and make it a difficult habit to break.

Some teen smokers argue inaccurately that smoking for a year or two and then quitting will have no effect on their long-term health, so why not enjoy smoking? In fact, teen smoking can have serious and immediate effects on the body since there is still some physical development taking place during these formative years. Teen smoking can cause a great deal of coughing, shortness of breath, poor lung function, respiratory problems, circulatory and hearing problems, and of course, addiction ("Effects of Teen Smoking").

Many teens also argue that they plan on quitting smoking after a year or two, which they can do easily. However, while most teens plan on quitting, over 60% are still smoking seven to nine years later, destroying the teen myth that it is easy to stop smoking ("Effects of Teen Smoking"). Finally, many teens simply ignore the long-term health effects of smoking, disinterested in what the distant future may hold for them, or are negatively fatalistic about their futures, particularly if they are among the high percentage of teen smokers from lower socio-economic backgrounds ("Teen Smoking: Statistics and Prevention").

The harmful effects of cigarette smoking are well known. One in two lifetime smokers will die from their habit, and many of these smokers begin in their teens. Tar coats the lungs of smokers and causes cancer. Men and women who smoke are ten times more likely to die from lung cancer than non-smokers ("Harmful Effects of Smoking Cigarettes"). Smoking is also associated with cancers of the mouth, pharynx, larynx, esophagus, stomach, pancreas, cervix, kidney, ureter, and bladder ("Nicotine").

Heart disease and strokes are also more common among smokers, and smoking causes one in five deaths from heart disease. In younger people, three out of four deaths from heart disease are caused by smoking. Emphysema is a common smoker's disease that slowly rots your lungs, leading to a long downward spiral ending in death. Cigarette smoking during pregnancy increases the risk of low birth weight, prematurity, spontaneous abortion, and perinatal mortality, referred to as the fetal tobacco syndrome ("Harmful Effects of Smoking Cigarettes"). Finally, smokers are not only ruining their own health, they are contributing to the bad health of those around them who suffer from second-hand smoke inhalation, which can lead to all of the problems that beset smokers. Some people make the argument that smoking around children is a form of child abuse, knowingly endangering the children's lives by subjecting them to second-hand smoke.

Knowing all of the horribly harmful effects of cigarette smoking is important for any teen smoker or potential smoker, and this knowledge will get some smokers to quit and others not to start. However, given that this information has been around for decades, the health message has not by itself gotten enough teens to stop smoking or never start. There has to be a greater attempt to address the root causes of smoking for most teens.

According to an online Mayo Clinic article, "Teens must be made more aware of the immediate negative effects of smoking, which may resonate more strongly than the later-life health issues they may to brush aside," ("Teen Smoking: How to Help Your Teen Quit"). For example, smoking gives you bad breath, stinky clothes and hair, yellow teeth and fingernails, a pale, unhealthy look, premature wrinkles, and a hacking cough, and saps your energy for sports and other activities ("Teen Smoking: How to Help Your Teen Quit").

Most teens do care about their appearance and the image they project, and if they understand that bad breath, stinky clothes, yellow teeth and wrinkles aren't cool, they may think twice about smoking. They also need to have the courage to quit something that their friends are doing, which may be easier said than done. Going along with their particular crowd is the way that most teens handle high school peer pressure, and it takes a lot of courage to swim against the tide. Any teen who faces rejection or ridicule from his or her "friends" for quitting smoking knows one thing: they aren't really your friends, and you are threatening their comfortable status quo.

Finally, teens who want to quit smoking need to know that they are dealing with a highly addictive drug and that quitting may take great willpower. If it didn't, the millions of smokers who confess that smoking is a dirty, unhealthy habit they would like to break would quit. However, according to the article "How Can I Quit Smoking?", there are some proven strategies that help teens kick the smoking habit:

Put it in writing. Teens who are successful at quitting smoking often put in writing that they want to quit and why. Putting it in writing makes the goal more real and binding.

Get support. Teens who quit smoking often are supported by friends and family. If this support isn't available, consider joining a support group either online or in person.

Set a quit date. Set a date when you are going to quit and let friends and family know. Mark the date on your calendar and stick to it ("How Can I Quit Smoking?" 1)

Throw away your cigarettes, along with ashtrays and lighters.

Wash all your clothes. Get the smoke smell out of all of your clothes and if you smoke in your car, have it cleaned out too.

Think about your triggers. Be aware of situations and times when you typically smoke - things that "trigger" your smoking - and avoid these situations as much as possible.

Substitute something else for cigarettes. You are used to having a cigarette in your hand and mouth, so substitute other things: gum, lollipops, tooth picks, mints ("How Can I Quit Smoking?" 2)

Expect some withdrawal symptoms. If you have smoked regularly, expect some nicotine withdrawal symptoms such as headaches, depression, sore throat, or the "munchies." These symptoms will pass, so be patient.

Keep yourself busy. The more distracted you are with activity, the less likely you'll be to crave cigarettes.

Quit gradually. While some people have success quitting "cold turkey," many others are successful by reducing the number of cigarettes they smoke daily until they get down to zero.

Use a nicotine replacement if necessary. If you find that none of these strategies is working, you might talk to your doctor about treatments. Using a nicotine replacement, such as gum, patches, inhalers, or nasal sprays, can be very helpful. Sprays and inhalers are available by prescription only, and it's important to see your doctor before buying the patch and gum over the counter so that he or she can help you find the solution that will work best for you ("How Can I Quit Smoking?" 3)

If you slip up, don't give up. If you slip up, it doesn't mean you've failed. You are overcoming a deadly, addictive habit, and you might suffer some lapses. The key is not to give up: the one thing that everyone who kicks the habit has in common ("How Can I Quit Smoking?" 4).

Smoking is a deadly, dirty, addictive habit that harms anyone who smokes, and 90% of life-long smokers begin in their teens ("The Tragedy of Teen Smoking"). If you begin smoking in your teens, there is a great likelihood that you will die well before your time from a horrible smoking-induced disease. The longer you smoke as a teen, the greater your addiction to nicotine and the greater the chance you will continue smoking.

Smoking isn't a cool or adult thing to do. Most adults who smoke wish they had never started. Smoking is, in fact, a stupid thing to do, ruining your health and creating a drug addiction. It takes courage to stop smoking when your peers smoke, but if you stop smoking, you may get others to stop also and get others not to start in the first place.

Quitting smoking may not be easy, but there are strategies that have worked for millions of former smokers. The small nicotine-induced pleasure you may get from smoking is nothing compared to the life-long damage you are doing to yourself, including drug addiction. Many former smokers say that the best day of their lives was when they kicked the habit. If you smoke, that day could be yours, and the sooner you quit, the easier it will be.

Works Cited

"Effects of Teen Smoking." *TeenSmoking.us* (May 2008) n. pag. Web 6 November 2011.

"Harmful Effects of Smoking Cigarettes." *QuitSmokingStop.com* (8 June 2009) 1-2. Web. 9 November 2011.

"How Can I Quit Smoking?" *KidsHealth.Org* (10 May 2010): 1-4. Web. 9 November 2011.

Laundry, Laura. "Nicotine." *HomeDrugTestingKit.com* (June 2010) n. pag. Web. 12 November 2011.

Chua, Amy. "Teen Smoking: How to Help Your Teen Quit." *MayoClinic.com* (August 2011) n. pag. Web. 12 November 2011.

"Teen Smoking: Statistics and Prevention." *FamilyFirstAid.org* (9 June 2009) 1-2. Web. 12 November 2011.

"The Tragedy of Teen Smoking." *TeenHelp.com* (August 2009) n. pag. Web. 15 November 2011.

Witmer, Denise. "Why Do Teens Start to Smoke?" *About.com.* (7 May 2011) 1-2. Web. 15 November 2011.

"Why Teens Smoke." *ThinkQuest.org* (9 September 2010) n. pag. Web. 18 November 2011.

Questions for Discussion

1. What, according to the essay, are the main reasons that teens smoke? Which do you feel are most responsible? Are there other reasons that teens smoke?

2. Why do you think that many teens continue smoking despite knowing of the dangerous consequences?

3. Evaluate the "strategies" in the essay to help teens quit smoking. Which do you feel would be most effective? Can you think of other strategies?

4. Discuss smoking experiences among your discussion group: why some continue smoking, how some quit, why some never started.

STDs: The Silent Epidemic
by Marianne Crowley

Julia Carter never imagined that she would ever contract a sexually transmitted disease. She had only slept with two men, one who was her current boyfriend, and both men practiced safe sex. Well, almost always. But one day Julia started getting sores in her genital area and went to her doctor immediately. She was diagnosed with genital herpes, a sexually transmitted disease with no cure. Julia will probably spend the rest of her life living with herpes and outbreaks of genital sores, a terrible price to pay for a few moments of indiscretion.

According to a State of the Nation report, sexually transmitted diseases (STDs) affect men and women of all backgrounds and economic levels ("Challenges Facing STD Prevention"). In the United States, the overall incidence of STDs has increased dramatically in recent years. The government's Center for Disease Control and Prevention (CDC) estimates that 19 million new infections occur each year, almost half of them among young people ages 15 to 24 (Weinstock, et al. 7). Despite the fact that STDs are extremely widespread and add an estimated 13 billion dollars to the nation's healthcare costs (Chesson, et al.), most people in the United States remain unaware of the risk and consequences of all but the most prominent STD -HIV, the virus that causes AIDS. STDs are not a common topic of conversation among young people, and those that contract a disease, often filled with guilt, shame, and embarrassment, seldom want anyone to know.

Sexually transmitted diseases are infections you can get by having sex with someone who has an infection ("STDs: Common Symptoms"). These infections are usually passed by having vaginal intercourse, but they can also be passed through anal sex, oral sex or skin-to-skin contact. STDs can be caused by either viruses or bacteria. STDs caused by viruses include hepatitis B, herpes, HIV and the human papilloma virus (HPV). STDs caused by bacteria include chlamydia, gonorrhea and syphilis ("STD: Common Symptoms"). Anyone who has had sexual relations may be at risk for having an STD. The risk is higher for those who have had many sex partners, who have had sex with someone who has had many partners, or who have had sex without using condoms.

Sexually Transmitted Diseases

Chlamydia is the most frequently reported bacterial STD in the United States. An estimated 2.8 million Americans are infected with chlamydia each year ("STDs Today"). However, under-reporting is substantial because most people with chlamydia are not aware of their infections and do not seek testing. The highest rates of chlamydial infection are in 15-to 19-year-old adolescents, regardless of demographics or location ("Sexually Transmitted Diseases").

Chlamydia can be transmitted during vaginal, oral, or anal sexual contact with an infected partner. A pregnant woman may pass the infection to her newborn during delivery, with subsequent neonatal eye infection or pneumonia. Even though symptoms of chlamydia are usually mild or absent, it can damage a woman's reproductive organs and cause serious complications. Irreversible damage, including infertility, can occur "silently" before a woman ever recognizes a problem ("STDs Today"). Chlamydia also can cause discharge from the penis of an infected man, although complications among men are rare. Although chlamydia can be easily treated and cured with antibiotics, the damage it may cause to a woman or her newborn are irreversible.

Genital herpes is a contagious viral infection caused by the herpes simplex virus (HSV) which has affected an astonishing one out of five (or 45 million) Americans ("STDs Today"). There are two types of HSV, and both can cause genital herpes. Genital HSV-2 infection is more common in women (approximately one out of four women) than in men (almost one out of five). Doctors estimate that as many as 500,000 new cases may occur each year. HSV type 1 most commonly causes sores on the lips (known as fever blisters or cold sores), but it can cause genital infections through oral-genital or genital-genital contact. HSV type 2 most often causes genital sores, but it also can infect the mouth.Both HSV 1 and 2 can produce sores in and around the vaginal area, on the penis, around the anal opening, and on the buttocks or thighs. Occasionally, sores also appear on other parts of the body where broken skin has come into contact with HSV. The virus remains in certain nerve cells of the body for life, causing periodic symptoms in some people ("STDs Today").

Genital herpes infection usually is acquired by sexual contact with someone who unknowingly is having an asymptomatic outbreak of herpes sores in the genital area. People with oral herpes can transmit the infection to the genital area of a partner during oral-genital sex. Herpes infections also can be transmitted by a person who is infected with HSV who has noticeable symptoms. The virus is spread only rarely, if at all, by contact with objects such as a toilet seat or hot tub ("STD's Today").

There is no treatment that can cure herpes, but antiviral medications can shorten and prevent outbreaks during the period of time the person takes the medication. Affecting one out of five Americans, genital herpes is a silent epidemic. It has been replaced in the public consciousness by the more life-threatening AIDS virus, but it remains nonetheless a terrible genital disease to live out one's life with, not to mention the effect it has on a person's partner or his or her future relationships.

Gonorrhea is caused by Neisseria Gonorrhoeae, a bacterium that can grow and multiply easily in the warm, moist areas of the reproductive tract. CDC estimates that more than 700,000 persons in the U.S. get new gonorrheal infections each year ("STDs Today"). The most common symptoms of infection are a discharge from the vagina or penis and painful or difficult urination. The most common and serious complications occur in women and, as with chalamydial infection, these complications include pelvic inflammatory disease (PID) ectopic (tubal) pregnancy, and infertility.

Gonorrhea can grow in the cervix, uterus, and fallopian tubes in women, and in the urethra in women and men. The bacterium can also grow in the mouth, throat, eyes, and anus. If it spreads to the blood or joints it can be life-threatening. In addition, people with gonorrhea can more easily contract HIV, the virus that causes AIDS. HIV-infected people with gonorrhea are also more likely to transmit HIV to someone else ("STDs Today"). Several antibiotics can successfully cure gonorrhea in adolescents and adults. However, drug-resistant strains of gonorrhea are increasing in many areas of the world, including the United States, and successful treatment of gonorrhea is becoming more difficult. New antibiotics or combinations of drugs must be used to treats these resistant strains.

Syphilis is caused by the bacterium Treponema Pallidum. The incidence of syphilis has increased and decreased dramatically in recent years, and in the United States, health officials reported over 32,000 cases of syphilis in 2002. Between 2001 and 2002, the number of reported primary and secondary syphilis cases increased 12.4 percent. Rates in women continued to decrease, and overall, the rate in men was 3.5 times that in women. This, in conjunction with reports of syphilis outbreaks in men who have sex with men (MSM), suggests that rates of syphilis in MSM are increasing ("STDs Today").

Syphilis is passed from person to person through direct contact with a syphilis sore. The first symptoms of syphilis infection may go undetected because they are very mild and disappear spontaneously. The initial symptom is a chancre (genital sore); it is usually a painless open sore that most often appears on the penis or around the vagina. It can also occur near the mouth, anus, or on the hands. Transmission of the organism occurs during vaginal, anal, or oral sex. Pregnant women with the disease can pass it to the babies they are carrying. If untreated, syphilis may go on to more advanced stages, including a transient rash and eventually, can cause serious involvement of the brain, nerves, eyes, heart, blood vessels, liver, bones, and joints. Chancres caused by syphilis make it easier to transmit HIV infection sexually. There is an estimated 2-5 fold risk of acquiring HIV infection when syphilis is present ("STDs Today"). The full course of the disease can take years. Penicillin remains the most effective drug to treat people with syphilis.

Trichomoniasis is caused by the single-celled protozoan parasite, Trichomonas vaginalis. It is the most common curable STD in young, sexually active women, and it affects men as well although symptoms are most common in women. An estimated 7.4 million new cases occur each year ("STDs Today").

The vagina is the most common site of infection in women, and the urethra (urine canal) is the most common site of infection in men. The parasite is sexually transmitted through penis-to-vagina intercourse or vulva-to-vulva (the genital area outside the vagina) contact with an infected partner. Women can acquire the disease from infected men or women, but men usually contract it only from infected women.

Most men with trichomoniasis do not have signs or symptoms; however, some men may temporarily have an irritation inside the penis, mild discharge, or slight burning after urination or ejaculation. Some women have signs or symptoms of infection which include a frothy, yellow-green vaginal discharge with a strong odor. The infection also may cause discomfort during intercourse and urination, as well as irritation and itching of the female genital area. Trichomoniasis can usually be cured with the prescription drug metronidazole, given by mouth in a single dose ("STDs Today").

AIDS (acquired immunodeficiency syndrome) was first reported in the United States in 1981. Since the beginning of the epidemic, an estimated 944,306 people have developed AIDS in the United States ("HIV/AIDS Surveillance Report"). AIDS is caused by the human immunodeficiency virus (HIV), a virus that destroys the body's ability to fight off infection.

People who have AIDS are susceptible to many life-threatening diseases, and to certain forms of cancer. Transmission of the virus primarily occurs during unprotected sexual activity and by sharing needles used to inject intravenous drugs.

Prevention
With the prevalence of sexually transmitted diseases in adolescents and young adults in the

United States, the devastating long-term damage STDs can cause their victims, and the ease with which people who have STDs can pass them on to others, it is imperative that all Americans become knowledgeable on sexually transmitted diseases and how they can be prevented. Not one adolescent or young adult should have to live with an STD, and no one has to. To dramatically decrease the chances of ever contracting an STD, the following practices should be embraced ("Sexually Transmitted Diseases Overview").

Don't have sex. The best way to prevent any STD is to practice abstinence, or not have vaginal, oral, or anal sex. While this may not be feasible advice for all young adults, it certainly is the best possible advice for adolescents.

Be faithful. Have a sexual relationship with one partner who has been tested for STDs and is not infected is another way to reduce your chances of getting infected. Having sex with a number of partners greatly increases a person's chances of contracting an STD, as does having sex with a person who has had a number of partners.

Use condoms. Protect yourself with a condom every time you have vaginal, anal, or oral sex. Condoms should be used for any type of sex with every partner. For vaginal sex, use a latex male condom or a female polyurethane condom. For anal sex, use a latex male condom. For oral sex, use a dental dam, a rubbery material that can be placed over the anus or the vagina before sexual contact. Condoms are by far the best way to prevent STDs, and it only takes one lapse to become infected.

Know that some methods of birth control, like birth control pills, shots, implants, or diaphragms, will not protect you from STDs. If you use one of these methods, be sure to also use a latex condom or dental dam (used for oral sex) correctly every time you have sex.

Talk with your sex partner(s) about STDs, their sexual history, and using condoms. It's up to each individual to make sure he or she is protected. Do not have sex with anyone who refuses to wear a condom.

Talk frankly with your doctor or nurse and your sex partner(s) about any STDs you or your partner have or had. Not only do you have a moral obligation to let your partner know if you have been infected with an STD, you may also have a legal obligation, as people who have been infected by an STD carrier who remained silent are testing their legal options, including filing lawsuits or criminal charges.

Have regular pelvic exams. Women should talk with their doctor about how often they need an exam. Many tests for STDs can be done during an exam. Women should ask their doctor to test them for STDs. The sooner an STD is found, the easier it is to treat ("Sexually Transmitted Diseases Overview").

Treatment
Any persons who have been sexually exposed to a person with an STD or who have symptoms

that they feel may derive from an STD should have a medical examination immediately. Seeing a doctor as soon as possible after exposure to an STD is important; these infections can easily spread to others and can have serious complications. Go to a hospital's emergency facility if an STD problem worsens, if a fever develops with other symptoms, or if it will be a few days before an appointment with a doctor can be scheduled ("Sexually Transmitted Diseases").

If a person is diagnosed with an STD, he or she should seek treatment immediately to stop the spread of the disease. It is important that all prescribed medicine is taken as directed. Sometimes follow-up tests are important, and future doctor's appointments need to be scheduled. In addition, it is important to avoid sexual contact while being treated for an STD. Finally, any person or persons that the infected person has had sexual contact with should be notified and urged to have a check-up ("Sexually Transmitted Diseases").

Sexually transmitted diseases will continue to infect million of adolescents and young adults every year, and if people remain ignorant to the risk of contracting an STD and the terrible consequences, including passing it on to a newborn child, the number of infections will continue to rise. That the chances of contracting genital herpes, a highly infectious disease with no cure, are one in five should strike enough fear in all young adults that they would do everything possible to avoid being infected.

However, it is up to our schools, the medical profession, and parents to educate all of our youth to the dangers of STDs and how to prevent them. This is not a problem without a solution, but as long as the spread of STDs among young people remains essentially a silent epidemic, millions of young lives will continue to be devastated by the effects.

Works Cited

"Challenges Facing STD Prevention in Youth." *State of the Nation Report* 2005. American Social Health Association: New York, 2005. Print.

Chesson H.W., Blandford J,M., Gift T.L., Tao G., Irwin K.L. "The Estimated Medical Cost of STDs Among American Youth." *National STD Prevention*, 11 March 2004: 11-12. Print.

"HIV/AIDS Surveillance Report 2004." *US Department of Health and Human Services, Center for Disease Control and Prevention.* 12 June 2005: 6. Print.

"Sexually Transmitted Diseases." *Sexual Health Center, WebMD.* (10 November 2008): n. pag. Web. 12 Nov. 2008.

"Sexually Transmitted Diseases: Overview." *WomensHealth.Gov* (May 2005): n. pag. Web. 8 August 2008.

"STDs Today." *National Prevention Education Network* (13 May 2008) n. pag. Web. 9 August 2008.

Weinstock H., Berman S., Cates W. "Sexually Transmitted Diseases Among American Youth." *Perspective on Sexual and Reproductive Health.* May 2004: 6-10. Print.

Questions for Discussion

1. What is the thesis of the essay: the main point that the author is conveying to readers? In what ways does she get this point across?

2. From the essay, what do adolescents and young adults need to know in order to avoid an STD infection?

3. What did you learn about STDs from the essay that you weren't aware of?

4. What do you think must be done to solve the problem of STD infection among young adults, and how do you think individuals can help?

Acknowledgements

Belanger, Jeff. "Dr. Hans Holzer - A Lifetime of Explaining the Unexplained." *Ghostvillage.com*, Feb. 7, 2005. Reprinted by permission of the author.

Carlin, George. "Baseball and Football." Print version of a George Carlin comedic routine. 1999.

Chang, William. "Teen Smoking." 2010. Reprinted by permission of the author.

Chua, Amy. "Why Chinese Mothers are Superior," *Huffington Post*, Jan. 8, 2011. Reprinted by permission of the author.

Collins, Lionel. "Getting Guys to the Altar. 2014. Reprinted by permission of the author.

Crowley, Marianne. "STDs: The Silent Epidemic." 2007. Reprinted by permission of the author.

Feeley, Malcolm. "Helping the Homeless." 2007. Reprinted by permission of the author.

Frey, Alicia. "Is College Worth It?" 2014. Reprinted by permission of the author.

Green, Lorna. "Giving Students Room to Run." *Teaching Tolerance*, Spring 2011. Reprinted by permission of *Teaching Tolerance* magazine.

Hout, Anton. "Cyber Bullying." *OvercomeBullying.org*, Nov. 6, 2013. Reprinted by permission of the author.

Ka-mei, Jes Yim. "Mama." 2007. Reprinted by permission of the author.

Karon, Jeff. "A Positive Solution for Plagiarism." *Chronicle of Higher Education*, Sept. 18, 2012. Reprinted by permission of the *Chronicle of Higher Education*.

Kaser, Paul. "Working on the Ranch." Reprinted by permission of the author.

Kuroda, Julianne. "Are You a Procrastinator?" 2007. Reprinted by permission of the author.

Mandela, Nelson. "In the Face of Adversity," from *Long Walk to Freedom*. Little, Brown, and Co., 1994. Reprinted by permission of Little, Brown, and Company.

Pitts, Leonard Jr. "How Black is Black Enough?" *Miami Herald*, Sept. 29, 2013. Reprinted by permission of the *Miami Herald*.

Platt, Shawna Platt. "Overcoming Abuse: My Story." *Wordpress.com*, 2007. Reprinted by permission of the author.

Rodriguez, Richard. "What a Wall Can't Stop." *Washington Post*, May 28, 2006. Reprinted by permission of the author.

Sander, Libby. "Colleges Confront a Gender Gap in Student Engagement." *Chronicle of Higher Education*, Oct. 29, 2012. Reprinted by permission of the *Chronicle of Higher Education*.

Sandoval, Ramon. "Wedding Bliss." 2014. Reprinted by permission of the author.

Snyder, Kurt. "My Personal Experience with Schizophrenia." *Schizoworld.com*, 2012. Reprinted by permission of the author.

Tisdale, Sallie. "Living with the Mystery of Headache." *Harper's*, May 2013. Reprinted by permission of *Harper's* magazine.

Walton, James A. "My Education Angel." From "First Generation College Graduates." California State University Fresno, 2012. Reprinted by permission of California State University, Fresno.

Wilder, Gretchen. "Vincent." 2014. Reprinted by permission of the author.

Woo, Park Ji. "Escape," *Gawker.com*, May, 2014. Reprinted by permission of the author.

Woodard, Colin. "The Intelligence of Beasts." *Chronicle of Higher Education*, June, 2011. Reprinted by permission of the *Chronicle of Higher Education*.

Index